# School-based Research

# School-based Research

## A guide for education students

Elaine Wilson

Los Angeles • London • New Delhi • Singapore • Washington DC

Introduction and editorial arrangement, Chapters 1, 2, 3, 11, and 12 © Elaine Wilson, 2009
Chapter 4 © Elaine Wilson and Kris Stutchbury, 2009
Chapter 5 and 6 © Elaine Wilson and Alison Fox, 2009
Chapters 7 and 8 © Michael Evans, 2009
Chapter 9 © Mark Winterbottom , 2009
Chapter 10 © Ros McLellan, 2009
Chapter 13 © Helen Demetriou, 2009
Chapters 14 and 15 © Keith, S. Taber, 2009
Chapter 16 © Christine Counsell, 2009

First published 2009

SAGE Publications Ltd
1 Oliver's Yard
55 City Road
London EC1Y 1SP

SAGE Publications Inc.
2455 Teller Road
Thousand Oaks, California 91320

SAGE Publications India Pvt Ltd
B 1/I 1 Mohan Cooperative Industrial Area
Mathura Road
New Delhi 110 044

SAGE Publications Asia-Pacific Pte Ltd
33 Pekin Street #02-01
Far East Square
Singapore 048763

**Library of Congress Control Number:**

**British Library Cataloguing in Publication data**

A catalogue record for this book is available from the British Library

ISBN 978-1-4129-4849-4
ISBN 978-1-4129-4850-0 (pbk)

Typeset by C&M Digitals (P) Ltd, Chennai, India
Printed in Great Britain by TJ International Ltd, Padstow, Cornwall
Printed on paper from sustainable resources

**Mixed Sources**
Product group from well-managed
forests and other controlled sources
www.fsc.org Cert no. SGS-COC-2482
© 1996 Forest Stewardship Council
FSC

# CONTENTS

# FOREWORD

Most teachers, in my experience, want to improve; it is part of the professional self. They differ, of course, in the routes they choose to take towards this goal. In the search for insights into how they can continue to develop, some become critical readers of other people's research and ideas. But, eventually, many conclude that the best way of understanding their own practice, and that of the institutions in which they work, is to engage in some kind of research. This book is intended to help teachers who want to embark on that journey.

Looking back, it is hard to believe that, less than thirty years ago, the idea of teachers researching their own practices was seen as controversial. Lawrence Stenhouse, who is widely recognized as the founding parent of teacher research, identified a number of objections to their involvement which were prevalent at that time. First, there were questions about 'the accuracy of teachers' self-reports' – 'teachers', some argued 'do not know what they do'. Second, they were likely to be 'biased' – they had too much of an interest in the outcomes to be objective. Third, they were 'theoretically innocent'. And fourth, put bluntly, they lacked the time – they 'taught too much' to achieve the kind of intellectual distance research required (reported in Rudduck and Hopkins, 1985, pp. 15–16).

This book is dedicated to the memory of Donald McIntyre and Jean Rudduck. Both were professors of education at Cambridge and both were convinced that teachers had crucial roles to play in research; indeed they dedicated their lives to this cause. As central architects of the revolution in education which took place here at the turn of the millennium they sought to harness the full weight of the university to this endeavour. Sadly, both died during 2007 (one of a heart attack and the other of cancer) but not before each, in their different way, had made major contributions to the development of research-based approaches in schools.

For McIntyre, the key to educational progress lay in developing teachers' 'craft knowledge' (Brown and McIntyre, 1993). By this, he meant the nexus of understandings which link teachers' knowledge of what to teach (their subject(s)), how to teach it (their pedagogical knowledge) and to whom (their understanding of their pupils). Researching these practices, rigorously and systematically, offered a way forward. In a series of action-based projects, he explored ways of engaging with teachers and schools around *their* concerns and, crucially, in partnership with them.

Rudduck started in a similar place. Her early work supported teachers in a variety of research endeavours, most notably in relation to understanding how to implement changes to classroom practice (Rudduck, 1991). Over time, however, she began to shift her attention from a teacher-centred view of educational innovation towards a more pupil-centred one. Her last book, written with Donald McIntyre shortly before she died, explored the numerous ways in which pupils and teachers can work together to bring about practical changes in classroom conditions. It is a powerful testimony to the importance both of taking teachers seriously and of giving weight to 'pupil voice' (Rudduck and McIntyre, 2007).

But can the insights of teachers and their pupils count as a contribution to knowledge, the central canon around which universities are organized? Or should teachers just sit back and let others determine how they teach? Stenhouse was adamant that teachers had a central role to play – and that governments and policy-makers neglected them at their peril.

He defined 'research' as 'systematic and sustained enquiry, planned and self-critical, which is subject to public criticism and to empirical tests where these are appropriate' (Rudduck and Hopkins, 1985: 19). After three decades of teacher-led research, his definition, and the challenges it implies, still ring true. If schools are to engage with their own futures in a planned and coherent way, they need the quiet but insistent voice of research. They need to invest in their own development by encouraging their members to acquire the basic tools – key ideas, key concepts and key methods.

As we move towards the vision of a research-based profession, there is quite a lot to learn and a great deal to fight for.

*John Gray*
*Cambridge, June 2008*

## References

Brown, S. and McIntyre, D. (1993) *Making Sense of Teaching*. Buckingham: Open University Press.

Rudduck, J. (1991) *Innovation and Change: Developing Involvement and Understanding*. Buckingham: Open University Press.

Rudduck, J. and Hopkins, D. (Eds.) (1985) *Research as a Basis for Teaching: Readings from the work of Lawrence Stenhouse*. London: Heinemann.

Rudduck, J. and McIntyre, D. (2007) *Improving Learning through Consulting Pupils*. London: Routledge.

# NOTES ON CONTRIBUTORS

**Christine Counsell** is Senior Lecturer at the University of Cambridge, Faculty of Education, where she has run the history PGCE course for ten years, and taught on Masters programmes. Christine taught history in state comprehensive schools, holding posts as Head of History, Head of Humanities and finally as deputy Head in Bristol. As Advisory Teacher for Gloucestershire LEA and later as PGCE tutor for the University of Gloucestershire, she broadened her expertise into primary education. Her best-selling pamphlet, *Analytical and Discursive Writing at Key Stage 3* (1997) enshrined her passion for developing language and literacy through history. She has carried out in-service training and consultancy for primary and secondary teachers in over 80 local authorities and has been invited to address teachers and teacher educators all over the UK and Europe, including Cyprus, Estonia, Ireland, Italy, Malta, the Netherlands and Norway. Christine is editor of the Historical Association's journal, *Teaching History*. She has published widely in history education and teacher education and is currently researching the experience of school-based PGCE mentors.

**Helen Demetriou** is a Research Associate at the Faculty of Education of the University of Cambridge since obtaining her PhD in developmental psychology from the Institute of Psychiatry, University of London in 1998. During this time, she has also lectured in developmental psychology at the University. Research has included *'Sustaining pupils' progress at Year 3* (for Ofsted); *Boy's performance in modern foreign languages* (for QCA); *Friendships and performance at transfer and transition* (for DfES); *Consulting pupils about teaching and learning* (ESRC-funded project); *How young children talk about fairness* (internally funded) Helen is currently working with Elaine Wilson on a Gatsby-funded project: *Supporting opportunities for new teachers' professional growth*.

**Michael Evans** is Senior Lecturer in Education and Deputy Head of Faculty at the University of Cambridge. He has extensive experience in foreign language teacher education and in the teaching and supervision of doctoral students in language education. He directs the MPhil in Research in Second Language Education. He is currently co-director of a national study of the impact of government initiatives on the provision and practice of language teaching at KS3 in England. He has published on a number of second language education topics, drawing on empirical research conducted in secondary schools. He is co-author of *Modern Foreign Languages: Teaching School Subjects 11–19* (London, RoutledgeFalmer, 2007).

**Alison Fox** is a Research Associate at the University of Cambridge and, until this year, has also been a practising teacher in secondary schools and in further education. Over the past eighteen years, she has worked as a researcher at both the University of Cambridge and the Open University. Projects have included a four-year project looking at educational networks as they relate to the developing assessment for learning practices in schools, an evaluation of the online learning components of leadership development programmes, an exploration of methods to understand professional learning at events, a longitudinal study of the professional learning of emergent leaders and an exploration of the pedagogic practices of higher-education lecturers. She is particularly interested in developing novel methods that allow new insights to be gained within case-study research frameworks.

**Ros McLellan** taught secondary mathematics and psychology for eight years prior to joining the Faculty of Education at the University of Cambridge in 2000. Since then, she has worked as a researcher on two externally funded research projects based in Faculty: 'Raising Boys' Achievement' (2000 to 2004) and 'Subject Leadership in Creativity in Secondary Design and Technology' (2005 to present). She was recently appointed a Lecturer in Teacher Education & Development/Pedagogical Innovation. Ros enjoys working collaboratively with practitioners to develop and refine strategies that make a real difference to teaching and learning in the classroom. Her research interests include achievement motivation (the focus of her PhD thesis), creativity, gender and achievement, and student attitudes and self-concepts.

**Kris Stutchbury** qualified as a teacher in 1982. She taught mainly chemistry at three different schools in Cheshire, also working on the SATIS project, Salter's A-level Chemistry and running courses for the LEA. Between 1992 and 2004, she was Head of Science and worked as a mentor with PGCE students from Manchester. In 2004, she moved to Cambridge and studied for an MEd. Her dissertation was on the impact of practitioner research in a local comprehensive school and during this time she also developed an interest in the ethics of educational research. She now works for the OU as a PGCE tutor, as a supervisor on the science MEd course at the University of Cambridge, Faculty of Education and part-time at Hills Road Sixth Form College.

**Keith S. Taber** qualified as a teacher of chemistry and physics in 1982. He taught science in comprehensive schools, and developed a taste for classroom research when he registered for a diploma course for science teachers. He undertook an action research project on girls' under-representation in physics in a school where he taught for his Masters degree dissertation. After moving into further education as a physics and chemistry lecturer, he registered for part-time doctoral study, exploring how his students' ideas developed during their college course. After completing his doctorate, Keith moved to Cambridge to join the Faculty of Education, where he works with those preparing to be teachers; with experienced teachers enquiring into aspects of teaching and learning; and with research students training to be educational researchers. His book, *Classroom-based Research and Evidence-based Practice: A Guide for Teachers*, is also published by Sage.

**Elaine Wilson** is a Senior Lecturer in Science Education at the University of Cambridge. She previously taught chemistry in a number of secondary schools. She teaches secondary science PGCE students, coordinates a blended learning science MEd course. Her research interests include collaborative online learning and new teacher education. Her publications include *The Non-Specialist Handbook: Teaching Chemistry to Key Stage 4* (Hodder), and *Teaching and Learning Primary Science with ICT* (Open University Press).

**Mark Winterbottom** is a lecturer in science education in the Faculty of Education, University of Cambridge. He previously taught in secondary schools. He teaches on undergraduate and Masters' level programmes, including the Postgraduate Certificate of Education and the science MEd course. His current research interests include teacher education, ICT and the classroom environment. His publications include *The Non-Specialist Handbook: Teaching Biology to Key Stage 4* (Hodder), and *Teaching and Learning Primary Science with ICT* (Open University Press).

the past eighteen years, she has worked as a researcher at both the University of Cambridge and the Open University. Projects have included a four-year project looking at educational networks as they relate to the developing assessment for learning practices in schools, an evaluation of the online learning components of leadership development programmes, an exploration of methods to understand professional learning at events, a longitudinal study of the professional learning of emergent leaders and an exploration of the pedagogic practices of higher-education lecturers. She is particularly interested in developing novel methods that allow new insights to be gained within case-study research frameworks.

**Ros McLellan** taught secondary mathematics and psychology for eight years prior to joining the Faculty of Education at the University of Cambridge in 2000. Since then, she has worked as a researcher on two externally funded research projects based in Faculty: 'Raising Boys' Achievement' (2000 to 2004) and 'Subject Leadership in Creativity in Secondary Design and Technology' (2005 to present). She was recently appointed a Lecturer in Teacher Education & Development/Pedagogical Innovation. Ros enjoys working collaboratively with practitioners to develop and refine strategies that make a real difference to teaching and learning in the classroom. Her research interests include achievement motivation (the focus of her PhD thesis), creativity, gender and achievement, and student attitudes and self-concepts.

**Kris Stutchbury** qualified as a teacher in 1982. She taught mainly chemistry at three different schools in Cheshire, also working on the SATIS project, Salter's A-level Chemistry and running courses for the LEA. Between 1992 and 2004, she was Head of Science and worked as a mentor with PGCE students from Manchester. In 2004, she moved to Cambridge and studied for an MEd. Her dissertation was on the impact of practitioner research in a local comprehensive school and during this time she also developed an interest in the ethics of educational research. She now works for the OU as a PGCE tutor, as a supervisor on the science MEd course at the University of Cambridge, Faculty of Education and part-time at Hills Road Sixth Form College.

**Keith S. Taber** qualified as a teacher of chemistry and physics in 1982. He taught science in comprehensive schools, and developed a taste for classroom research when he registered for a diploma course for science teachers. He undertook an action research project on girls' under-representation in physics in a school where he taught for his Masters degree dissertation. After moving into further education as a physics and chemistry lecturer, he registered for part-time doctoral study, exploring how his students' ideas developed during their college course. After completing his doctorate, Keith moved to Cambridge to join the Faculty of Education, where he works with those preparing to be teachers; with experienced teachers enquiring into aspects of teaching and learning; and with research students training to be educational researchers. His book, *Classroom-based Research and Evidence-based Practice: A Guide for Teachers*, is also published by Sage.

**Elaine Wilson** is a Senior Lecturer in Science Education at the University of Cambridge. She previously taught chemistry in a number of secondary schools. She teaches secondary science PGCE students, coordinates a blended learning science MEd course. Her research interests include collaborative online learning and new teacher education. Her publications include *The Non-Specialist Handbook: Teaching Chemistry to Key Stage 4* (Hodder), and *Teaching and Learning Primary Science with ICT* (Open University Press).

**Mark Winterbottom** is a lecturer in science education in the Faculty of Education, University of Cambridge. He previously taught in secondary schools. He teaches on undergraduate and Masters' level programmes, including the Postgraduate Certificate of Education and the science MEd course. His current research interests include teacher education, ICT and the classroom environment. His publications include *The Non-Specialist Handbook: Teaching Biology to Key Stage 4* (Hodder), and *Teaching and Learning Primary Science with ICT* (Open University Press).

# INTRODUCTION: PGCE – M LEVEL: WHY SHOULD TEACHERS DO SCHOOL-BASED RESEARCH?

In short, the outstanding characteristics of the extended professional is a capacity for autonomous professional self-development through systematic self-study, through the study of the work of other teachers and through the testing of ideas by classroom research procedures. (Stenhouse, 1985)

## WHY ARE THERE PGCE – M LEVEL COURSES?

The Quality Assurance Agency (QAA) for higher education was established in 1997 as an independent body funded by subscriptions from UK universities and colleges of higher education, and through contracts with the main UK higher education funding bodies. In 1998, the QAA undertook an extensive consultation process involving all higher education institutes in an attempt to rationalize the frameworks on which all qualifications were based. At the time, there were many postgraduate awards and degree subjects on offer.

Following this consultation and within a wider European context following the Bologna agreement in 1999, the National Framework for Higher Education Qualifications (FHEQ) was introduced in 2004 in England, Scotland and Northern Ireland, with a version also available for Scotland to reflect the differences in undergraduate awards there. These frameworks provide the basis for much of the work done since on postgraduate awards, including the Postgraduate Certificate in Education.

In April 2005, Universities UK (UUK), QAA, the Standing Conference of Principals (SCOP) and Universities Council for the Education of Teachers (UCET) issued the following statement:

1. The PGCE is a well-established and internationally recognized qualification undertaken by graduates to prepare them for a career in teaching. Over time, a number of PGCE models have been developed to meet the different needs of learners and the profession. However, the essential characteristics of the PGCE have remained constant – an HE programme providing both professional training leading to QTS and a course of academic study leading to an academic qualification.
2. The qualification acronym 'PGCE' has traditionally been understood to stand for 'Post-Graduate Certificate in Education'. However, the academic level of PGCE courses does vary. Some institutions run PGCE courses which aim for the academic equivalent of the final year of an undergraduate honours degree, with QTS. Other courses, however, are pitched beyond Honours level, incorporate subject or

specialist work in greater detail, and include consideration of research methods. Such courses may form a progression route within a framework which ultimately leads to a Masters degree.

3. In line with the principles underpinning the Framework for HE Qualifications (FHEQ) (QAA, 2001), the full qualification title for 'PGCE' courses should represent accurately the expected level of achievement, and should be aligned with the most appropriate qualification descriptor. It will be a matter for Higher Education Institutions (HEIs) to determine the appropriate level of their qualifications and to assign the appropriate title, in line with the following guidance:

   • Professional Graduate Certificate in Education for those PGCE qualifications which are pitched at Honours level, and align with the FHEQ qualification descriptor at H (honours) level
   • Postgraduate Certificate in Education titles for those PGCE qualifications which are pitched beyond Honours level and align with the FHEQ qualification descriptor at M (masters) level.

4. Institutions should continue to ensure that the level of their qualification(s) is clear and transparent to all applicants, students and other stakeholders. References to the level and full title of the PGCE should be made in course publications, admissions materials, programme specifications, transcripts and certificates. Institutions were expected to identify clearly the level and associated nomenclature of their PGCE programmes, and their subsequent awards, from 1 September 2006.

## A POSTGRADUATE, AS OPPOSED TO A PROFESSIONAL, CERTIFICATE IN EDUCATION AT M (MASTERS) LEVEL

The challenge for education departments will be to persuade and convince other faculties within their own universities that PGCE – M level courses are as intellectually demanding as other Masters courses in other subjects while also ensuring that beginning teachers start their first post well equipped to teach. The Joint Quality Initiative (JQI), a group of UK and European educational organizations, has produced a set of statements to articulate what Bachelor, Masters and Doctorate level study might entail, which may be helpful in identifying what 'm levelness' might be on PGCE courses (see Box I.1).

---

### BOX I.1

#### 'Dublin' descriptors for masters level work

1. Knowledge and understanding provide a basis or opportunity for originality in developing or applying ideas often in a research context.
2. Applying knowledge and understanding through problem-solving abilities [applied] in new or unfamiliar environments within broader or multidisciplinary contexts.
3. Making judgements by demonstrating the ability to integrate knowledge and handle complexity, and formulate judgements with incomplete data.
4. Communications of their conclusions and the underpinning knowledge and rationale (restricted scope) to specialist and non-specialist audiences.
5. Learning skills: study in a manner that may be largely self-directed or autonomous.

## Why should beginning teachers do PGCE – M level courses?

At the 2007 UCET conference, Furlong suggested that 'more than ever before, we need to educate young people to think critically about knowledge and about values, to recognize differences in interpretation, to develop the skills needed to form their own judgments in a rapidly changing world' (Furlong, 2007). Consequently, if those who teach are to be 'critical educators', then part of their own professional education must be based on the same approach to teaching and learning. To this end, Initial Teacher Education must provide high-quality practical training relevant to institutional and national need. The university education departments will be key contributors but will work in close partnership with a network of schools.

This book has been produced to support Postgraduate Certificate of Education and Masters students while they work in schools on individual research projects and goes some way to meeting the challenges set out in the 'Dublin' descriptors in Box I.1.

## WHY SHOULD TEACHERS DO SCHOOL-BASED RESEARCH?

Teachers constantly reflect on classroom interactions and question why students behave and perform in a particular way. However, in order to understand why things happen in the way they do, this necessitates standing back and taking time to deliberate more explicitly about practice. This requires the conscious management of thinking and activity through setting aside time to:

- learn about theories or codified explicit knowledge
- engage in activities and make explicit tacit knowledge
- justify and develop new knowledge
- subject new ideas to the critical scrutiny of other practitioners.

## TYPES OF KNOWLEDGE ABOUT TEACHING AND LEARNING

Knowledge about teaching and learning is constantly developing and evolving and can be classified into three broad categories:

Firstly, we have explicit knowledge that has been codified formally using a system of symbols and language which can be easily communicated or diffused. This codified academic knowledge may be object-based or rule-based. For example, we have come to understand the nature of the chemical bond and know a fair amount about our own human development and we were probably introduced to this in secondary school science lessons. This sort of knowledge is found in textbooks. Furthermore, it is related to our ongoing intellectual development and progresses through a hierarchy leading to greater levels of abstraction. In a school context, codified knowledge can also take the form of organization-specific, rule-based information such as records, correspondence and manuals.

There is also a vast educational research literature of well-grounded propositions which, although abstract in nature, have the potential value to be highly applicable in classrooms.

The second form of knowledge which is tacit, practical and implicit is used by teachers to perform their job and make sense of classrooms. This knowledge is hard to verbalize because it is expressed through action-based skills, is difficult to make explicit or to represent in a textual form because it is largely acquired informally through participation in teaching situations, and it is often so 'taken for granted' that teachers are unaware of its influence on their behaviour. This knowledge is context-specific and is not easily codified but nonetheless also plays a key role in school-based practices and activities.

The third form of knowledge is cultural knowledge which is also context-specific and is associated with the shared assumptions and beliefs that are used to perceive and explain classroom reality and to assign value and significance to new information and ideas.

The curriculum is imbued with cultural values and the translation of this into teaching episodes will also be value-laden with the thoughts behind the choice of words, tone, storylines, and other elements which are not explicitly articulated but can be picked up by the learners nonetheless.

Donald McIntyre argued that there is a gap between the first type of codified research knowledge and the second type – teachers' everyday practice knowledge – which he presented on a continuum (see Figure I.1).

McIntyre suggested that this is not:

> primarily because educational researchers are self-indulgent or irresponsible in the kinds of research that they do or in the ways that they report it, nor because teachers are unprofessional or anti-intellectual in their approach to practice, nor even because of inappropriate organizational arrangements, but primarily because the kind of knowledge that research can offer is of a very different kind from the knowledge that classroom teachers need to use. (McIntyre, 2005, p. 358)

McIntyre also argued that codified research knowledge is not easily translated into practical knowledge because what works for one teacher, or in one school, or with one class, or on one occasion, may not translate directly into action in another. This is because each school is unique, each classroom different by the hour and each teacher has their own 'individual "schemata" for recognizing classes or pupils or situations as being similar to others they have dealt with before, each schema incorporating a range of more or less remembered individual cases, and on corresponding repertoires of actions that have seemed to work in some circumstances in the past'. (McIntyre, 2005)

In other words, teachers make judgements based on their beliefs and values and these have developed through a range of experience. The role of the teacher/researcher is to try to bridge the gap between codified research knowledge and the everyday 'craft' knowledge of teachers. So researching practice is about challenging beliefs and values through encountering new ideas from other teachers and codified research knowledge, so that well-informed judgements can be made in classrooms which ultimately increase the well-being and attainment of every student in each class. Box 2 uses Donald McIntyre's (2005) words to summarize the reasons why teachers ought to engage in school-based research.

Figure I.1    McIntyre's Knowledge Continuum

## BOX I.2

A first suggested way of dealing with the gap starts from the understanding that the two contrasting kinds of knowledge at the ends of the spectrum both have inevitable limitations but also have considerable and mutually complementary strengths. This first way of dealing with the gap is in my view well conceived but has not received the attention it deserves.

Three elements are necessarily involved in this way of dealing with the gap. First, there has to be a recognition – which we shall assume here – that the characteristics of classroom teachers' craft knowledge and of research-based knowledge, as we have described them, are in no way inappropriate but, on the contrary, are in both cases necessary for their purpose, and also mutually complementary in potentially highly fruitful ways.

Second, realization of the potential value of their complementarity depends upon some movement, in both cases, from the extreme ends of the continuum. Third, time, energy and helpful procedures are needed to foster effective dialogue, exploring relationships between their two kinds of knowledge, including the development of new syntheses of the

*(Continued)*

*(Continued)*

two kinds of knowledge. When productive, this process of dialogue – which might be either metaphorical or literal – should culminate in classroom teachers themselves investigating the merits of research-based proposals by testing them through action research in their own teaching. This approach is based therefore on the premise that research can be helpful in improving the quality of classroom teaching, but equally on a second premise that research cannot be helpful except through quite complex processes culminating in classroom teachers engaging in dialogue with research-based proposals.

(McIntyre, 2005)

Furthermore, Zeichner (2003) also identified several conditions under which school-based teacher research can be a transformative professional development activity for teachers. These are:

- creating a culture of enquiry and respect for teacher knowledge
- encouraging learner-centred instruction
- teachers developing and controlling their own foci for enquiries
- engaging in collaborative work and study groups for intellectual challenge and stimulation.

## RESEARCHING PRACTICE AND CREATING KNOWLEDGE ABOUT TEACHING AND LEARNING

To research classroom practice involves searching for information and in the process creating new knowledge about particular teaching situations. In this way, teachers' personal tacit knowledge is extended through their daily experiences both inside and outside classrooms. However, for this tacit knowledge to be made explicit so that it can be shared with other practitioners, it must be articulated through dialogue and reflection and presented in a way that is meaningful to other practitioners and researchers, so that it will contribute to our understanding about how children learn and develop or better understand how schools function. Alternatively, this knowledge might involve the development of new ideas about innovative teaching approaches which might inform what other teachers do.

## Making more informed judgements through classroom-based research

Teachers choose how to act and decide what to do – that is, they exercise judgements. These judgements may be <u>intuitive</u> or explicit, often have important consequences and are not only driven by rational thinking but to a large degree by human experiences and emotions. Moreover, this professional judgement is always value-laden and not based simply on technical judgement. Becoming involved in classroom-based research involves standing back and identifying what your personal values are so that you can take these into account when interpreting what you see in classrooms. In other words, we learn to be teachers through the growing capacity to make appropriate judgements in the changing, and often unique, circumstances that occur in our different classrooms. However, with time, teachers become more familiar with classroom situations and there is a danger that we may come to react in ways we have always done instead of responding sensitively to situations. Having the opportunity to stand back and think about an issue or problem can aid such sensitivity.

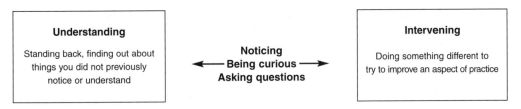

Figure I.2    Ways of researching schools

Researching our practice presents the opportunity to problem-solve more intelligently through drawing on existing research findings and by using rigorous methods to collect evidence which helps clarify our thinking. Experiences of participating in an informed way, and acting freshly, offer the teacher for whom teaching has become a routine a sense of freedom, of meaning, of worthiness and consequently increased self-esteem. Therefore, generating practice-based knowledge can often be liberating for the individual teacher while not necessarily being directly transferable to other classrooms.

It could be argued that the real value of classroom-based research is in the process of building the capacity to reflect critically on your own practice so that more students learn and that you better understand this process.

## Reflection and Reflexivity

The notion of reflection-in-action, and the term *reflective practitioner*, were first posited by Donald Schön in 1983 when he described how reflection-in-action could be used by professionals as a tool to improve their practice. He argued that reflection-in-action involves teachers retrospectively analysing their own actions and attempting to determine how these actions influence classroom events.

The notion of *reflexivity* goes further and requires more deliberative thinking. In other words, reflexivity is an interactive process that takes into consideration the relationship between the teacher, the students and the learning context, and also examines the underlying assumptions and priorities that shape interaction within a given time, place and situation. Furthermore, the process can also be transformative, in that, by definition, it requires a teacher to make a major shift in their understanding of classrooms. It is also integrative in that it involves interrogating taken-for-granted topics such as gender, policy or power. At its heart is the idea that practice is rooted in the same skills of critical thinking and sceptical inquiry that underlie most scientific and critical disciplines. Finally, it is certainly a problematic concept because it is always difficult to think reflexively and to challenge one's own presuppositions in relation to seemingly fundamental topics like assessment and gender.

To sum up, reflection is related to self and improving future practice through a retrospective analysis of action. Even in the reflection-in-action process, reflection is post facto, relating to completed stages and analysing them before taking the next step. Reflection is future-focused in that it seeks to improve practice through an understanding of the relative successes and failures of previous events. However, it remains connected to the past focusing on completed stages: reflection takes the form of a cumulative body of knowledge that can then be used to improve practice. Although reflection influences the development of reflexive practice, there are profound differences.

Being reflexive involves a teacher also being pro-active through explicitly requiring the re-evaluation of assumptions and priorities that shape classroom interactions. Reflexivity can be used to provide insight into priorities before the teacher reacts inappropriately. Reflexive practice in this manner can have an immediate impact in improving practice, as practitioners are able to incorporate new insights into each interaction.

Hence, one key difference relates to when the process of introspection takes place. In reflection, it takes place after an interaction, whereas the reflexive process incorporates interactive introspection into each interaction.

## CREATING NEW KNOWLEDGE ABOUT TEACHING AND LEARNING

In published educational literature about teaching and learning, the direction taken by professional researchers seems to follow two basic approaches. In simple terms, the first is educational research which is concerned with understanding how children learn and develop, and which is carried out through both empirical and theoretical studies. The outcome of this work is published in educational journals and textbooks.

Secondly and equally important to the classroom practitioner is classroom-based research which uses ideas often generated through knowledge created through empirical and theoretical work which are then used to inform what teachers do in their specific classrooms.

Both types of research are usually undertaken by large well-funded research groups and the outcomes are disseminated though conferences and journal articles. Examples of both sorts of approaches are given in the next two paragraphs.

### Research that contributes to understanding

Professor Neil Mercer, at the University of Cambridge, is a very experienced, prolific educational researcher and in the following extract he explains the rationale for a recent research project he undertook, which contributed to our understanding of how children learn through the use of dialogue. In an interview with the author he describes his research rationale:

> we realized that we wanted to know whether the kind of claims that were becoming common, based on Vygotsky's research back in the '30s, about the relationship between social interaction and children's cognitive development, were justified. It seemed to us that there wasn't actually any empirical evidence to show that Vygotsky's claim that children's interactions, with adults especially, and other people, shape the way they think. It seemed plausible and sensible, but was there any strong evidence? And we thought, well, we should try and look at whether there is, by setting up some sort of conditions in which we would say, well, children are given a special quality of interaction, a certain quality of interaction. We will then see if that affects what they learn and how well they understand things. And we will compare them systematically with children who are just going about life in a sort of ordinary way. So we had that theoretical interest — was Vygotsky right about the relationship between what he called the intra-mental or psychological, and the intermental or social?

The outcome of this particular research project has been published in a very influential book, *Words and Minds* (Mercer, 2000) – in other words, it has now become explicit, codified knowledge which is now considered to be essential subject knowledge for aspiring teachers.

## Creating practical knowledge based on an intervention

In a different research project, Professor Mercer and Doctor Lyn Dawes worked together on a classroom-based intervention in which teachers introduced group work to investigate what would happen if students were given more opportunity to engage in dialogue. Professor Mercer describes the research rationale for this practical-based, knowledge-generating project:

> We also were motivated by some practical questions, which was that people were concerned about the quality of groupwork in school, when children work together. One lot were saying 'groupwork's great', while another lot of people were saying 'it seems to be a bit of a waste of time. They should be sitting more and listening to teacher and so on, getting a lot more out of it'. And we thought, can we show that if you set up groupwork in a certain structured, organized way, it achieves certain sorts of goals, that you can say make it worthwhile?

The outcomes of both projects are published in the educational literature and while both projects are very relevant to classroom teaching, the work remains largely inaccessible to most school-based teachers.

Part of the process of teachers accessing this literature is to attempt to bridge the gap between such important codified knowledge and teachers' tacit everyday knowledge.

## TEACHERS CREATING NEW KNOWLEDGE ABOUT TEACHING AND LEARNING

Teachers can also create new knowledge which will be invaluable to them personally and to other practitioners in similar educational contexts. In the process of undertaking such research, a teacher will also come to better understand the dynamics of their classroom.

Finally, a further concern is the perceived imprecise nature of research undertaken by teachers. Teachers themselves often believe, together with other critics of small-scale qualitative studies, that the only legitimate research is large-scale and quantitative, seeking clear-cut conclusions and a steer for future strategies and policies.

Campbell and Jacques (2003) identified the key factors and issues in quality and economy from work with teacher/researchers in the Best Practice Research Scholarship (BPRS) projects as:

1. the autonomy and control of the research questioned by researchers
2. the quality of support for research projects in their design and implementation
3. robust self-monitoring, critical reflection and evaluation aimed at supporting the quality of research
4. transparent procedures for the dissemination and debate of research projects.

## HOW THIS BOOK WILL HELP

Written by members of the PGCE – M Level teaching team who cross the boundaries between academic research and classroom teaching as part of their role as teacher educators, each author has been a classroom teacher and so understands the complexity and tensions of being in the classroom from firsthand experience, but also contributes to the generation of academic codified research knowledge.

This book is aimed at beginning teachers involved in classroom research as part of their M-level initial teacher education as well as serving teachers completing Masters courses.

Our aim is to try to demystify the research process so that teachers can systematically research their classrooms in a rigorous way. To this end, we have illustrated the principles by exemplifying each stage using existing M-level and expert researchers' published work set in school contexts.

Box 3 shows the layout of the book.

## THE STRUCTURE OF THE BOOK

Section 1 is about critically engaging with the existing research literature and planning classroom-based research. Chapter 1 introduces the idea of becoming a reflexive teacher and guides the novice researcher through the process of critically reading existing literature. Chapter 2 provides help with refining the area of research into a research question

# BOX I.3

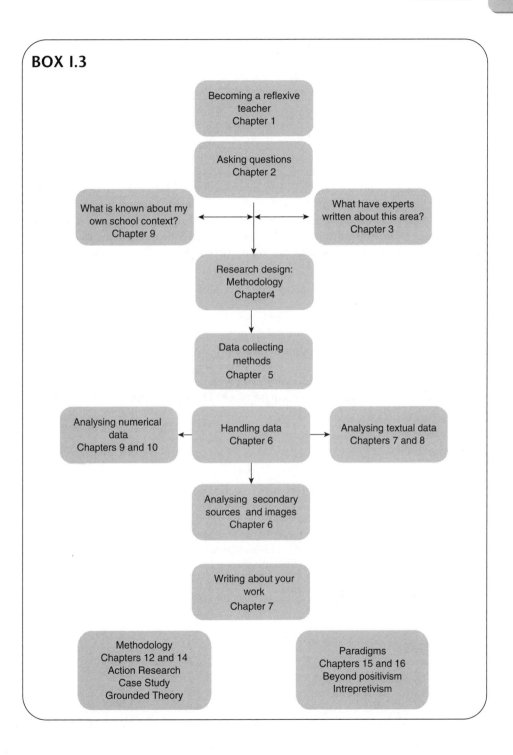

using examples of PGCE M-level work. Chapter 3 discusses how to review literature so that you can produce a literature review.

Section 2 is about carrying out and reporting on classroom-based research. Chapter 4 introduces methodology but from a research design perspective and finding the best methods to answer your question. Later on, when you come to write a thesis, you can extend your understanding of other possible methodology through reading Chapters 12–14 in Section 3, which look in depth at Action Research, using case studies and grounded theory.

Chapter 5 summarizes the limitations and strengths of each data collection method and Chapter 6 considers how to handle and analyse data. Chapters 7 and 8 deal with qualitative data which is mainly in the form of words and Chapters 9 and 10 look at quantitative data which is mainly in the form of numbers. The final part of Section 2, Chapter 11, provides advice on the difficult task of writing about your work.

Section 4 builds on the ideas of paradigms mentioned superficially in Chapter 1.

## Further Reading

Campbell, A. and Jacques, K. ( 2003) 'Best practice researched: teachers' perceptions of the impact of doing research in their classrooms and schools', *Teacher Development*, 7 (1): 75–90.

Furlong, J. (2007) 'Universities and Education', universities council for the Education of Teacher conference proceedings http://escalate.ac.uk/4154 (accessed 14 July 2008).

## References

McIntyre, D. (2005) 'Bridging the gap between research and practice', *Cambridge Journal of Education*, 35 (3): 357–82.

Mercer, N. (2000) *Words and Minds: How we Use Language Together*. London: Routledge.

Stenhouse, L. (1985) 'How teachers use research – an example', in J. Rudduck and D. Hopkins (eds) *Research as a Basis for Teaching*. London: Heinemann.

Zeichner, K. M. (2003) 'The adequacies and inadequacies of three current strategies to recruit, prepare, and retain the best teachers for all students', *Teachers College Record,* 105 (3): 490–519.

Schön, D. (1983) *The Reflective Practitioner: How professionals think in action*. London: Temple Smith.

# SECTION 1

## USING EXISTING RESEARCH TO UNDERSTAND AND PLAN YOUR OWN CLASSROOM-BASED RESEARCH

# BECOMING A REFLEXIVE TEACHER

## Elaine Wilson

Becoming a teacher involves more that just being 'told what to do', developing skills or mimicking other teachers. Therefore, reflecting *on* and *in* classrooms is an important part of becoming a teacher and is the essence of researching practice. Through the process of researching classroom practice, teachers come to recognize the depth and quality of their individual and collective expertise. Writing about this research is a way of articulating, sharing and examining practice which will also extend knowledge about teaching.

*practice => theory*
*reflection*

## TEACHING IS ABOUT INTERACTION

Teaching is an action which firstly aims to bring about learning, secondly takes account of where the learner is at, thirdly has regard for the nature of that which has to be learnt. Therefore, teaching chemistry is different from teaching swimming; teaching how to ride a bicycle is different from teaching how to be virtuous. Each activity requires a different knowledge base on the part of the teacher and a different approach to helping students learn. Indeed, it is difficult to justify an action which disregards either the state of readiness of a learner or the nature of the subject matter as teaching.

> The lecture on a complex scientific topic which pays no regard to the level of understanding of the audience could hardly be called teaching. (Pring, 2000, p. 23)

*really important*

Consequently, it seems to be the case that obtaining information about the state of readiness of the learner is as important as having extensive subject-specific knowledge. Furthermore, the three components of teaching are more likely to be realized through reflecting *in* and *on* actual classrooms, by teachers finding out about learners in those classrooms and through the subsequent adoption of appropriate approaches to bridge the knowledge gap between learner and teacher.

> **BOX 1.1**
>
> Teaching therefore is the conscious effort to bridge the gap between the state of mind of the learner and the subject matter (the public forms of knowledge and understanding) which is to be learnt, and as such the teacher's expertise lies in understanding both.

It is possible for a teacher to use a wide range of activities, for example: instruction, questioning, arranging practical experiences or through structuring the classroom in a particular way, as long as students learn what the teacher intended.

Therefore, becoming a teacher initially involves questioning how expert classroom teachers:

1. decide on how to bring about learning
2. ensure that the chosen activities are relevant to the kind of learning to be brought about
3. ensure that these activities are relevant to the state of mind and motivation of the learner.

However, teachers do not act on their own. They are part of a larger enterprise, and their authority derives from their participation in communicating to another generation the public understandings and procedures we have inherited. Consequently, teachers ought to be aware of the origins of their specific area of public understanding and how the procedures in operation have come about.

## EDUCATIONAL DISCOURSE

To engage in dialogue with other teachers, parents and students involves using educational discourse, that is, the way in which we talk about educational practice. However, educational discourse, like other forms of specialist discourse, is constructed by the specialist group and serves the interests of the particular group. In some situations, where such discourse remains unchallenged, it comes to be perceived and experienced by groups as though it offers an explanation of a natural, shared process or common sense wisdom. An example of this is pupil grouping in secondary schools where the common practice is to group students according to 'ability'. In this case, 'ability' has become a 'common sense' concept that in the UK is seen as a natural way of talking about children. However, there are those who dispute this – for example, Bourne and Moon (1995) argue that although we have words such as intelligence and ability, this 'does not mean that they exist any more than the unicorn does'. Talking about ability seems a natural way of talking and so people do not normally challenge this idea, although there is considerable scope for confusion. For instance, Hart et al. (2004) pose the following questions:

- When young people are identified as 'more able' or 'less able' than others, are we saying something about innate intelligence or the inherent capacity to learn?
- Are we implying a fixed or stable difference in degree between those deemed more able and those deemed less able?
- Or are we simply saying something about differences in their current ability to perform certain tasks, their observable ability to do certain things – like reading or mathematical calculations – according to agreed criteria?

Furthermore, if it is important that teaching activities are related to the state of mind and readiness of our students to learn, ought we not to examine this 'common sense' idea of 'ability' more closely? To do this may require us to open our minds to new ideas, to become a reflexive teacher.

## BECOMING A REFLEXIVE TEACHER

Reflexivity is an interactive process which takes into consideration the relationship between the teacher, the students and the learning context, and also examines the underlying assumptions and priorities that shape interaction within a given time, place and situation. In other words, a reflexive teacher can stand back and examine the underlying beliefs and values which are informing decision-making and actions in classroom situations (see Figure 1.1). These 'hidden' beliefs and values influence our interpretation of 'grey, common sense ' areas such as ability labelling, but it is the ability to be reflexive that will enable us to look at situations, ask further questions and find alternate interpretations.

## CHALLENGING 'COMMON SENSE' IDEAS

A feature of common sense is its changing content. What is common sense at one time may no longer be so at another; what is not known at one time might become part of the unquestioned folklore later. On the other hand, common sense understanding also includes beliefs which seem undeniable, particularly in relation to the physical, personal and social worlds that we live in. To differentiate between ideas which might be classified as part of an indispensable framework within which we identify and think about the physical and social world and the second category which are part of a shared discourse of unquestioned beliefs about education, it requires that we test out these ideas. Teacher-led, classroom-based research may provide an authentic way of testing out such ideas. Pring (2000) argues that classroom-based research 'percolates down to the unquestioned assumptions of everyday life' (p. 84) and that the 'education of common sense' lies in the acquisition of a questioning and critical approach to ideas which appear to be accepted uncritically. Moreover, this framework of ordinary language, together with the accompanying beliefs about the world of education, provides both the

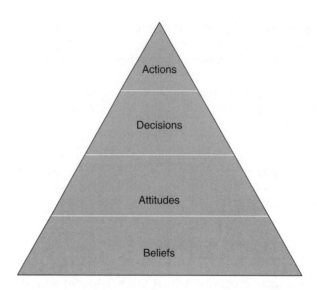

Figure 1.1   Becoming self-aware

starting point and the point of application of existing theoretical knowledge about teaching. In other words, to try to address Hart's questions, we must recognize that ideas emerge from different disciplines and that different theoretical accounts help us to arrive at a clearer understanding of the various perspectives held.

---

## BOX 1.2

### Establishing your world view

How you try to understand the world around you will colour what you consider to be evidence. Searle's big question below brings this point across well:

> How can we square the self-conception of ourselves as mindful, meaning-creating, free, rational, etc., agents with a universe that consists entirely of mindless, meaningless, unfree, non-rational, brute physical particles? (Searle, 2007)

Searle's question confronts us with ideas that we don't usually stop to think about in the rush of everyday life. Nonetheless, these 'hidden' views influence how we think about complex issues and raise further questions. What is your world view? How does your world view influence how you behave in your everyday and professional life? How will you study the world? Are the rules for studying the natural or social world the same? (See Chapters 15 and 16.)

| Knowledge is objective | Knowledge is constructed |
|---|---|
| Objects are independent of our perspective | We all see things from different perspectives |
| Knowledge is accumulated through measurement | Knowledge is constructed through social interaction |

Figure 1.2    What is your world view?

Positivist ← World view → Intrepretivist

World view → How will you study the world ?

Figure 1.3    Positivist of Interpretivist?

## USING EXISTING RESEARCH LITERATURE

A trawl of educational literature about teaching will illustrate just how complex class-rooms are and the diverse ways in which research about them is conducted. In some work, people are the 'objects of science' where the researchers attempt to draw general-ized and causal explanations. In other work, researchers try to explain what is happen-ing through interpreting the world in their own personal ways. Understanding human beings, and thus researching into what they do and how they behave, calls upon many different methods, each making complex assumptions about what it means to explain behaviours and personal and social activities.

Furthermore, all forms of research are informed by underlying theoretical perspec-tives. Each of us has a theoretical perspective, even though this may not always be immediately apparent. When we read experts' work, we ought to be aware of the theo-retical perspectives informing their viewpoint and appreciate the methods used to col-lect the evidence, interpret findings and draw conclusions. The various methods used will make claims to generating knowledge about aspects of the area of study but each method will have a different role, position and purpose. Accordingly, work published from disparate studies will need different types of critical appraisal, be brought together and interrelated with great care; and will need to be selected and combined in response to the kind of question being asked.

## CRITICAL READING ACTIVITY

In this section, examples of papers representing three different theoretical perspectives to pupil grouping are used to illustrate the points made in the previous section. This chapter will serve as an introduction to theoretical perspectives which will be explored in more detail later in the book. Table 1.1 (page 22) summarizes the approaches used by the three theoretical perspectives drawn on in the reading activity. This activity will also help you to read educational research critically.

*find*

### Activity 1.1    Tips for reading the text

As you read the work, you will <u>find</u> that some parts of the text contain critical, conceptual or causal arguments which should be read very carefully and repeatedly if necessary; others contain illustrative materials and empirical elaborations which can be read more rapidly.

Annotate the text as you read it marking the progression, twists and turns of the argument as it unfolds. You can devise your own stenographic system (arrows, stars, circling, underlining, etc.) to highlight in a consistent and economical manner the main definitions, logical turning points, conclusions and implications. Don't highlight too much text as this will be unhelpful.

Pay attention to passages that confuse. It may be, as you begin to read educational research literature, that the terms or language used by an author may seem confusing, or that the writing may be impenetrable. With patience and perseverance, you will come to be able to read texts critically but they will take a bit more time than reading prose that is written to be more accessible. Note down the source of confusion. Is there a key term being used in an unfamiliar or unclear way? If so, revisit the beginning of the text (or any other passages that set up the framework of the argument) to see if there are helpful definitions.

Try untangling complex syntax to see if the writer's meaning becomes clear (and then, having learned a bit about the writer's habits, learn what you know to unravel other difficult passages). Ignoring difficult vocabulary or passages will likely leave you unclear about the author's overall work.

Use whatever devices (tables, lists, bullets, diagrams, etc.) give you the best synoptic and synthetic view of the piece you've read. Try to represent the major argument in another form, perhaps as a diagram. Your reading notes will be an invaluable self-teaching and learning aid later.

The first paper by Wiliam and Bartholomew (2004) (1) is an example of work under-pinned by what are termed positivist/objectivist theoretical perspectives where the methodological approach is based on the scientific method. The knowledge reported in the work is based on an assumption that the world exists in an objectively knowable, singular, natural law-abiding reality. The goal of this method is to predict and control in ways that apply across all contexts. The researcher's perspective is distant and removed from the object of the research.

The second paper by Bolaer, Wiliam and Brown (2000) (2) is underpinned by what are termed constructionist/intrepretivist theoretical perspectives where the method-ological approach is based on interpreting the views and experiences of students in classrooms. The researcher reduces the complex responses which are not easily quan-tifiable and interprets these within the contexts of the schools involved in the research.

The third paper by Cremin and Thomas (2005) (3) is informed by critical theory which calls for a radical restructuring of grouping toward the ends of social justice. Whereas critical theory does not dictate a particular methodology, the focus on eman-cipation is congruent with the same ideas about how we come to know and how ideas come into existence as that which underpins constructionism.

## Activity 1.2

Read all three articles and while you are reading the work, consider the following questions:

- What do the authors intend to do in the writing?
- What is the problem the authors are trying to resolve?
- What concepts are being used to develop a solution to the problem?
- What evidence do the authors bring to bear on the issue?
- Do the authors argue the points well? Is the work logically consistent and empirically adequate, plausible or convincing and why (not)? What alternative or rival arguments come to mind?
- How does this work fit in with your views of your own education so far?
- How does this work fit in with your views of what you have observed in classrooms so far?
- How does this work fit in with other work that you may have read about the subject so far?
- What are your views about grouping? Have these views altered after reading this work?
- Why do you think that grouping in secondary schools is common practice?

All three papers are available online using an Athens password to log in. See the refer-ences for details.

Table 1.1 Comparing three papers from different theoretical perspectives based on ideas about ability grouping

| Type | Empirical Studies | | Theoretical Study |
|---|---|---|---|
| Paper | 1. Wiliam and Bartholomew (2004) | 2. Boaler, Wiliam and Brown (2000) | 3. Cremin and Thomas (2005) |
| Aim | To investigate the influence of ability grouping on student progress. | To investigate the experiences of pupils in ability groups. | To challenge the idea that comparison of students is a major factor in the alienation and exclusion experienced by students in schools. |
| Stance of the researcher | Analysing the outcomes of teaching so the researcher is distanced from the subject of the research. | Observing in classrooms, so involved in and aware of the students' experience. | Completely removed from actual schools approaching the issue from a theoretical stance. |
| Type of reasoning | *Deductive:* that is the conclusions are reached by using 'factual' data, such as student examination performance. Therefore, if the premises are true, i.e. test scores, then the conclusions must also be true. | *Inductive:* that is the premise of the argument, the students' views, support the inferred conclusions that there is disaffection and polarization among students. | *Inductive:* the argument that self-comparison of each student and the endorsement of such a comparison by schools support the conclusion that students are segregated and therefore feel alienated and excluded in schools. |
| Research plan | Longitudinal study over four years following the progress of a large sample of students moving through KS3 testing and through to GCSE examinations. | Part of a longer study. This work focuses on the experiences of Y8 students moving into Y9 and beyond. | Historical account of contrastive judgements and the presentation of a theoretical model to account for the root of difficulty in schools. |
| Methods used and analysis | Large-scale questionnaire, using 955 students in six schools. Information collected about: socio-economic status of parents, pupil outcome data for KS3 tests and GCSE examinations. Results analysed using statistical methods to investigate correlations. | Classroom observation of lessons and questionnaire about student attitudes and beliefs about lessons. Interviews with pairs of students. Data is analysed and ascribed properties related to types identified from observation and students' responses. | Review of existing literature to support a theoretical model. |
| Theoretical perspective | The world exists in objectively knowable natural law-abiding reality. | The human world is socially constructed. | Society organizes itself in oppressive ways and should be transformed. |
| Ideas about the nature of knowledge | Things exist as meaningful entities; they have truth and meaning residing within them and can be measured. | Knowledge and therefore meaningful reality are constructed in and out of interaction between humans. | Research knowledge serves the interests of particular groups. |

## KEY IDEAS

Becoming a teacher involves learning how to bridge the gap between the state of mind of the learner and the subject matter which is to be learnt. This can be done through questioning expert teachers, and through reflecting *on* and *in* classrooms. To teach requires cognizance about how to bring about learning; choose activities that are relevant to the kind of learning to be brought about and ensure that activities are relevant to the state of mind and motivation of the learner.

However, teachers work within larger schools which are bound by procedures and expectations. These procedures and expectations are determined by the wider educational world. Within this educational world, people have a shared discourse which includes common sense wisdom which may contradict the requirements of the classroom teacher for matching the state of mind and motivation of students but which nonetheless has become part of the procedures. One example of this is the practice of grouping pupils according to a notion of 'ability'. To fully engage with all the views about this issue requires awareness that we all have theoretical perspectives on which our beliefs are based. Additionally, we need to understand the basis on which these views have been formed. The final section of the chapter explores three different theoretical perspectives on grouping, summarizing the differences in approach and also providing guidance on how to critically read research literature.

## *References*

Bolaer, J., Wiliam, D. and Brown, M. (2000) 'Students' experiences of ability grouping: disaffection, polarisation and the construction of failure', *British Educational Research Journal*, 26 (5) 631–48.

Bourne, J. and Moon, B. (1995) 'A question of ability?', in B. Moon and A. Shelton Mayes (eds) *Teaching and Learning in the Secondary School*. London: Routledge.

Cremin, H. and Thomas, G. (2005) 'Maintaining under classes via contrastive judgement: can inclusive education ever happen?', *British Journal of Educational Studies*, 53 (4), 431–46.

Hart, S., Dixon, A., Drummond, M. and McIntyre, D. (2004) *Learning without Limits*. Maidenhead: Open University Press/McGraw-Hill.

Pring, R. (2000) *Philosophy of Educational Research*. London: Continuum.

Searle, J. (2007) *Freedom and Neurobiology: Reflections on Free Will, Language, and Political Power*. New York: Columbia Press.

Wiliam, D. and Bartholomew, H. (2004) 'It's not which school but which set you're in that matters: the influence of ability grouping practices on students' progress in mathematics', *British Educational Research Journal*, 30 (2), 279–93.

# 2 REFINING THE FOCUS FOR RESEARCH AND FORMULATING A RESEARCH QUESTION

Elaine Wilson

## Hints

- Investigate something that you are genuinely interested in researching.
- Situate your inquiry in your own workplace if possible.
- Narrow the focus of your research down to something that is manageable.
- Formulate your research area into a question or questions which can then be answered.

## INTRODUCTION

It is really important that you refine your initial research concern into precisely formulated research questions. However, this process is not straightforward or linear. Indeed, you may well change direction once you start to read more and talk with colleagues. Nonetheless, you must start off by trying to narrow your focus if your research is to be worthwhile. It is also important to recognize that undertaking a research enquiry will make extra demands on your time, energy and resources, so your enquiry must be realistically manageable on top of your teaching role and where possible be seen as no more than extending the activities you are already engaged in within your own classroom or school. The further removed your research is from your usual professional work, the more difficult it will be to undertake. Furthermore, carrying out an enquiry which is not directly related to your own interest or professional work will be less useful to you. Ideas for research will emerge from your own interests and experiences. This might be a new curriculum development, a recurring difficulty, an idea you encountered on a course or as a result of reading a research paper. Moving from a research topic to a research question is an important next step.

**Activity 2.1**

**Generating ideas**

Brainstorming is a free-association technique of spontaneously listing all words, concepts, ideas, questions and knowledge about a topic. Start by making a lengthy list about the areas you are interested in researching.

**Sorting ideas**

Next, sort these ideas into categories. This allows you to sort out your current awareness of the area, decide what perspectives are most interesting and/or relevant, and decide in which direction to steer your research. Create a concept map from the categories you arrived at in the brainstorming stage. Concept maps may be elaborate or simple and are designed to help you organize your thinking about a topic, recognize where you have gaps in your knowledge, and help to generate specific questions that may guide your research. Having done that, decide if you now know enough about the area. Do you need to do further reading? Are you ready to go onto the next stage of 'drilling down' to the core of the problem?

'Drilling down' is a term taken from management literature and simply involves analysing the research area from various perspectives to help narrow the focus. Figure 2.1 provides an example in an educational context where a teacher identified her area of interest as characteristics of successful lessons. This is a huge and complex area so the teacher first considered what a successful lesson might look like from her own perspective as the teacher, then from the school perspective and finally from the students' perspective. This led on to a series of second-level questions such as: how will I know if the students are learning? As a result of this process, the teacher decided to focus on the students' perspectives of successful lessons. This helped to identify other ideas and raised further questions such as: Are the students able to do the work I set? Do they believe they are able to do the work I set? How do students perceive my role? Do students think the work is worthwhile? Do they enjoy the work? In this case, the teacher decided to explore this aspect further through asking a few students for their ideas, talking to colleagues and searching out recent research in the area of student voice and motivation before attempting to formulate her research question. In the next section, I will introduce other strategies that might help you to formulate your questions.

## FORMULATING THE RESEARCH QUESTION

Having decided on and refined your research area, you then need to narrow this down into a researchable question. For example, talk in class is a good area for research but

Figure 2.1    Drilling down to the core of the issue

still needs turning into a narrower research question, such as: what sort of talk do students engage in during groupwork in science lessons?

To start out, you might also find it helpful to ask yourself the following questions (see also Figure 2.2):

1.  What is known already about this area and what have experts already written about this area? (See Chapter 3 on reviewing literature.)
2.  What do colleagues in my school think about this area? What does my higher-degree tutor advise me to do?
3.  Why am I doing this research?

## RESEARCH PURPOSE: WHY ARE YOU DOING THE RESEARCH?

Having a clear idea about the rationale for doing your research is important. The main reasons teachers give for undertaking research are listed in Box 2.1.

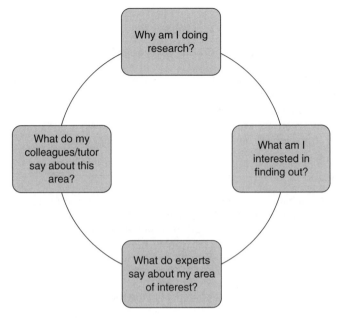

Figure 2.2   Formulating a research question

---

## BOX 2.1

### Teachers' classroom-based research

Firstly, to explore what is happening in your classroom or to seek new insights into your classrooms. For example:

- How do teachers manage their classes? What are the classroom rules? How are elements such as time, space, pupil behaviour or their own strategies managed?
- How are classroom decisions made: by the teacher, by pupils, or by both by negotiation?
- How is pupils' work monitored and assessed in the classroom?
- How do teachers explain new topics to pupils?

Secondly, to describe or portray an accurate profile of persons, events or situations which will require extensive knowledge of the situation. For example:

- What do teachers and pupils do in the classroom? How do they spend their time?
- What kind of interaction takes place, who talks to whom and about what?

*(Continued)*

*(Continued)*

- What do pupils learn, what tasks do they engage in, and with what degree of involvement and success?
- What is a school day or a lesson like from a pupil's point of view? Are any individuals or groups getting a relatively poor deal out of schooling?
- What happens when pupils disrupt lessons or behave in an anti-social manner?
- What happens when children work in small groups? What sorts of assignments are undertaken? Who decides what? Are the groups collaborative?

Thirdly, to explain a situation or problem, account for patterns relating to the phenomena being researched, or to identify relationships. For example:

- Do teachers and children perceive the same events in different or similar ways?
- Do children read better as a result of a new programme?
- Do children read better in this programme compared with the standard programme?
- Do teachers in the same school or department have similar or different practices, beliefs, expectations, rewards and punishments, and conventions, and how are these understood by the pupils?

Fourthly, to intervene to bring about changes in your classroom. For example:

- Can I raise students' self-esteem in my lessons?
- How can I improve my own teaching?
- What happens in the classroom when there is a change of policy, a new curriculum, work scheme, textbook, course, or new forms of assessment?

For example, a secondary school English teacher was dissatisfied with the way her students wrote biographical sketches and on 'drilling down' found that her students did not know how to structure or correct their writing. She decided that she would intervene to develop and evaluate a new teaching approach. The teacher's key research question was 'What teaching strategies will help my students recognize the gaps and mistakes in their writing?', and a sub-question was 'How can I help my students write better transitions?'. The new approach involved setting up situations for her students to do peer editing using a new guide designed to help them locate transitions and missing transitions in the text. She monitored the students' work during and following the intervention.

Formulating a clearly stated question will help you to decide on the most useful data to collect to answer your research question. Moreover having a clear focus will also prevent you stashing away too much information that *may* be vaguely relevant. Having too broad an approach is more likely to cause you angst because of the sheer volume and complexity of information available. In the example given in Figure 2.3 the teacher has narrowed her original very broad approach to a much narrower and manageable question: 'How can I increase students' self-esteem in my lessons?'.

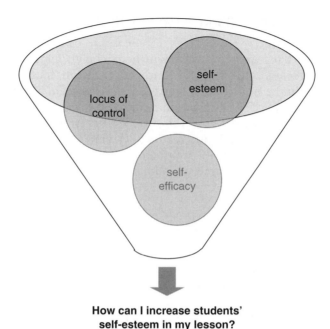

How can I increase students'
self-esteem in my lesson?

Figure 2.3    Narrowing your focus

Additionally, having a clear open-ended research question calls for deep thinking about issues and makes it easier to know when you have done enough reading.

Furthermore, it is vital that you focus on a research area that is manageable in the timescale you have available to you and that what you set out to find what is measurable. For instance, it is very difficult to measure understanding directly as in the case of students' understanding of addition and subtraction. This is because understanding these concepts, facts and skills occurs within the student and requires probing more explicitly; therefore a more useful variable to investigate would be to measure student accuracy in applying addition and subtraction by counting the number of times each student answered subtraction and addition problems correctly.

Finally, beware of trying to measure impact or of trying to attribute increased understanding or better pupil test performance directly to your new teaching approach, because there are many variables in each very different classroom. Be cautious in making such causal claims. There is a tendency to want to link pupils' outcomes directly to teaching approaches, however, there are many mediating factors in operation such as the motivation and aptitude of individual students, the mix of students in your class and the resultant classroom dynamics which could account for changes.

## LOOKING AT EXPERT RESEARCHERS' QUESTIONS

Reading more expert researchers' work will help you to learn how to undertake classroom-based research. Identify the authors' research focus and locate their research questions. In the final published paper this will seem like a straightforward linear process moving effortlessly from identifying a focus through to formulating the question, but as you now know this was probably not the case. The expert researchers will also have spent hours reading relevant literature, thought long and hard about the purpose of their research before finally framing the research questions. Consider the style of research questions that expert researchers use in their work set out in Box 2.2.

---

### BOX 2.2

**An example of an expert researcher's school-based research**

Paper used: O'Brien, C. (2007) 'Peer devaluation in British secondary schools: young people's comparisons of group-based and individual-based bullying', *Educational Research*, 49 (3), 297–324.

O'Brien sets out her research area early in the opening pages; this is to focus on young adolescents' perceptions of two distinguishable bases for being bullied:

1. For group membership, such as one's race or sex as a whole.
2. For individual, unique differences.

At the end of her literature review and before her methods section, she also clearly states her research questions.

This exploratory study has a threefold aim:

1. Do students evaluate pejorative names differentially?
2. How do students justify their value judgements? On what dimensions are group and individual-based name-calling perceived as similar and different?
3. Are appraisals comparable? Are we comparing 'apples and oranges'?

---

### Activity 2.2

Use the grid in Figure 2.4 below to help you clarify your thoughts about your focus and research question.

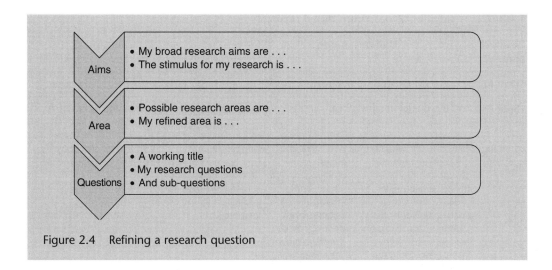

Figure 2.4    Refining a research question

## FURTHER EXAMPLES OF CLASSROOM-BASED RESEARCH PROJECTS

Table 2.1 below shows four further examples of classroom-based research. In these examples, the work was undertaken by beginning teachers during their initial teacher education. Two research projects were stimulated by a developing awareness of practice through exposure to new ideas, and the broad research aims were to better understand history teaching and student motivation. The history teacher set out 'primarily to problematize or characterize an aspect of subject learning', while the motivation study was an attempt at understanding why a small group of boys were disaffected in science lessons.

The other two projects took the form of an intervention whereby both teachers tried a new approach and monitored the effect on student learning.

## THE M-LEVELNESS OF PGCE WORK

Each university will have specific criteria for judging M-level work which is used to assess and make judgements about students' work. However, in the introduction we set out generic descriptors for Masters level work which I will use here to illustrate how PGCE school-based research can met these requirements.

In essence, these require that Masters level work demonstrates:

- knowledge and understanding
- the application of knowledge and understanding through problem-solving abilities
- the ability to integrate knowledge and handle complexity by making judgements

**Table 2.1  Examples of classroom-based research**

| Research aim | Understanding | | Intervention | |
|---|---|---|---|---|
| Stimulus | Develop new awareness | | Dissatisfaction with practice | |
| Topic area | History teaching | Motivation | Modern languages | Group work |
| Emerging questions | Elaborate the working conceptual apparatus around moral vs. historical debate, in order to strengthen the analytic power of the definitions/goals history teachers work with. What concerns in my own practice am I seeking to address and illuminate? Justify and define focus on pupil *experience*. | Why are some pupils disengaged with school work? What prevents students from working? What is work-avoidant behaviour? | Differentiation? Can teachers of MFL differentiate lessons? Is there evidence of impact on FL learning? | Can A-level chemistry teaching be less didactic? |
| Working title | A critical analysis of commonality and divergence across moral reasoning and causal reasoning, drawing upon a study of four Year 9 pupils' experience of constructing causal explanations of the Holocaust. | A case study of Y9 examining pupils' self-perceptions towards learning in a science classroom. | A critical analysis of the impact of teaching strategies that cater for differentiation in a class of Y9 pupils of French learning the perfect tense. | Does the use of active teaching approaches to encourage independent learning increase students' understanding in Year 12 chemistry lessons? |
| Research questions | What forms did pupils' reasoning (oral and written) take? How might those forms be classified? What *counts* as 'reasoning' for me as a history teacher? How adequate is the existing conceptual apparatus for framing these pupils' reasoning experiences? | Why do pupils display work-avoidant behaviour in my Y9 class? | How does the use of different modes of differentiation impact on individual learning? What are the key features of an effective differentiated approach? What are the pupils' perceptions of the differentiated teaching approach? | (1) As far as the pupils themselves are concerned, are lessons dominated by symmetrical dialogue more effective at developing their understanding than lessons without such a bias? (2) Does a topic taught through symmetrical dialogue result in enhanced test performances, compared to a topic taught without such a bias? |

- the communication of conclusions and underpinning knowledge and rationale to specialist and non-specialist audiences
- the ability to study in a manner that may be largely self-directed or autonomous.

In the next section, I will use a further example of PGCE – M level work to illustrate how school-based research can meet these descriptors of M 'levelness'. Further examples will be continually added to the website. (See http://www. schoolbasedresearch.co.uk)

The work used was submitted by Owain, a beginning teacher completing a one-year PGCE M-level secondary science course. This work is the final 8500-word report of a classroom-based case study undertaken in the second and third terms of his professional school placement.

The title of his work is: 'A Case Study of Assessment for Learning: A Critical Analysis of the Perceptions and Interactions of Science Students Engaged in Peer-Assessment Exercises in a Year 10 Triple Set *Living and Growing* Teaching Episode'.

This work extends Owain's knowledge and understanding through applying ideas in a research context. It also illustrates how Owain applies knowledge and understanding through problem-solving in a new classroom environment within broader multidisciplinary contexts. Box 2.3 provides Owain's rationale for undertaking this work.

---

## Box 2.3    Introduction

Assessment, the judgement or evaluation of students' learning and understanding [Sadler, 1989], is traditionally associated with testing and examination or a sequence of teacher-led questions. With the inception of league tables, emphasis on summative assessment in schooling has increased. Arguably this is detrimental to learning and understanding, which the summative method, by definition, contributes little to [Black and Wiliam, 1998b]. However, assessment need not exclusively be summative, an assessment *of* learning, but rather may be used to inform and enhance understanding: an assessment *for* learning (AfL). This enables students to become aware of the quality of understanding they demonstrate and how they can improve, a process more efficacious than trial-and-error learning, constituting an evaluative feedback loop [Sadler, 1989]. Using formative assessment effectively could therefore bring learning to learn, rather than learning to be tested to the forefront of education [Black and Wiliam, 1998b; Black, McCormick, James and Pedder, 2006]. Interest in using AfL strategies is evident from the numerous research articles, which examine their effects on students and teachers at all educational levels.

Given the learning benefits that AfL strategies may provide, I undertook a case study investigating the classroom use of peer-assessment in a context under-explored in the existing literature. The participants were members of my Year 10 triple award class, at a Suffolk upper school, studying a GCSE biology module. I first aimed to describe the students' perceptions of peer-assessment and the relationship between how they thought it had affected their learning, and their assessed understanding of the material. Secondly, exploring the process, rather than the outcome, I examined the intra-peer-assessment student interactions. This research was carried out in accordance with the ethical guidelines specified by the British Educational Research Association [BERA, 2004: 4], with the participants' informed, voluntary consent. Only students' first names are used in this report.

To help orientate/his thinking, Owain read about existing research in his area of interest – assessment for learning – and wrote a literature review (see Chapter 3). The summary of this review is set out in Box 2.4. This review provides evidence of Owain's extended knowledge and understanding of the area of assessment for learning.

---

### Box 2.4

### Summary (of the literature review)

This review demonstrates the large extent to which the study of formative assessment is influenced by theoretical perspectives. Peer-assessment has been identified as one method by which formative assessment may be facilitated. Studies of classroom implementation show it to be a practicable option that has met with the approval of teachers. However, relatively little investigation has focused on how peer-assessment in science lessons, or indeed in secondary education, in this country is seen by the individuals most intimately involved in the process. Neither has the nature of the exchanges that occur between the students, which contribute to the theorised effects of peer-assessment, been examined. As Cowie comments: 'Despite the need for active pupil participation, very little is known about pupil perceptions and experiences of assessment for learning' [Cowie, 2005: 138]. These issues will be considered in the establishing of my research focus in the following section.

---

Owain then identified three research questions which he proposed investigating in his placement schools.

---

### Box 2.5

### Research Sub-questions

To achieve a more holistic understanding of the peer-assessment, more emphasis on analysing the process from the learners' perspectives is needed. Three research sub-questions (RQs) are therefore proposed for investigation in my case study to fulfil this overarching analytical aim:

- RQ1: What are the students' perceptions of peer-assessment?
- RQ2: How do the students interact with each other during peer-assessment exercises?
- RQ3: Is there parity between the students' perceptions of the effectiveness of peer-assessment with regard to their learning and their actual attainment?

---

In his final report, he discussed how he went about answering his research questions. He set out his research design (see Chapter 4) and explained how he would collect and analyse data.

This report provides evidence of Owain making judgements by demonstrating the ability to integrate knowledge and handle complexity, and formulate judgements with incomplete data.

His written report communicated his conclusions, underpinning knowledge and rationale to other teachers and colleagues in his placement school. Although he worked with a university-based tutor and school-based mentor, he did undertake the study in a manner that was largely self-directed or autonomous. Owain's final summary is set out in Box 2.5.

---

## BOX 2.6

This case study found that students' perceptions of peer-assessment encompassed a broad range of positive and negative aspects, depending on the individual, that were largely consistent with those documented in the literature. A key issue for some students was their unfamiliarity with peer-assessment and consequent difficulty in carrying out the protocol, which led them to perceive it as ineffective. To some extent this may explain the findings regarding the students' interactions when engaged in peer-assessment. These were characterised by their briefness and limited exchange of formative verbal feedback. The evidence regarding the relationship between students' perceptions of their understanding and the understanding they demonstrate is limited by the validity of the measures used and the complexities of performing such a comparison.

While these conclusions have validity in the ecological and methodological context of the present study, caution should be taken in generalisation, given I) the peer-assessment protocol's specificity and II) the composition, age and attainment range of the class. There are many different ways of implementing peer-assessment and an even larger suite of AfL strategies. My findings should thus be used as a tentative indicator for how students *might* respond, given a sufficient degree of similarity to the research context described here. Next steps in this research area could be to investigate differences in perceptions and interactions between different groups of students, introduce further methods of formative assessment and investigate how they are received or begin to consider how the protocol employed could be modified to increase its effectiveness, approaching the enquiry as action research.

The aim of this study was to investigate how peer-assessment is viewed and enacted by students, breaking from the tendency of writings on assessment to focus on the teacher's role [Brookhart, 2001]. However, in my own role as a teacher, the experience of teaching a peer-assessment episode has been valuable for informing my practice. I have learned that the exercise *may* be perceived as a positive educational experience and can be successful, provided that necessarily clear instructions and sufficient time are given and that students are familiar with AfL strategies. I would consider using peer-assessment less often, introducing it gradually over an extended time period with simpler methods of self- and peer-assessment, as recommended by both the literature and the participating students. This leads on to my final point, regarding student voice. Some of the comments received from students relating to peer-assessment were

*(Continued)*

*(Continued)*

remarkably perceptive, demonstrating a good awareness of what helped and hindered their learning and how activities could be modified and improved to further facilitate this. With the caveat of class composition, I will endeavour in the future to provide the opportunity for students to give oral and written feedback on 'the process' of their classroom learning and use this to inform and adapt my teaching to produce improved outcomes for all.

## KEY IDEAS

It is likely that your research will solve significant problems in your own classroom and expand your knowledge base of teaching and learning, therefore it is going to be a demanding process. Moreover, such an enquiry will require discipline, stamina and hard work on your part, but as a result of engaging in meaningful activity of community and scholarship, you will come to understand your practice better. In order that you can do this well, it is really important that you start the research process by refining your initial research concern into precisely formulated research questions. Your research will be more relevant, useful and manageable if it is closely related to an area of interest, does not overly extend your everyday role and can be done within the time constraints. Additionally, when designing the research and defining the data collection methods, try to manage any potential biases/subjectivities you may have. Furthermore, to be useful, your work ought to make a contribution to teacher knowledge so to this end seek the support and guidance of a critical friend if you feel you do not have the skills and expertise necessary to carry out the research.

 *Further Reading*

Bell, J. (1999) *Doing your Research Project*. Buckingham: Open University Press.

Denscombe, M. (1998) *The Good Research Guide for Small-scale Social Research Projects*. Buckingham: Open University Press.

# USING AND REVIEWING LITERATURE
## Elaine Wilson

**Hints**

- The literature review stage of a research project is very important, so don't rush this part.
- Search as many sources as you can but have a rationale for what you keep.
- Make sure you have clear search parameters.
- Set up reference management systems right at the beginning of your research project.
- Read efficiently and effectively.
- Don't ignore work that seems to contradict your ideas; consider the counter arguments.

## INTRODUCTION

A literature review should meet three criteria: firstly, to present results of similar studies; secondly, to relate your study to the ongoing dialogue in the literature; and thirdly, to provide a framework for comparing the results of a study with other studies. To accomplish this, you will need to: identify suitable search terms; locate appropriate literature; read and check the relevance of the literature; organize the literature you have selected; and, finally, write a literature review.

Set out in the five stages, it may look like a straightforward process, however, there are many steps involved. Indeed, more experienced researchers often assume that these steps are obvious and straightforward for a novice. This is not the case. Consequently, this chapter is written with the complete novice in mind. The structure of this chapter will follow the five stages mentioned earlier, although the writing stage will be discussed in Chapter 7. I will start by considering the purpose of reviewing the literature and of writing a literature review.

# WHAT IS THE PURPOSE OF REVIEWING THE LITERATURE?

Working with literature is an essential part of the research process. If you do this thoroughly and critically, the process will help you to generate new ideas and direct your research questions while also being an integral part of planning your research design.

In other words, the actual process of doing a review is an initial important step in carrying out good research and the outcome of this process, in the form of a written literature review, will provide the evidence that you have been thorough in situating your own work.

Moreover, the purposes of undertaking a literature review are threefold. The first purpose is to inform you of what is already known about your area of interest and to help identify the key ideas in the field. This means developing a good knowledge of the key thinkers in the subject area along with an understanding of the significance of their work. It will be through getting to know who is doing what, and where they are doing this, that you will be able to evaluate the relevance of literature encountered in your search. As you become familiar with specific knowledge areas and vocabulary, it will become apparent where the ideas originated and how they have been developed. Secondly, during the process of searching existing literature, you will also gain an understanding of the interrelationships between the subject being considered and other subject areas. As you become more knowledgeable about a topic, you might identify other new areas worth studying which will advance your knowledge on that topic.

Thirdly, as you engage with the work and methods of others who are researching the same area, you will become familiar with the contributions others have made to the knowledge pool. In addition, you will also come to understand how each researcher has studied the topic. Consequently, the ideas and work of others may also provide you with the framework for your own work, which includes methodological assumptions, data-collection techniques, key concepts and structuring the research into a conventional academic thesis.

Reviewing the literature on a topic can therefore provide an academically enriching experience, but only if it is done properly. Figure 3.1 also summarizes these ideas.

The final outcome of the process will take the form of a written literature review which will go some way to informing your audience of what is happening in the area. It will also establish you as a credible, well-informed and capable researcher. Additionally, if well constructed, it will help provide a context for your own approach, argue for the relevance and significance of your research question, and justify the appropriateness of your approach.

# STAGES OF REVIEWING LITERATURE

The process of reviewing the literature can be broken down into four stages. Firstly, actually finding sources will require careful searching and when you do find material which might look useful, you will need to discriminate between the various literature types. Secondly, it is important that you set up a management system to store and catalogue all the sources you find.

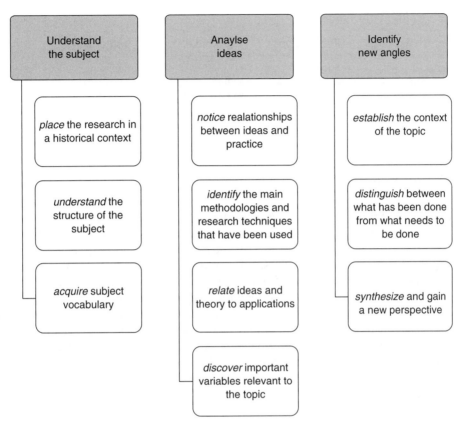

Figure 3.1    The purposes of reviewing literature

Thirdly, you will need to decide which of the many sources you find are relevant and then be able to read these efficiently, making judgements about which papers you will use and why.

Finally, having read widely, you will choose your research focus, develop your question, argue your rationale and design your method.

This chapter will focus on the first three points and Chapter 4 will help you with research design.

## FINDING LITERATURE

In this section, I will discuss where you might look for sources of ideas, what types of literature might be useful and how to search electronic databases.

Table 3.1   Information sources

| Collaborative groups | Publications | The Media | Individuals |
|---|---|---|---|
| Chat rooms | Books | TV | Colleagues |
| Blogs and wikis | Papers | Radio | Librarians |
| Email lists | Magazines | Videos | Experts/Tutors |
| | Journals | DVDs | Friends |
| | Reports | Podcasts | |
| | Pictures | | |

## Searching for literature

There are several ways of identifying potentially useful literature, such as doing hand searches, using sources recommended in course texts and by personal professional contacts within your field of study. If you are studying for a higher degree, your tutor will probably point you towards the 'classic' material in your area, to get you started. Don't overlook your colleagues and other more immediate contacts. Contact with experts in your chosen field is another recommended method of finding material as they can often help identify work that has yet to be published. This can be done either personally or through an email discussion list. Contact with others working in the same field may lead to literature that you have not uncovered in other ways. In summary then, information can come from many sources as Table 3.1 illustrates.

## Using the internet

The internet provides an amazing array of information but you must be very discriminating in what and how you use sources found using web search engines. Nonetheless there are many useful, reputable and freely available sources online which are linked on the SAGE website (www.sagepub.co.uk/wilson). (Six helpful sources are suggested in Box 3.1.)

### BOX 3.1

- The British Education Internet Resource Catalogue (BEIRC) is a freely accessible, indexed database of evaluated and described internet sites and resources which support educational research, policy and practice.
- The Directory of Open Access Journals on Education includes a selection of peer-reviewed titles offering full-text content.
- Education-line is a searchable collection of conference papers, reports, speeches and other full-text documents about education since 1997.
- Google Scholar may link to the full text of articles found through a web search.

*(Continued)*

*(Continued)*

- The General Teaching Council's research activity includes appraising and utilizing the fruits of others' research, as well as sponsoring or directly commissioning new studies.
- The Teacher Training Resource Bank has an e-Librarian who can help with research questions.

## TYPES OF LITERATURE

A literature review for the purposes of a dissertation or thesis should be based primarily in the academic literature. This does not mean that there is not a role for sources such as government documents, working papers, conference papers and publications with short print runs. This is often referred to as grey literature. However, you should be clear in your own mind and in the written review about the role of non-academic sources. For example, does a newspaper article or series contribute specific highly relevant information or flag up concern from the community concern? You must not use academic journal articles and grey literature as if they are the same kind of reference with equal status. Academic in this context means peer-reviewed work published in scholarly journals.

Furthermore, you need to be confident that you have found as much of the available evidence as possible by searching the literature on your chosen topic in a systematic way. Your search must also be open to scrutiny so it can be replicated and updated.

## USING ELECTRONIC DATABASES

This section will consider searching in electronic databases, as these are often the main starting point for literature searches. (See Box 3.2 – these are linked via the website.)

### BOX 3.2

**Electronic databases**

- British Education Index: the BEI will provide you with references to articles in almost 400 journals and is a vital tool for almost every student, teacher or researcher in education. It provides direct links to the full text of articles where possible. To gain full access to the complete database, you will need to use your library's subscription.
- ERIC is the much larger US equivalent of BEI, allowing the searching of nearly 1.2 million citations and free access to 110,000 full-text materials. To gain full access to the complete database, you will need to use your library's subscription.
- Intute is a free online service providing you with access to the very best web resources for education and research. The service is created by a network of UK universities and partners. Subject specialists select and evaluate the websites in the database and write descriptions of the resources. The database contains 121,632 records.

Your tutor will advise you on the key journals in your field, although all journals and articles are not automatically included in electronic databases, and even then you are dependent on studies being indexed correctly. Electronic databases focus on a particular topic or discipline, and it is always a good idea to search as many of these sources as possible, depending on time and resources available.

## Search Strategy

If you use the British Education Index, your search strategy can often be less closely defined, simply because the BEI is a specialized education database. When using a multidisciplinary database, such as the International Bibliography of the Social Sciences, more care will be needed to achieve the necessary focus in your search strategy itself.

The British Education Index contains less than 100,000 items, ERIC has almost 800,000, so if you search the BEI you can also be more adventurous without the fear of being overwhelmed with results.

In addition, if you access the British Education Index through Dialog DataStar, you will also be able to look at the thesaurus, although this requires a rather cumbersome Zmethod to select all the terms of use for your search strategy, whereas the Cambridge Scientific Abstracts interface for ERIC, Sociological Abstracts, Linguistics and Language Behavior Abstracts, etc., present the thesaurus very clearly and in a way which helps you easily select all the appropriate terms to include in your search.

In general, the larger the database, the more abstracts there are and the more important it is to use the thesaurus or set of subject headings, if it is available to you.

## Searching databases

To carry out an effective search of an electronic database, you need to understand how these systems work, and how to plan a search to take full advantage of them. The British Education Index (BEI) is based on Boolean logic which uses two main logical operators.

It is probably easier to understand this if you have an actual example to look at. For example, Figure 3.2 shows the preliminary stages of a search carried out by Atkinson et al. in their published literature review.

Atkinson, M., Springate, I., Johnson, F. and Halsey, K. (2007) *Inter-school Collaboration: A Literature Review*. Slough: NFER.

In Appendix 6 of the report, the authors tell us that they searched the following sources:

- the NFER Library bibliographical databases
- the current educational research in the UK database (CERUK)
- AEI (Australian Education Index)
- BEI (British Education Index)
- CBCA Fulltext Education (Canadian Business and Current Affairs)
- ERIC (Education Resources Information Center).

When they searched the BEI, they used a number of terms and Figure 3.2 uses the very first stages of their search to illustrate the difference between Boolean Or/And statements.

In the search, the shaded circle with the words 'educational cooperation' represents all the records that contain these words. This search found 1351 results for these words. The other shaded circles with the words 'cooperative programmes' and 'school' represent all the records that contain 'cooperative programmes' and 'school'. In this case, the database has 373 and 43,786 records respectively. OR logic is most commonly used to search for

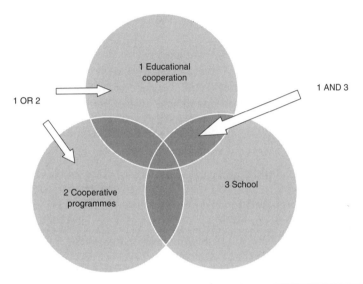

| Search history | | | | | | |
|---|---|---|---|---|---|---|
| **No. Database** | | **Search term** | **Info added since** | **Results** | | |
| **CP** | | **Clipboard** | | **0** | | |
| 1 | British Education Index 1975 to date | Educational AD3 Cooperation | unrestricted | 1351 | Show titles | ☐ |
| 2 | British Education Index 1975 to date | Cooperative AD3 programmes | unrestricted | 373 | Show titles | ☐ |
| 3 | British Education Index 1975 to date | School | unrestricted | 43786 | Show titles | ☐ |
| 4 | British Education Index 1975 to date | 1 OR 2 | unrestricted | 1594 | Show titles | ☐ |
| 5 | British Education Index 1975 to date | 3 AND 4 | unrestricted | 661 | Show titles | ☐ |

Figure 3.2    Boolean Logic and search history

synonymous terms or concepts and will broaden your search. OR logic collates the results to retrieve all the unique records containing one term, the other, or both. The more terms or concepts we combine in a search with OR logic, the more records we will retrieve. In this search, 1594 records were located for the search '1 OR 2'.

The authors wanted to retrieve records in which all the search terms are present and this is illustrated by the shaded area overlapping the three circles, representing all the records that contain all three search terms. So they used the AND operator which restricts the numbers of records located by combining each term. The more terms or concepts combined in a search with AND logic, the fewer records we will retrieve.

## SETTING SEARCH PARAMETERS

Once you have identified your sources, you also need to decide on the search parameters, such as timescale, geographical scope, age range, types of literature and date of publication.

### What is the timescale of your research?

In general, your sources should be recent and if many of your sources are over 10–15 years old, you must explain why this is. You may of course have chosen to use older ideas and theories and, if so, be prepared to explain why. Researchers often use older references when they are 'classic' works or establish a benchmark against which you are comparing things. For example, you may want to trace literature published after an important piece of legislation was introduced.

### What is the geographical scope of your review?

It is likely that you will focus on work carried out in the UK, but limiting your review to studies written in English is a recognized source of bias, so this must be clearly stated in your search strategy.

### What is the age range or educational level of your study population?

If your research is limited to one educational level, this will help to narrow down the search results.

### What types of literature will your review cover?

Decide if you are going to restrict your search to published studies only or if you will also want to use unpublished theses, newspaper articles, opinion pieces, other grey literature and current research too. Including different types of literature in the review will give different viewpoints, but excluding them will narrow your search and make it more focused.

*→ Important*

**Activity 3.1    Developing your own search strategy**

It is much better if you can spend some time thinking about the best keywords and search terms before you start your search. To help you do this, consider the following questions:

1. What is your research question? Break this down into its component parts, mapping out all the different subject elements.
2. Compile a list of keywords and phrases that describe these different elements and that you can use as keywords in your search.
3. Are there similar words that describe each of these concepts?
4. Are there any other more specific keywords that could limit your search?
5. How can you combine these keywords together to search? For example, 'Gender AND Science' returns results containing both words. 'Gender OR Science' returns results containing either the word gender or the word science. Use uppercase letters for OR and AND when using search engines.
6. If you don't find the information you need quickly, try using different keywords.

## PUBLISHED META-ANALYSIS LITERATURE REVIEWS

Since 1993, the Evidence for Policy and Practice Information and Co-ordinating Centre (EPPI-Centre) at the Institute of Education, University of London has coordinated systematic reviews in a range of school-based areas. Review teams based in university departments in the UK conduct extensive searches of literature relevant to particular research questions, and use explicit methods to identify what can be reliably claimed on the basis of the chosen studies. This web-based repository also has a searchable thesaurus and database. Box 3.3 includes a summary report for a recent EPPI review from the online database which reports on learning skills.

---

### BOX 3.3

**EPPI Review 1501R (Report) and 1501T (Technical Report):**

Higgins, S., Baumfield, V. and Hall, E. (2007) 'Learning skills and the development of learning capabilities', in *Research Evidence in Education Library*. London: EPPI-Centre, Social Science Research Unit, Institute of Education, University of London.

**What do we want to know?**

Which teaching approaches that aim to develop pupils' learning capabilities show evidence of the improved learning of pupils?

*(Continued)*

*(Continued)*

**Who wants to know and why?**

The key aim of this review was to support current policy initiatives: specifically, to support the development of personalized learning by identifying teaching and learning strategies which actively engage and challenge learners, which develop their ability to focus on their learning skills and their capacity to take ownership of their own progress. A second aim was to identify evidence from research which helps teachers to understand not just what works in terms of specific teaching approaches in specific contexts but why different approaches are successful. This can support teachers in making informed choices about what is likely to be effective in their own context.

**What did we find?**

There is a tension between approaches to learning skills which emphasize content – in terms of mastery of specific skills – and process – in terms of locating skills within an overall understanding of learning approaches. In the short term, the most effective means to improve performance where the assessment focuses on content knowledge is likely to be direct instruction. In the longer term, or where assessment focuses on conceptual understanding, metacognitive or strategic approaches are likely to be more effective.

Effective approaches are those which explicitly develop the awareness of learning strategies and techniques, particularly when these are targeted at the metacognitive level. The characteristics of these approaches identified by the review include:

- structured tasks which focus on specific and explicit strategies in the subject context
- the capacity in lessons for more effective exchanges between the learner and the teacher concerning the purpose of the activity
- small group interactions promoting articulation about the use of learning strategies
- mechanisms built into learning tasks to promote checking for mutual understanding of learning goals by peers and with the teacher
- enhanced opportunities for the learner to receive diagnostic feedback linked directly to the content of the task.

We can also identify some necessary conditions for these approaches to be successful:

- The teacher needs to have a good understanding of the subject, of different approaches to learning and be sensitive to the demands of different types of learners.
- Teachers should have a repertoire of practical tools and strategies to guide the learner and enhance opportunities for feedback about learning.
- Both teachers and learners should have an orientation towards learning characterized by a willingness to engage in dialogue and negotiation regarding the intent and purpose of a particular teaching and learning activity.
- The focus of learning should be on how to succeed through effort rather than ability and through the selection of appropriate strategies by the learner.

*(Continued)*

*(Continued)*

**How did we get these results?**

From the electronic databases and full-text collections, we identified 1379 citations. A total of 146 reports were obtained, of which 80 studies were selected for inclusion in the review. The in-depth review focused on a subgroup of 10 studies.

## MANAGING LITERATURE

### Storing the literature you find

You must be organized and diligent when it comes to keeping references. It is a good idea to set up a system to help you to track and catalogue the sources that you find right from the start of your research project. Retaining and subsequently retrieving the literature will be important at all stages of the process. The system you use will depend on your personal choice. In the past, researchers used handwritten card indexes but more recently bibliographic software has become more readily available. There are a number of widely used commercial packages that you may want to buy. EndNote® is used widely in university departments and is a powerful database package which enables you to organize, store and search references and abstracts of research literature. It can save you time when writing papers or your thesis, allowing you to input citations directly from EndNote into a Word document, and to create a bibliography without having to type out all the references. You can also use it to access, search and download references directly from online bibliographic databases or library catalogues.

Zotero is a free online package which also allows for the storage of bibliographic information, user notes, and attachments of electronic documents or screen captures which integrates with popular academic databases, pulling information related to articles such as citation information and abstracts.

The larger databases, such as the BEI, AEI and ERIC, have a variety of options for saving and transmitting search results to these commercial packages, which may be very useful. Make sure that you can keep track of what you've found and keep your own record of how you completed the searches and the literature that you found. The search terms and combinations of terms that have been used for each individual database should be documented as you may later need to make these explicit. Moreover, this will also be useful if you want to replicate a search you have completed in one database in another. Consequently, when you come to write up your results, you will be able to show the systematic and thorough nature of your search.

Likewise, keep and file copies of relevant books, and above all, find out what the recommended referencing style is and use it from the start. See the website for links to how to reference your work.

## Keeping on top of reading

You will probably find lots of sources which will be quite rewarding and the tendency will be to stash these away to be read later. However, this can be daunting and may put you off reading all the material you find, so I would recommend that you sort through all the references as you find them. Therefore, try to develop efficient reading strategies – by this, I mean making good use of your valuable time by avoiding reading irrelevant papers. In addition, try to develop effective reading strategies, which means that when you subsequently set aside the time to read the selected papers that you are successful in understanding what you read.

## Efficient Reading

### *Read the abstract*

The first thing to do is to read the abstract carefully. If the abstract is well constructed, then this will give you a good idea of whether it is worth your while reading the whole article. Reading the abstracts and discarding those that are not appropriate will reduce the number of articles on the pile of things to be read or stored in your bibliographic database.

However, sometimes the abstract is not very helpful, so if this is the case, try reading the introduction, key findings or conclusions instead. These sections should give you enough information for you to decide whether it is worth reading the whole article. Box 3.4 provides a simplified description of the basic structure of most empirical research articles.

---

### BOX 3.4

**The layout of a journal article**

Although the exact layout of peer-reviewed journal articles will be determined by the author and the specific journal, most articles reporting on empirical findings will adhere to the following structure:

1. Introduction/Background: a statement concerning the context of the study, a review of relevant literature and other research in the field, the identification of some area that has not yet been studied.
2. Purpose: the main research aims/questions addressed in the article, a statement of what was studied. It can be in the form of a thesis statement which makes a claim of some kind but this is not always the case.

*(Continued)*

---

*(Continued)*

3. Programme description: brief details of the programme or intervention under investigation (if relevant).
4. Sample: sample details, including the number of participants, geographical location/type of setting, age and stage of education and other demographic information pertinent to the study (e.g. gender, ability/attainment, ethnicity, special educational needs).
5. Design and methods: the study design and methods, including dates of data collection, sampling method, methods of data collection and analysis.
6. Results: the main findings in relation to the research aims/questions.
7. Discussion: the interpretation and evaluation of your findings, problems encountered in carrying out the research, implications of the results obtained.
8. Conclusions: the main conclusions arising from the research, possible applications and further research needed.

## Selecting articles for careful study

Don't try to read an academic journal article in the same way as you would a newspaper report or novel. If you just start at the beginning and try to read through to the end, you will get frustrated and may even get the wrong idea that the ideas are too complicated for you to bother with. Most academic articles can't be grasped in a single reading and you may have to engage with them several times, but in different ways.

To quickly gain an overview, familiarize yourself with a chapter or article so that you understand the structure for later note-taking by looking at summaries, headings, sub-headings, tables, diagrams and illustrations. Then read the first sentences of paragraphs to see what they are about and to gauge if the material is useful or interesting, so that you can decide whether just some sections are relevant or whether you need to read it all.

## Effective reading

Reading at speed is fine for scanning and skim-reading, but is unlikely to work for reflective, critical reading. The more you read, the faster you will become as you grow more familiar with specialist vocabulary, academic language and reading about theories and ideas.

Nonetheless, even if you have followed the advice given in the previous section, it is likely that you will still have a large number of articles to read so it would be a good idea to have a systematic strategy for reading these.

1. Sorting papers into categories – sort the articles into piles that are all related to each strand of your research or sub-question. Alternatively, you might want to rank them in order of importance, or even rank each pile.

2. Note-taking – create a table before you start to read the papers, so that you can write down notes as you read. Table 3.2 gives an example of such a template and is the structure used by Atkinson in the literature review referred to earlier in this chapter. It is worthwhile spending time before you start creating a relevant straightforward table for you to use as you read so that you can go back to these notes at a later time. Make a note of pertinent quotations or extracts as you read, in case you want to use these later.

**Table 3.2    Literature summary template**

Title:
Author(s):
Date:

**REVIEW OF SOURCE**

Purpose/focus of literature
Type of collaboration, e.g. no. of schools, etc.
Description of collaboration and its operation/processes
Aims/purpose/intended outcomes (why collaborate)
Conditions/factors which drive collaboration
Conditions/factors which facilitate collaboration (during)
Recommendations/key factors for best practice
Conditions/factors which inhibit collaboration
Challenges/concerns
Role of LA/government/other organizations in
    supporting collaboration
Evidence of gains/benefits arising from
    collaboration

**DESCRIPTION OF SOURCE**

Sector
Country/area
Participants
Method(s)
When data collected and duration
Source/document type
Key references

**REVIEWER'S COMMENTS**

Is the reported analysis adequate and correct?
Are the author's interpretations supported by the evidence?
Are there any biases/caveats raised or to be aware of?
Is there a corroboration or triangulation of sources?
Relevance to review (high, medium or low)
Date of review

*Source*: Atkinson, M., Springate, I., Johnson, F. and Halsey, K. (2007). *Inter-school Collaboration: A Literature Review*. Slough: NFER.

**Activity 3.2**

Create a personalized table to use when you are reading your chosen articles. Table 3.3 provides some suggestions but you will need to adapt these to suit your research question.

## Critical reading

It will be helpful if you can use active reading techniques when you come to read the papers carefully. You ought to have thought about the questions you want to answer already when you devised your reading template in Activity 3.2. The next stage is to try to understand what the author is saying and to challenge the claims being made in each paper. While you read each paper, ask the following questions.

## *Purpose of the work*

- What is the author's purpose in writing the paper?
- Does this fit in with the area you are interested in? If not, then omit this from your review.
- What is the problem or issue and is this clearly defined?
- Is the significance of the work clearly established?
- Could the problem have been approached more effectively from another perspective?

## *Structure of the Work*

Examine the structure of the paper account to help you understand how the authors develop their argument.

**Table 3.3    Organizing note-taking**

| Citation | RQ | Key findings | Design and Methods | Sample | Extracts or Quotes | Comments | Rank 1–5 |
|---|---|---|---|---|---|---|---|
| E.g. Author, date, title, journal, volume, issue, pages | Related to your research question | Related to your research question | What kind of research? How was it done? | Who was involved? How many? | Page numbers | Anything else of note | 1 very important<br><br>5 interesting but not important |

- How does the author structure the argument?
- Identify the main claims the author makes in putting forward their argument.
- Deconstruct the flow of the argument to see whether or where it breaks down logically; see Box 3.5 which uses Fisher's analysis of an argument.

---

## BOX 3.5

Extracts from the discussion section from: Pedder, D. (2006) 'Are small classes better? Understanding relationships between class size, classroom processes and pupils' learning', *Oxford Review of Education*, 32 (2): 213–234.

The text has been annotated with <u>conclusions underlined</u>, (reasons) in brackets and inference indicators in italics.

The secondary school study (Pedder, 2001) <u>developed no evidence of simple one-way relationships between class size and optimum conditions for all kinds of teaching and learning. This is a key finding</u>. <Different teachers recognised increased opportunities for promoting and supporting learning in large as well as in small classes; they also recognised constraints in small as well as in large classes>. Politicians therefore need to be <u>receptive</u> to *the possibility that benefits to pupils' learning arise in large as well as in small classes* and thus need to promote frameworks within which schools can adopt more flexible approaches to allocating pupils to learning groups of different size for different teaching and learning purposes.

---

## Challenging the claims made by the author

Adopt a sceptical stance towards the author's claims, checking whether they support convincingly what they assert.

- Does the author have sufficient backing for the generalizations they make in a research study?
- How robust are the basic components of the study design (e.g. sample size, intervention and outcome)?
- How accurate and valid are the measurements?
- Is the analysis of the data accurate and relevant to the research question?
- Are the conclusions validly based upon the data and analysis?

## Check for biases

Consider whether and how any values guiding the author's work may affect what they claim. Distinguish between respecting the authors as people and being sceptical about what they write. Keep an open mind, retaining a conditional willingness to be convinced.

- Has the author evaluated the literature relevant to the problem or issue?
- Does the author include literature taking positions she or he does not agree with?

## Check for relevance

Check that everything the authors have written is relevant to their purpose in writing the account and the argument they develop.

- In material written for a popular readership, does the author use appeals to emotion, one-sided examples, or rhetorically charged language and tone?
- Is there an objective basis to the reasoning, or is the author merely 'proving' what he or she already believes?

## KEY IDEAS

Setting your own research in the context of other literature on the same or similar subject adds credibility to your work. It broadens your awareness of other research in the area and provides background information and data that corroborate what you've found. It also ensures that you are not duplicating research that has already been done by someone else. Searching the literature may also challenge your assumptions – you may find that the literature contradicts commonly held points of view or says exactly the opposite to what you were hoping to find. Sometimes, researchers decide to revise their original line of enquiry to take account of new information that has been found during the literature search.

## Further Reading

Harlen, W. and Schlapp, U. (1998) Literature Reviews, Scottish Council for Research in Education. www.scre.ac.uk (retrieved January 2008)

Hart, C. (1998) *Doing a Literature Review*. London: Sage.

## References

Atkinson, M., Springate, I., Johnson, F. and Halsey, K. (2007) *Inter-school Collaboration: A Literature Review*. Slough: NFER.

# SECTION 2

## CARRYING OUT AND REPORTING ON CLASSROOM-BASED RESEARCH

# 4

# RESEARCH DESIGN AND ETHICS

## Elaine Wilson and Kris Stutchbury

## THEORETICAL PERSPECTIVES

Chapter 1 introduced the notion that philosophical ideas often remain largely 'hidden' although these have a profound influence on the actual practice of research. However, the methodology you choose to adopt will be coloured by these 'hidden' beliefs. Therefore, for this reason, you will need to be clear about this yourself and be able to make your own theoretical perspective explicit, particularly when you write a thesis.

This chapter will focus on methods, that is how to collect evidence to answer your research question, what data to collect and from whom. Methodology consists of the overarching ideas about how a research study is designed, and the research design is the strategy which integrates the different components of the research project in a cohesive and coherent way so that your research questions can be answered.

## WHICH RESEARCH APPROACH WILL YOU USE?

Once you have decided on a general area of interest and have narrowed your research into a manageable question or hypothesis, you will have a clearer idea of the aims and objectives of the research. The next stage will be to decide on an appropriate research approach which is most likely to provide you with evidence to help answer your question or test out your hypothesis. The approach you adopt will be specific to the problem or question you have identified, so it is helpful to think in terms of identifying the best strategy for you, rather than starting with the idea that you are going to do action research. Once you start to plan the process and become clearer about the purpose of your research, it will be easier to identify your methodology and what the most appropriate data-collection methods are.

There is however some directionality about this whole process (see Figure 4.1). Research design is not only influenced by the overall research purposes but also by the underpinning ideas driving your research. As you read more about your substantive area of study, you will become more familiar with what is already known about your area of study and also be in a much better position to be able to make decisions about the methods to be used and the sample size to work with.

Unless you are working with a fixed, quantitative design, such as a tightly pre-specified hypothesis-testing process, then it is acceptable to go back and modify your design once you start. It might well be the case that by the end of the research programme, you will have modified your original plan and collected further data. Indeed, some research approaches develop theory during the research process, which means having to be responsive to emerging data to follow up interesting lines, or to look for answers to rather different questions. You may even review the purpose of your study in light of a changed context arising from the way in which the other aspects are developing.

Nevertheless, as a novice, it is a good idea to have some ideas at the start of the process about the nature of the data you need to collect and when you should do this.

## WHAT IS METHODOLOGY?

Methodology is the plan of action which informs and links the methods used to collect and analyse data to answer the original research question. Your essay or thesis will include a substantial section about the methodology you have adopted, together with a rationale for the particular methods being used. As you read more about expert work, it will become apparent that some methodological approaches depend heavily on one type of data although increasingly researchers are using a mix of approaches. Nonetheless, it is fair to say that most research methodologies tend to be either largely quantitative in nature, that is they set out to answer 'how many', 'how much', 'who' or 'where' style questions and generate mainly numerical data. Conversely, other researchers use a more qualitative approach, that is they ask 'what is happening here' type questions which are answered mainly in the form of words.

School-based research tends not to adopt such a polarized stance to methodology and is more likely to be situated in the middle of this continuum. Table 4.1 provides examples (Cotton and Ivens) at either end of the qualitative–quantitative continuum

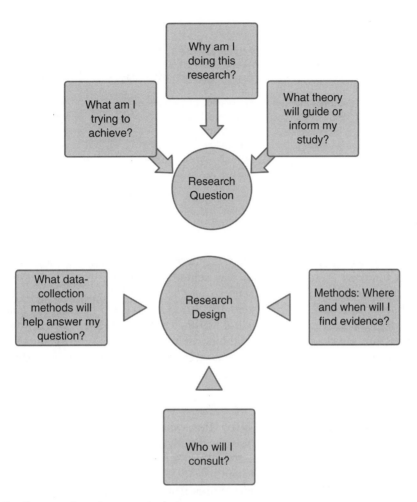

Figure 4.1   Key questions in research design

and also provides an example (Hayes et al.) which uses what has come to be termed mixed methods.

When you start out, it is helpful to analyse the research designs used by more experienced researchers. This will not only help you to see what is possible, but will also give you a good insight into the strengths and limitations of the various methodologies and methods being used. To help illustrate this, Table 4.2 presents a summary of the methods and sample sizes used for each research project reported in the three exemplar papers. An analysis of the purpose of the research and theoretical underpinning for each paper is also summarized on the SAGE website for information, www.sagepub.co.uk/wilson.

**Table 4.1 Methodology continuum**

| Qualitative study | Mixed Methods Study | Quantitative Study |
|---|---|---|
| *Cotton (2006)* Teaching controversial environmental issues: neutrality and balance in the reality of the classroom. *Educational Research,* 48 (2): 223–41. | *Hayes, Hindle and Withington (2007)* Strategies for developing positive behaviour management. *Educational Psychology in Practice,* 23 (2): 161–75. | *Ivens (2007)* The development of a happiness measure in school children. *Educational Psychology in Practice,* 23 (3): 221–39. |

## Qualitative studies

Cotton's qualitative paper investigated teachers' beliefs about teaching controversial issues and matched these with what was actually happening in their classrooms. She observed three teachers in different schools over a 5–6 week period and also interviewed both teachers and students using a semi-structured interview schedule. She analysed the themes and issues emerging from a close reading of the interview transcripts and lesson observations, and checked the trustworthiness of her data by collecting extensive data and by verifying the accuracy of her interpretation by consulting the teachers concerned.

## Quantitative studies

Ivens's quantitative paper investigated the validity and reliability of a modified Subjective Well-Being (SWB) inventory originally used with adults. He modified the psychometric test so that it could be used with school-aged students and renamed the test School Children's Happiness Inventory (SCHI). He subsequently collected data through a series of self-report questionnaires from a large number of students. These data were validated by using statistical correlation.

## Mixed Methods

The final example is a paper by Hayes, Hindle and Withington which is a mixed method study carried out in one large secondary school over an 18-month period. This study investigated how teacher behaviour was modified during and after a developmental intervention. The research team used a range of methods including classroom observation, questionnaires and interviews. Hayes et al. analysed the classroom interactions and teachers' responses and ensured the trustworthiness of their interpretations through 'triangulating' the data between researcher, teachers and students.

Table 4.2    Methods and sample sizes

| | Ivens (2007) Quantitative Study, Fixed Design | Hayes et al. (2007) Mixed Methods Study | Cotton (2006) Qualitative Study Flexible Design |
|---|---|---|---|
| **Research Question(s)** | | | |
| | Is the School Children's Happiness Inventory (SCHI) a valid and reliable psychometric test? | How is teacher behaviour modified by a development intervention? | Do teachers believe that they should take a balanced or neutral view when teaching about controversial issues? What actually happens in their classroom? |
| **Methods** | | | |
| What specific techniques were used? | Series of self-report questionnaires for students | Classroom observation of teachers and pupils, questionnaires, interview | Lesson observations, semi-structured interviews with teachers and students |
| How are the data analysed? | Look for correlation, tested against standardized psychometric test(s) | Classroom interactions, teacher responses | Themes and issues emerging from close reading of interview transcripts and lesson observations |
| How are the data shown to be trustworthy? | Large enough sample | Data 'triangulated' between researchers', teachers' and students' interpretation | In-depth, rich data collected |
| **Sampling strategy** | | | |
| From whom did the researchers seek data? | One discreet study of 771 8–15 yr old students, 77 8–11 yr old students as part of larger study, 41 8–14 yr old students as an interview transcript. | One school – large secondary school | Three experienced teachers |
| Where and when? | In school during a research project | In school over an 18-month period | Three schools for a 5–6 week period |

## ANALYSING METHODOLOGY

Activity 4.1 asks you to analyse three further examples to establish what the researchers' questions are and what techniques were used to answer these questions. How are the data analysed? How are the data shown to be trustworthy? And finally from whom were the data collected, where and when?

These six papers, three in Table 4.2 and the three used in Activity 4.1, will also be used in the next chapters about data collecting and data handling to illustrate the diverse approaches researchers use to investigate schools and classrooms.

**Activity 4.1**

Read the three further papers suggested in the table below and then produce a similar analysis using the categories in the table. See the SAGE website (www.sagepub.co.uk/wilson) for more information.

## WHICH METHODOLOGY IS USEFUL FOR SCHOOL-BASED RESEARCH?

The methodological approach adopted will be dependent on the time and resources available to you to undertake school-based research. You are likely to be engaged in a small-scale, short-term, classroom-based project so using either a case-study or action-research approach is likely to be the most appropriate.

### Case study

Cotton's paper is an example of a case study. Case studies provide detailed knowledge about a single 'case' or small number of cases. In Cotton's paper, the cases are three classroom teachers within the context of different schools. She collected detailed information about each teacher and school through lesson observations, semi-structured interviews with teachers and students, and looks for patterns across the cases. Chapter 13 provides further detailed information about carrying out case studies.

### Action research

Hayes, Hindle and Withington's paper is an example of researchers directly participating in the process of initiating change, while at the same time researching the effects of such changes on the school. Chapter 12 provides more detailed guidance if you intend to use an action-research approach.

**Table 4.3    Analysing research design**

| Paper | Nardi, E. and Steward, S. (2003) 'Is Mathematics T.I.R.E.D? A profile of quiet disaffection in the secondary mathematics classroom', *British Educational Research Journal*, 29 (3): 345–66. | Syh-Jong, J. (2007) 'A study of students' construction of science knowledge: talk and writing in collaborative groups', *Educational Research*, 49 (1): 65–81. | Hidi, S., Berndorff, D. and Ainley, M. (2002) 'Children's argument writing, interest and self-efficacy: an intervention study', *Learning and Instruction*, 12: 429–46. |
|---|---|---|---|
| Research Question(s) | | | |
| What specific techniques were used? How are the data analysed? How are the data shown to be trustworthy? | | | |
| From whom did the researchers seek data? Where and when? | | | |

## OTHER METHODOLOGIES

If you have an extended period of time available to carry out your research, you may be able to use a grounded theory or an ethnographic approach if this is appropriate to the aims of your project.

### Grounded theory

Nardi and Steward and Syh-Jong's papers are examples of grounded theory. This approach involves generating theory from data collected during the study and is particularly useful in new, applied areas of research where there is a lack of theory and concepts to describe and explain what is going on. Nardi and Steward collected extensive data and proposed a 'profile of quiet disaffection' to describe secondary school students' responses in mathematics lessons. The researchers characterize these as: tedium, isolation, rote learning, elitism and depersonalization through an inductive approach. Chapter 14, provides detailed guidance about carrying out a grounded-theory study.

### Ethnography

Ethnographic methodology has arisen from the field of anthropology which describes people and their cultures. In a school context, an ethnographic study would provide a summary of the extensive rich data collected about the participants over an extended, extensive period of observation, while at the same time being culturally immersed in the classrooms. Ethnographers are constantly aware of their own interpretation of situations and try to overcome this by verifying and incorporating the perspectives of the participants to validate emerging ideas.

For example, in the paper 'Climbing over the rocks in the road to student engagement and learning in a challenging high school in Australia' (*Educational Research*, 2007, 49 (3): 273–95), Smith and Fasoli report on an ethnographic case study of a single secondary school conducted over a 5-week continuous period. They used 'embedded interviews' involving observation of in-class teaching prior to extensive one-hour interviews with teachers and students' focus groups. All interviews were recorded. Detailed field notes were kept of classroom observations and other activities, including school assemblies, staff meetings and reflections on informal conversations held during teaching breaks in the staffroom. Activity 4.2 uses criteria to help judge this ethnographic study and further information can be found in the SAGE website (www.sagepub.co.uk/wilson).

**Activity 4.2**

Read Smyth and Fasoli's paper. Use the criteria set out below in the form of a series of questions to analyse the ethnographic study and write down what evidence there is for this in the paper.

## Ethnographic approach

- Does the research avoid disrupting the *natural* setting?
- How does the research focus on *lifestyle* and *meaning*?
- How have the researchers negotiated access to the school?
- How much time have the researchers spent in the classroom?
- How much data have they collected?
- Have the researchers considered both *processes* and *relationships*?
- Do the researchers take account of their own *beliefs, interests, experience* and *expertise* in drawing conclusions?
- Do the researchers describe how their work builds on or contradicts other explanations?
- Do the researchers acknowledge that their findings are their *interpretation* rather than a *literal* description?

## LARGE-SCALE QUANTITATIVE STUDIES

When the aim of the research is to seek patterns and the researcher has access to large numbers of participants, perhaps at a whole school level, then you could use either an experimental or non-experimental fixed research design. Chapters 9 and 10 provide details of these approaches.

1. Experimental design: Hidi, Berndorff and Ainley's paper is an example of an experimental strategy. The central feature of this approach is that the researcher actively and deliberately introduces a change in the situation of the participants with a view to producing and measuring a resultant change in their behaviour. This is an example of a researcher manipulating one variable on another variable – in this case, the detailed design was pre-specified before the main data collection began.
2. Non-experimental design: Ivens's paper, on the other hand, uses a non-experimental strategy. Although Ivens draws on a large sample, his approach is different from the experimental approach in that he does not attempt to change the participants' circumstances but rather looks for patterns on the data.

## HOW BIG SHOULD YOUR SAMPLE BE?

Before starting to collect data for all methodological approaches, you should define the population of your area of interest and determine the size of your sample by using an appropriate sampling strategy. In other words, start by considering who you will include in your research project and why, and be able to justify the selection of this sample.

If you intend to generate big numerical data sets to look for patterns and correlations, you should read Chapter 9 which will explain the different approaches you could take.

If, on the other hand, you are interested in what is going on in a particular setting, then the sampling approach will be different and will be determined by the scope of your study. To this end, your research approach should be either very thorough or confirmed by triangulation. Being thorough involves *saturation*, that is continuing to gather information until you reach a point where you are not adding any new data. This is more likely to happen through prolonged engagement with your research, persistent observation, broad representation of the area of study and through dialogue with a critical friend. Triangulation might involve confirming your findings with participants or through using a range of methods to provide different perspectives. Chapters 7 and 8 extend these ideas further.

As an individual classroom practitioner, it is advisable for you to keep your study narrowly bound with a clear manageable focus because the broader the scope, the longer it will take you to collect sufficient data to be confident about the validity and reliability of the claims being made, so that your work will be credible. For example, planning repeated interviews using semi-structured interviews, which produce a small amount of data per interview question, will need a large number of participants, while in-depth interviews producing much richer data can be fewer in number.

## IS WHAT YOU ARE PROPOSING TO DO ETHICAL?

All research involving groups of people interacting with each other has an ethical dimension; educational research is no exception and the ethical issues are often complex. They are likely to emerge and may change as the research proceeds. On one level, ethics is about obvious things like acting with honesty and integrity, acting within the law and 'doing the right thing'. However, in qualitative research, it is also about the integrity of your research. It is about ensuring that you have enough data to draw conclusions, reporting the evidence accurately, and being open about your assumptions and the limitations of your conclusions. It is about 'doing things right'. As researchers, we have a duty to act ethically and to make sure that in reporting our research, the reasoning behind ethical decisions is recoverable by the reader. It is important that the decisions that we make have a defensible moral basis and that the process of making those decisions is transparent. In this section, we describe an ethical tool – a framework for making sense of ethical issues. It takes into account the fact that as you deliberate on the ethical issues associated with a project, you will find that the ideas are connected to each other and that it can be difficult to be logical, consistent and sure that everything has been covered. It covers both 'doing the right thing' and 'doing things right'.

The framework that we describe prompts you to think about your situation at different levels. By using the grid to analyse a situation, the ethical issues can be tackled *systematically*, within a moral framework. The grid does not provide solutions, but through its use, the researcher is more likely to act ethically and can present the decisions in such a way that the decision-making process is transparent and can be discussed. It has been developed from the work of Seedhouse (1998a) and Flinders (1992). Seedhouse is a philosopher and developed what he calls a 'grid' based on moral theory in order to support the work of healthcare professionals involved in ethical decision-making. Flinders argues that discussion of ethics in qualitative research is often characterized by a lack of models that might help researchers to anticipate and better recognize dilemmas. He proposes four 'ethical frameworks' (based on moral theory) that can be used as a basis for discussion of ethical dilemmas in qualitative research. Seedhouse's grid has been successfully applied to action-research projects in the field of management science (Atkinson, 1989). In this section, we will describe and explain the framework and suggest a methodology for its use in educational research (see Figure 4.2).

Imagine you are looking down on a pyramid. Each layer represents an area of moral theory that should be taken into consideration when dealing with a situation with an ethical dimension. (A brief introduction to moral theory can be found at www.st-andrews.ac.uk/~ea10/theory.htm.) Within each layer, Seedhouse identified a set of boxes; we have used Flinders's ideas to adapt these boxes to make the grid more applicable to educational research.

## An Explanation of the Layers

The external or ecological layer: This layer invites us to consider the wishes of people external to the situation, the culture of the institution in which you are working and the relationship between the part of the institution in which you are working and the institution as a whole.

| The consequential layer or framework: | This layer encourages reflection on whether the 'good' attached to our anticipations for action is increased for humanity as a whole, for a particular group, for the individual or for the researcher personally. We need to consider the effects that the research might have on the participants, the consequences of suggested actions on a school, teachers or students and consideration of anyone else who might be affected by the results or carrying out of this research. |
| --- | --- |
| The deontological layer/duties and motives: | This layer considers the duties and motives of the research. Deontologists either decide on a single overriding duty (e.g. never breaking promises), a range of duties or a hierarchy of duties to guide their actions. It is about avoiding doing wrong. Seedhouse invites us to consider whether our proposed cause of action 'is the right thing to do'. It covers things like not doing harm, beneficence and acting with integrity, truth-telling and promise-keeping. This would include consideration of the way in which the research was carried out, informing participants and interested parties of the outcomes at an appropriate stage and consideration of how we might deal with sensitive information that emerges. This incorporates the 'situationist' approach to ethics (Oliver, 2003). |
| Individual layer/relational ethics: | In this layer, we are invited to focus on the 'core rationale' of the project and to consider the needs of the individuals involved. We need to focus on the relationships at the heart of the research. In healthcare, autonomy is an over-riding theme; in educational research, Bond (2005) argues that it should be 'trust'. |

## Using the grid

Seedhouse divides each layer into a set of boxes (Seedhouse, 1998b) which embrace key issues appropriate to that 'layer' of thinking. Using the work of Flinders and Seedhouse together, we have modified these boxes from the original grid to make them more appropriate for educational research. The idea is that the 'boxes' can be used to generate a set of questions that you can use to interrogate your situation. Some possible questions are suggested, but you might find it more appropriate to focus on the left-hand column and devise your own set of questions that apply to your situation.

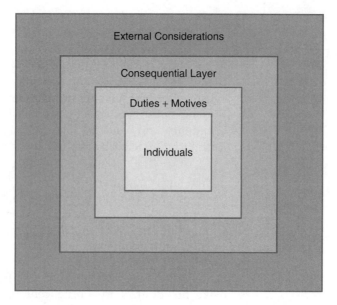

Figure 4.2    Seedhouse ethical grid

A few points arise in using this grid in this way that it is worth highlighting.

• In your situation, some of the issues might not apply. Don't feel you have to answer every question at every level.
• As you apply this grid to your own research, there will inevitably be some repetition and overlap. This is not a problem and is inevitable in the complex situations that arise. In fact, this is why linear organizing principles are often difficult to apply. For example, you are invited to focus on the implications for the individuals concerned in the 'consequential layer' and the 'individual layer'. This is entirely appropriate, as on one level you need to consider practical things like 'do they understand my project?' and 'how much time have they got available?', as well as the deeper, emotional implications of what you are asking them to do.
• In his paper, Flinders applies his frameworks to each stage of the research, recognizing that the dilemmas and issues will change as the project progresses. You need to be mindful of the grid and revisit the questions as your focus shifts from gathering data to analysis and interpretation.
• The questions incorporate big ethical questions that might arise (such as the implications of videoing or photographing children, reporting unpopular findings, ensuring confidentiality), as well as issues around the integrity of your research (such as getting enough data, making efficient use of resources and reporting your findings appropriately).
• Any decisions that you make during this process can be traced back to one of the questions within a particular layer. The decision-making process is therefore recoverable and has a moral basis.

**Table 4.4    Ethical questions**

| External/Ecological | Questions to consider |
| --- | --- |
| Cultural sensitivity | What are the values, norms and roles in the environment in which I am working? |
| Awareness of all parts of the institution | What is the relationship between the group I am working with and the institution as a whole? How does it affect the participants? |
| Responsive communication – awareness of the wishes of others | How might my work be viewed/interpreted by others in the institution? How will the language I use be interpreted? |
| Responsibilities to sponsors | What are my responsibilities to the people paying for this research (local authority, my school)? |
| BERA codes | Have I stuck to the BERA guidelines? |
| Efficiency/use of resources | Have I made efficient use of the resources available to me – including people's time? |
| Quality of evidence on which conclusions are based | Have I got enough evidence to back up my conclusions and recommendations? |
| The law | What are the implications of what I want to do within the ECM agenda? Do I need written permissions? Is anyone at risk as a result of my research? |
| **Consequential/Utilitarian** | |
| Benefits for individuals – informed consent | Have I made sure that all the people involved know what I am doing and why? Are they aware that they can withdraw if they wish? How will I ensure confidentiality? |
| Benefits for particular groups/ organization | What are the benefits of me doing my research to the school/department? Could these be increased in any way? How will I ensure that they know about my findings? Is my work relevant to the school development plan? |
| Most benefits for society | Is this a worthwhile area to research? Am I contributing to the 'greater good'? |
| Benefits for the researcher | Am I going to be able to get enough data to write a good thesis? |
| **Deontological** | |
| Avoidance of wrong – honesty and candour | Have I been open and honest with everyone who might be affected by this research? |
| Minimization of harm – be fair | Have I treated all participants fairly? |
| Reciprocity – do they really understand what I am doing? | What will I do if I find out something that the participants/school/department do not like? How will I report unpopular findings? |
| Doing the most positive good | Is there any other way I could carry out this research that would bring more benefits to those involved? |
| **Relational/Individual** | |
| Genuine collaboration/trust established | Who are the key people involved? How can I build a constructive relationship with them? |

*(Continued)*

**Table 4.4** *(Continued)*

| External/Ecological | Questions to consider |
|---|---|
| Avoiding imposition/respecting autonomy | Am I making unreasonable demands on any individuals? Do they appreciate that participation is voluntary? Am I acting in a way that might constitute an imposition? |
| Confirmation of findings | What steps will I take in my methodology to ensure the validity and reliability of my findings? |
| Respecting persons equally | How will I demonstrate my respect for all participants? Have I treated pupils in the same way as teachers? |

Likewise, any decisions that are forced on you as a result of changing circumstances can be checked alongside the grid to ensure the integrity of your research is maintained. For example, you may plan to interview six people for an hour each. It turns out that cover is not available and that you are limited to 20-minute interviews. This can be justified in terms of making use of available resources and not imposing on the participants, but will it generate enough data? By thinking it through in the context of the grid, you should be able to come to a sensible decision about how to proceed. Instead of just settling for what you can get, the grid prompts you to maybe find an alternative source of data.

• Very often in educational research, decisions are made on a reactive basis. The application of this grid encourages you to be proactive in identifying dilemmas before you get into difficulties.

## Links with the literature from educational research

In educational research, as you immerse yourself in the literature of your chosen area you find, after a while, references to things you have already read and the literature begins to take on some sort of 'shape'. The field of 'ethics', however, is so complex that it is difficult to achieve this in the timescale of a small-scale study. A strength of this grid is that it embraces many of the ideas in the literature in a form that they can all be considered. Without the grid, the temptation is to adopt one particular approach and there is a risk of not considering all the angles. Also, most of what is written in this field makes good sense, and there is very little with which one could disagree, but there is a distinct absence of unifying principles, presented in a useful manner (Flinders, 1992; Small, 2001). There is a set of comprehensive guidelines from BERA but as Homan (1991) argues, 'the notion of an ethical code does not easily fit the conditions which apply in social research' (p. 36). The grid incorporates BERA's guidelines as part of a comprehensive and systematic analysis of your situation. At the end of this chapter, there is a bibliography including accounts of ethics that might apply to small-scale research projects. By applying the grid, you will have incorporated many of the ideas presented.

In small-scale educational research projects conducted in school by practising teachers, it is unlikely that huge ethical dilemmas will arise. However, by applying this grid to your work, any that there are will be identified and the implications of methodological decisions can be checked. Hence the integrity of your research will be maintained; you will be 'doing the right thing' as well as 'doing things right'.

## PLANNING THE DATA-COLLECTION PROCESS

Having decided on your approach and the data you want to collect, it is a good idea to plan each stage carefully.

### Activity 4.3    Planning your research

Plaut's paper provides a good illustration of the planning process and she explains the stages that she went through to collect the data in her paper 'I just don't get it': Teachers' and students' conceptions of confusion and implications and learning in the high school English classroom (*Curriculum Inquiry*, 2006, 36 (4): 391–421), in Figure 4.3. Use this example along with the questions in Table 4.4 to plan your own sequence of data-collecting events. You may want to have more than one research question and subdivide this into a series of sub-questions, as suggested in the grid in Table 4.5. What is important is that you have clear questions and that the research process is about trying to answer these with the best data sources available. Chapter 5 will focus on how to collect valid and reliable data. There are other visual tools available on the website to help you structure your plan.

Figure 4.3    Plaut's data-collection plan

**Table 4.5  Planning data collection**

| Title | | | | |
|---|---|---|---|---|
| Research question | | | | |
| Sub-questions | Data Source | Data Source | Data Source | Data Source |
| 1. | | | | |
| 2. | | | | |
| 3. | | | | |

**When do I need to collect the data?**

| | Pre-intervention? | During | Post-intervention |
|---|---|---|---|
| Sub-Q1 | | | |
| Sub-Q2 | | | |

**An example timescale**

| Jan. – Apr. | | Apr. – Jun. | | Jul. – Aug. | Sept. |
|---|---|---|---|---|---|
| Review literature | Essay 1 | Methods/pilot study | | Writing up | Essay 2 |
| Data collection | Lit. rev. chapter | Data analysis | Method chapter | | Thesis |

# RECORDING EVENTS – USING A RESEARCH DIARY

Finally, writing a research diary is a very effective way of keeping control of the information your research generates. You could also use the contents of your diary as a source of data, although this will be different from the information, observations, records or other data which you collect. The diary contains information about you and what you do, and will provide an accurate record of the process of research. It complements the data yielded by the research methodology.

Some people use a highly structured format using prepared forms. However, this is not essential provided you can find your way around your own diary. It is very useful to leave space for later comments or additions, either in wide margins, on the backs of pages, or in good spaces between entries.

There are no hard and fast rules about style, language and spelling. Keep your diary in the style which you find useful, and which helps you to reflect on what you are doing. Critically reflect on your own diary keeping.

> **Activity 4.4    Keeping a Research Diary**
>
> **What goes in your diary?**
>
> 1. A summary of what happens each day you work on the project.
> 2. Stories of conversations, discussions, interviews, planning sessions, and so on with peers, co-researchers, teachers, supervisors and participants.
> 3. Questions and topics for further study or investigation.
> 4. Hunches and thoughts.
> 5. Diagrams, drawings and mind-maps.
> 6. Observations.
> 7. Reflections on what you saw.
> 8. Reflections on re-reading the diary.
> 9. Plans for future action or research.

## KEY IDEAS

The key ideas introduced here are presented in the form of a checklist below to help you design and plan the data-collection stages of your own research.

1. Negotiating access
   (a) Do you have formal permission to carry out your investigation?
   (b) Have the participants agreed to be involved?
2. Ethics
   (c) Is what you are proposing to do ethical?
   (d) Have you read the BERA guidelines?
3. Information for participants
   (e) Have you discussed what you intend to do with your participants?
   (f) Have you discussed what the outcome of the research will be?
   (g) Will you provide the participants with a copy of the final report?
4. What information?
   (h) What hunches and thoughts arise during the research?
   (i) Is the context or background information important?
   (j) Is it likely that there is a wide range of views and of practice?
5. Why collect this information?
   (k) How will the kinds of information identified in 1, above, help you answer a particular research question?
   (l) Do you need to collect data from all the possible sources available?
   (m) Are some more vital than others?

6. When do you need it?
   (n) Is there an order of priorities for data collection?
   (o) Is certain information only available at particular times in the school year?
   (p) Do you need to collect baseline data before you start with your intervention?
7. How do you collect it? Will you need to:
   (q) observe situations?
   (r) sit in on discussions?
   (s) interview those involved?
   (t) use a questionnaire?
8. Where can you find the information?
   (u) Should you look in classrooms, staffrooms, corridors, meetings, filing cabinets, official documents, through private contact with individuals?
9. From whom?
   (v) Are you clear about who all the participants are?
   (w) Has every possibility been identified?

## *Further Reading*

Anderson, G. and Arsenault, N. (1998) *Fundamentals of Educational Research.* London: The Falmer Press.

Bridges, D. (2001) 'The ethics of outsider research', *Journal of Philosophy of Education.* 35(3): 371–87.

Busher, H. (2002) 'Ethics of research in education', in M. Coleman and A. R. J. Briggs (eds) *Research Methods in Educational Leadership and Management.* London: Paul Chapman.

Cohen, L., Manion, L. and Morrison, K. (2000) *Research Methods in Education.* London: RoutledgeFalmer.

Denscombe, M. (2003) *The Good Research Guide.* Maidenhead: McGraw-Hill (Open University Press).

Pendlebury, S. and Enslin, P. (2001) 'Representation, identification and trust: Towards an ethics of educational research', *Journal of Philosophy of Education*, 35(3): 361–70.

Pring, R. (2004) *Philosophy of Educational Research.* London: Continuum.

Simons, H. and Usher, R. (eds) (2000) *Situated Ethics in Educational Research.* London: RoutledgeFalmer.

Taskakkori, A. and Teddlie, C. (1998) *Mixed Methodology: Combining Qualitative and Quantative Approaches.* Thousand Oaks, CA: Sage.

# *References*

Atkinson, C. J. (1989) 'A lost dimension in Soft Systems Practice', *Journal of Applied Systems Analysis*, 16: 43–53.

BERA (2004) www.bera.ac.uk/publications/guides.php (downloaded on 21/05/2007).

Bond, T. (2005) 'Researching education: A question of trust?'. Keynote lecture given on the MEd course, University of Cambridge, Faculty of Education, 2 March.

Cresswell, J. (2003) *Research Design*. London: Sage.

Flinders, D. J. (1992) 'In search of ethical guidance: Constructing a basis for dialogue', *Qualitative Studies in Education*, 5(2): 101–15.

Homan, R. (1991) *The Ethics of Social Research*. Harlow: Longman.

Oliver, P. (2003) *A Student's Guide to Research Ethics*. Maidenhead: Open University Press/ McGraw-Hill.

Seedhouse, D. (1998a) *Ethics: The Heart of Healthcare*. Chichester: Wiley.

Seedhouse, D. (1998b) Ethical Grid, downloaded on 21/05/2007 from www.priory.com/ images/ethicgrid.JPG

Small, R. (2001) 'Codes are not enough: What philosophy can contribute to the ethics of educational research', *Journal of Philosophy of Education*, 35(3): 387–405.

# COLLECTING DATA

## Elaine Wilson and Alison Fox

---

**Hints**

- Remember that data selectively represents events so try to record these as faithfully as possible.
- Be aware too that what data you select also adds to this interpretative process.

---

This chapter builds on the ideas about research design introduced in Chapter 4 and will offer advice on the strengths and limitations of each data-collection method to help guide your collection of data. If the methods you propose involve mainly words, then you should also read Chapters 7 and 8 before you start. Alternatively, if you want to collect data involving mainly numbers, then also read Chapters 9 and 10.

Table 5.1 summarizes the relevant information about each of the examples used in the chapter to illustrate the data-collection method.

## DECIDING ON DATA-COLLECTION METHODS

Having decided on the focus of your research, the research questions you want to answer, the overall strategy you want to use, then the next stage is to consider what data you need to collect to help you to answer the research questions.

There are three possible approaches to obtaining evidence about schools and classrooms. Firstly, you can observe students and teachers at work to find out what is going on. Secondly, you could ask students or teachers about what they think is going on and, thirdly, you could look for traces of other evidence to verify that whatever you were investigating has taken place. Table 5.1 provides examples of how expert researchers involved in school-based research collect data to answer a wide range of school-focused questions. Examples of each of these approaches will be introduced in the next sections.

There are no rules which say you must only use one method in an investigation. In classroom-based research, using more than one method will be an advantage although

**Table 5.1** Examples of school-based research

| Published Example | Research Question(s) | Data Type | Sample Timescale | Data Source 1 | Data Source 2 | Data Source 3 |
|---|---|---|---|---|---|---|
| Cotton, D. (2006) Teaching controversial environmental issues: neutrality and balance in the reality of the classroom. *Educational Research*, 48 (2): 223–41 | 1. Do teachers believe that they should take a balanced or neutral view when teaching about controversial issues? 2. What actually happens in their classroom? | Qualitative | 3 teachers 5–6 week period | Semi-structured interviews with individual teachers | Semi-structured interviews with individual students | Classroom observation |
| Hawkey, K. (2007) 'Could you just tell us the story?' Pedagogical approaches to introducing narrative in history classes. *Curriculum Inquiry*, 37 (3) | 1. How are narratives introduced within the history classroom? 2. What models of good practice underpin these classroom approaches? | Qualitative | 5 schools 5 teachers 20 lessons | Lesson observation | Interviews with individual teachers | Focus group interviews with teachers |
| Hayes, B., Hindle, S. and Withington, P. (2007) Strategies for developing positive behaviour management. Teacher behaviour outcomes and attitudes to the change process. *Educational Psychology in Practice*, 23 (2): 161–75 | How is teacher behaviour modified by development intervention? | Mixed | 1 school | Lesson observation | Pre- and post-intervention surveys | Individual teacher interviews |
| Hidi, S., Berndorff, D. and Ainley, M. (2002) Children's argument writing, interest and self-efficacy: an intervention study. *Learning and Instruction*, 12: 429–46 | Can students' writing be enhanced by increasing motivation and cognitive support? | Quantitative | 177 students | Pre- and post-intervention survey | Self-report test | |

*(Continued)*

Table 5.1 (Continued)

| Published Example | Research Question(s) | Data Type | Sample Timescale | Data Source 1 | Data Source 2 | Data Source 3 |
|---|---|---|---|---|---|---|
| Ivens, J. (2007) The development of a happiness measure in school children. *Educational Psychology in Practice*, 23 (3): 221–39 | Is the School Children's Happiness Inventory (SCHI) a valid and reliable psychometric test? | Quantitative | 771 students | Series of self-report questionnaires | | |
| Maloney, J. (2007) Children's role and use of evidence in science: an analysis of decision-making in small groups. *British Educational Research Journal*, 33 (3): 371–401. | How do children use evidence to engage in argumentation? | Qualitative | 1 class | Lesson observation | Video recordings of groups of children | |
| Nardi, E. and Steward, S. (2003) Is mathematics T.I.R.E.D? A profile of quiet disaffection in the secondary mathematics classroom. *British Educational Research Journal*, 29 (3): 345–66 | 1. What is going on in Maths classrooms? 2. What are the students' views? 3. What actually happens in the classrooms? | Qualitative | 70 students 7 weeks | Classroom observation | Interviews with groups of up to four students | |
| Noyes, A. (2004) Video diary: a method for exploring learning dispositions. *Cambridge Journal of Education*, 34 (2): 193–204. | An analysis of the diary entries to map types and quantities of (cultural, economic and social) capital, the dispositions of the habitus and an examination of the structuring effect of the three fields, school, family and youth cultures. | Qualitative | 'A few' children | Video diaries | | |
| O'Brien, C. (2007) Peer devaluation in British secondary | 1. Do students evaluate pejorative names differentially? | Mixed | 471 students 8 schools | Tape-recorded group interviews | Stimulated open-ended interviews | |

*(Continued)*

**Table 5.1**  (Continued)

| Published Example | Research Question(s) | Data Type | Sample Timescale | Data Source 1 | Data Source 2 | Data Source 3 |
|---|---|---|---|---|---|---|
| schools: young people's comparisons of group-based and individual-based bullying. *Educational Research*, 49 (3): 297–324 | 2. How do students justify their value judgements? On what dimensions are group and individual-based name-calling perceived as similar and different? 3. Are appraisals comparable? Are we comparing 'apples and oranges'? | | focus group interviews | | | |
| Plaut, S. (2006) 'I just don't get it': teachers' and students' conceptions of confusion and implications and learning in the high school English classroom. *Curriculum Inquiry*, 36 (4) | 1. What sources of information do secondary school writing teachers and their students rely on to identify student confusion? 2. What do teachers' and students' interpretations of that information reveal about their conceptions of confusion, of teaching and earning, and of learning to write persuasive essays about l terature? 3. How is each teacher's conception of confusion similar to or different from his students' conceptions? | Qualitative | 2 teachers 6 students A series of lessons | Video-taped lessons | Stimulated recall interviews with individual teachers | Stimulated recall interview with individual students |
| Syh-Jong, J. (2007) A study of students' construction of science knowledge: talk and writing in collaborative groups. *Educational Research*, 49 (1) 65–81 | 1. Does working in collaborative groups help students construct science knowledge? | Mixed | 19 Students 1 year | Students' reflective journals | Likert/open-question survey | Paired student interviews |

*(Continued)*

**Table 5.1** *(Continued)*

| Published Example | Research Question(s) | Data Type | Sample Timescale | Data Source 1 | Data Source 2 | Data Source 3 |
|---|---|---|---|---|---|---|
| | 2. Does the process of working and talking help students construct science knowledge? | Qualitative | 1 school 5 weeks | Classroom observation | Interviews with individual teachers | Interviews with individual students |
| Smyth, J. and Fasoli, L. N. (2007) Climbing over the rocks in the road to student engagement and learning in a challenging high school in Australia. *Educational Research*, 49 (3): 273–95 | 1. What are the conditions that occur in a school and its community that amount to new ways of understanding and addressing the barriers to school engagement? 2. How can a school reconfigure and reinterpret itself to ensure that students do not become 'exiles'? | | | | | |

it will add to the time needed to carry out your research. Indeed, by using only one source, you may miss key ideas or worse be lulled into thinking your survey has discovered the 'right' answer about the issue in your classroom. Using more than one source of data will help you take into account other perspectives in your developing understanding of the situation.

It may be the case that you have devised more than one research question or subdivided your question into smaller, more measurable parts which will automatically lead you to more than one method. For example, Syh-Jong and O'Brien have investigated more than one question and both have used a mixture of data-collection methods. Whichever approach you decide to use, you must always make it clear that you are aware of the threats to the reliability and validity of your data-collection methods and tell the reader how you have minimized this. Chapter 7 discusses this in more detail.

## REDUCING THREATS TO THE VALIDITY AND RELIABILITY OF YOUR DATA-COLLECTION METHODS

Whichever method you choose will selectively represent events. During the process of becoming data, either by being written down as on observation transcript or recorded during an interview, some element of selection will have taken place. Indeed, focusing on a particular approach means that you have already selected some aspect of reality as important while at the same time ignoring other parts. To some extent, you will have made a conscious decision to ignore some aspects of the classroom dynamic as part of interpreting the research question or choosing a particular methodology. However, it may also be the case that you have done this accidentally, as a result of your own unconscious prejudices, or some known or unknown bias of the methods chosen. There may also be some form of restriction in the research context, such as a timetabling issue which has made it impossible for you to interview a particular pupil, thus alerting your sample strategy which will also introduce further bias to the process.

Furthermore, having collected the data, you will still need to be vigilant of the fact that selecting the source of data is in itself an interpretative process and that the next stages of making meaning from the data will extend this interpretation process even further, particularly if you intend to transform your own personal experiences into data. So there are many pitfalls along the way which will compromise the reliability and validity of your data-collection process.

The next sections will set out the advantages and disadvantages of the various data-collection methods which you could use in school-based research. The nature of your research question will determine what the most appropriate method is, and Table 5.1 provides examples of how expert researchers have used a range of methods to answer their research questions. This might help you in your choice of methods. Finally avoid the tendency of collecting too much data as it will probably be just you who will have to analyse it subsequently. Activity 5.1 will help guide the planning stage.

Figure 5.1   Data-collection methods

## Activity 5.1

**Data-collection checklist**

**Planning: Who, where, when, how and what?**

Have you considered the following?

1. Who or what are you going to include in the data-collection process and why?
2. Do you have a clear plan for where and when you will collect data?
3. Will you collect data in your own classroom or that of a colleague? Have you established what your role will be during the data-collection process? Are you a teacher or researcher or both?
4. Have you identified and set in place measures to help you control your own possible subjectivities?
5. Have you consulted the BERA ethical guidelines? Are you aware of any potential ethical dilemmas?
6. Have you read the relevant sections in this chapter on how to collect each data source?
7. Have you considered how you will minimize the threats to the validity of your data-collection methods?
8. Are you sure that the data you intend to collect will help you answer your research question?
9. Do you have a back-up plan in case there are last minute changes in school?

**Preparing and piloting the data-collection tools**

10. Can you use an existing standardized test, survey or questionnaire?
11. Have you prepared your interview schedule, if applicable?

*(Continued)*

*(Continued)*

12. Have you checked that your audio-visual equipment is working, if you intend to use this approach?
13. Have you tried out your survey or interview question on a small pilot group?
14. Do you need to modify your data-collection plan in light of your pilot?

## RECORDING WHAT IS HAPPENING

## Observations

Observation is a normal process for teachers. Indeed, teachers are continually monitoring what is going on in classrooms and constantly questioning what is happening. Reactions and responses are often informed by teachers' tacit experiential knowledge which helps to interpret what is going on. This tacit experiential knowledge is constantly being developed and indeed this may well be why you are embarking on a classroom-based research project. Consequently, if you want to research your own classroom, you will need to be able to stand back and open your mind to other ways of interpreting what is going on in your classroom. In other words, you will need to be systematic in how you collect evidence about what is happening in your classroom.

Evidence collected through observation will rely on your ability to gather data through using all your senses and to do this you might use checklists, inventories or narrative descriptions as tools to help your analysis.

Classrooms are very complex social settings and there are many things going on at once. You need to have a clear purpose when you come to observe the classroom, otherwise you might end up with a very superficial analysis if you try to record everything. On the other hand, if you limit your focus too much, there is a danger that you only see what you want to see. Remember that when you observe a classroom you are selecting from an ongoing sequence of events so plan carefully for this opportunity. Activity 5.2 provides a checklist of points to consider before you carry out an observation.

**Activity 5.2**

**Preparing to Observe**

1. What are you going to observe? Will you focus on a particular aspect of practice? Will this allow you to collect enough data to answer your question?
2. Why are you carrying out the observation? What are the assumptions and expectations on which it is based? Are you sure your biases are not ruling out another interpretation of the situation?
3. When will the observation be carried out, and how long will it take? Will this fit in with the timetabling schedule and other whole school events?

## Recording Observations

Several of the expert researchers whose work is summarized in Table 5.1 have used classroom observation methods. Nardi and Steward used a highly structured observation schedule which they devised for their study to record the classroom behaviours of students in Maths classes. Hayes et al. used a published schedule called Observing Pupils and Teachers in Class (OPTIC) to record the number of positive and negative feedback statements made by teachers.

Cotton used a much more open-ended approach to record how teachers taught students about controversial issues, while Smyth et al. observed classes to look for changes in student behaviour before and after an intervention programme.

Classroom observations are most reliable when they are conducted over a period of time or on more than one occasion so as to minimize the chances of the observation lesson being atypical. Figure 5.2 provides an example of a structured observation schedule used to analyse talk in science lessons. Other schedules and links can be found on the SAGE website (www.sagepub.co.uk/wilson).

## Challenges

Constructing a classroom observation schedule is quite a difficult process, especially if you are going to ask someone else to use your schedule. This is because each observer will approach the classroom with his or her own experiences and biases. As a result, two observers may interpret what is going on differently and may then record different responses to the same lesson.

Moreover, the presence of one or more observers may interrupt the normal class environment which can lead to lessons that do not represent the norm. Table 5.2 summarizes the advantages and disadvantages of observing lessons.

## SUPPORTING AND SUPPLEMENTING OBSERVATION

It is good practice to record information about the context in which you undertook your observations, for example you ought to note how many students were involved, what the seating arrangements were and perhaps also write a chronology of the events that took place during the observation. Making an audio or video recording will capture some of the classroom interaction in a more permanent form.

### Making audio recordings

Tape recordings capture the sounds of a situation – although information about the classroom surroundings together with the non-verbal cues and gestures will be lost, the technique does enable you to collect a more complete record than just direct classroom observations. You might want to supplement your classroom observation with a tape recording of certain selected parts of the lesson. This is a relatively straightforward

**Lesson aims:**      **Year group:**      **Number of students:**

| | Teacher–student interaction | | | | | | | | | | | | What students are doing | | | | | | | How students are grouped | | |
|---|---|---|---|---|---|---|---|---|---|---|---|---|---|---|---|---|---|---|---|---|---|---|
| | Key: Mgt = management or admin, Inst = Giving instructions, A, B, C or D type dialogue, Demo = demonstrating, Explan = explaining, Quest = questioning | | | | | | | | | | | | | | | | | | | | | |
| Time | Whole class: Teacher addressing the whole class | | | | | | | | Teacher interacting with small groups of students or individuals | | | | | | | | | | | | | |
| | Mgt | Inst | A | B | C | D | Demo | Mgt | Inst | Explan | Quest | O | Write | Listen | Talk | Read | Practical | Other | individual | Pair | Group |
| 0–5 mins | | | | | | | | | | | | | | | | | | | | | |
| | | | | | | | | | | | | | | | | | | | | | |
| | | | | | | | | | | | | | | | | | | | | | |
| | | | | | | | | | | | | | | | | | | | | | |
| | | | | | | | | | | | | | | | | | | | | | |
| | | | | | | | | | | | | | | | | | | | | | |
| | | | | | | | | | | | | | | | | | | | | | |
| | | | | | | | | | | | | | | | | | | | | | |
| | | | | | | | | | | | | | | | | | | | | | |
| | | | | | | | | | | | | | | | | | | | | | |
| | | | | | | | | | | | | | | | | | | | | | |
| | | | | | | | | | | | | | | | | | | | | | |

Figure 5.2   An example of a structured observation schedule

**Table 5.2 Advantages and disadvantages of using observation and audio/video recording**

|  | Advantages of this approach | Disadvantages of this approach |
| --- | --- | --- |
| **Written observations** | Immediate account available; observer actually sees what is happening; account can be available for discussion immediately after observation; full view of the classroom or school setting available to the observer at time of observation. | Observer must make immediate decisions about what to record, so may be superficial or unreliable account; no chance of 'action replay'; some effects on class behaviour because of observer's presence. |
| **Video recording** | Both visual and sound record of the lesson which can be replayed several times; no pressure to take instant decisions; focus can be on teacher only or on individual or group of pupils; lesson can be discussed with participants. | Loss of information such as room temperature, smells, events out of camera shot; effects on class of presence of camera; time-consuming analysis; one camera provides one perspective. |
| **Audio recording** | Sound recording can be replayed several times for discussion, analysis, or corroboration of written account; radio microphone can be used to obtain high quality record of what the teacher says; observer's comments can be recorded simultaneously on twin-track tape; allows lesson to be subsequently transcribed. | Loss of important visual cues such as facial expressions, gesture, body language, movement; sound quality can be poor without radio microphone, especially if acoustics are poor; difficult to identify individual children who speak; analysis time substantially increased. |

process although listening to these later and making notes about the recording will take a substantial amount of time. Transcribed classroom dialogue is a really useful data source but it is probably only necessary for you to transcribe short extracts of the dialogue unless the focus of the research is on classroom dialogue.

## Making video recordings

Video recordings are a good way of collecting both the dialogue of the lesson as well as many of the details recorded in direct lesson observation. By representing the sequence of events in time, video recordings can make the context and causal relationships more accessible than other methods of data collection. Student behaviour patterns can also be recorded including the relationship between verbal and non-verbal behaviour. Additionally, videotapes are also an excellent way of presenting a situation to others to open up discussion.

However, there are also disadvantages. Although video recordings can provide a relatively holistic record of the lesson, the sequences only show the view seen from the perspective of the camera. In addition, good quality video recordings involve the use of a lot of equipment which can be very distracting in a classroom, although the use of smaller webcams has minimized this problem. The main difficulty lies in using the camera in a static position and using it sufficiently frequently for it to become routine. More seriously, video recordings can be misleading because they give the appearance of being a complete record of events when, in fact, they are highly selective (the camera has been pointed in one direction and there is no indication of periods of time when it has not been recording).

Making good use of video recordings takes a lot of time. A careful analysis concentrating on events that appear to be essential in terms of the research question requires repeated showing of the tape.

Sometimes a fixed camera is sufficient, positioned on a tripod at the (window) side of the classroom and allowed to run for the whole session without pause. It can be focused on a whole area of the room, on a group of pupils, or on one pupil. Recordings of this kind make rather boring viewing for people not involved, but they provide a more complete record of the session for purposes of analysis or discussion.

Maloney used video to complement her direct lesson observation of students engaged in argumentation, Noyes collected video diaries from students and Plaut used video recordings of lessons as a stimulus for follow-up interviews with teachers and students.

## ASKING PEOPLE ABOUT WHAT IS GOING ON

### Surveys

Surveying involves gathering information from individuals using a questionnaire. Surveys can be descriptive or explanatory, involve entire populations or samples of populations, capture a moment or map trends and can be administered in a number of ways. Another advantage is that this approach offers a degree of confidentiality and anonymity to the person taking part in the research.

Using a survey means that you are able to reach a large number of respondents and generate standardized, quantifiable, empirical data in the process. The use of closed questions forces respondents to choose from a range of predetermined responses, which are generally easy to code and analyse. For example, Hidi et al. and Syh-Jong both used closed-question surveys to collect numerical data from large samples.

You can also use open questions which ask respondents to construct answers using their own words. Such survey questions can generate rich and candid data, but it can be difficult to code and analyse.

Although using a survey can generate large amounts of credible data, it is difficult to construct the actual survey. The overall process involves formulating questions, response categories, writing up background information and giving clear instructions. Getting the layout and setting right as well as getting the right length and organization are also tricky. It can be difficult getting the questions just right and you must always try them out on a small group before going wider. There are several excellent short guides aimed at small-scale researchers listed in the Further Reading section at the end of this chapter.

It is best to keep the language simple and ask a critical friend to look out for poorly worded questions, and statements that use complex terms and language. Avoid using ambiguous questions, and statements with double negatives. Try not to 'lead' the respondent by using loaded, 'ring true' and hard-to-disagree-with statements or questions.

Surveys and questionnaires are usually administered mainly on paper but data can also be collected online using open source software such as SurveyMonkey.

## Standardized tests

Psychologists and other social scientists have developed a wide range of self-report measuring instruments to assess attributes such as attitudes to learning or cognitive ability tests used by some schools to measure students on entry to a school.

Technically, such tests provide a scale on which you would assess an individual's performance. You do need specialized training to develop such tests, so it is more sensible for you to use a recognized standardized test to supplement your own data, provided you can obtain details of the scoring system and are able to analyse the data collected (see Chapters 9 and 10). For example, Hidi has used an existing standardized test to measure self-efficacy and Ivens has modified a test scale to measure the subjective well-being of school-age students.

Table 5.3 summarizes the advantages and disadvantages of using surveys and standardized tests.

## Interviews and Focus Groups

Strictly speaking, an interview is a conversation between two people and focus groups are conducted in small groups. The principles involved in both approaches are the same although using focus groups can add further complications to the process which will be examined later. Both interviews and focus groups are communications that aim to consult teachers and students about their points of view, interpretations and meanings to help understand classroom dynamics. They are most often used to gather detailed, qualitative descriptions, although even when done carefully, you will only be able to establish what the interviewee thinks of his/her perceptions at a particular time.

**Table 5.3    Advantages and disadvantages of using surveys and standardized tests**

|  | Advantages of this approach | Disadvantages of this approach |
| --- | --- | --- |
| **Questionnaire-based surveys** | Surveys are relatively easy to administer, on paper or online. | The overall usefulness will be determined by the quality of the questions. |
|  | Surveys are useful for collecting information from large samples. | You need to ensure that a large number of the selected sample will reply. |
|  | Many questions can be asked about a given area. | Participants may not recall information or tell the truth about a controversial question. |
|  |  | Surveys are inflexible in that they require that the survey remains unchanged throughout the data collection. |
| **Tests and scales** | Standardization ensures that similar data can be collected from groups and then interpreted comparatively. | Tests are difficult to develop and need considerable expertise to write and analyse. |
|  | The tests are usually reliable and data is easy to obtain, so observer subjectivity is eliminated. |  |

## Establishing trust

In both cases, you need to establish trust and build confidence before you start and this can be done by reassuring the interviewees that their views are important. The relationship between you and the person you are interviewing will influence how they understand what is being said and vice versa. If you are interviewing one of your own students, this might be problematic as you and the student will have already developed a relationship and with this various attitudes towards each other. This may range from a completely trusting relationship to one of mistrust or one of affection to outright animosity. It may be the case that carrying out an interview with a student who you find difficult might actually improve your relationship, if as a result you come to understand them and their behaviour better. However, if the student perceives that you are only interested in reinforcing your negative impressions, then this may make things worse and because the student will assume that you are not interested in their own personal perceptions. In this case, it may be better if you could ask a colleague who does not know the students to do the interviews.

## Focus Groups

Focus groups are useful for revealing, through interaction, the beliefs, attitudes, experiences and feelings of participants.

Focus groups can provide an insight into multiple and different views and on the dynamics of interaction within the group context, such as consensus, disagreement and power differences between the participants. O'Brien (see Table 5.1) used a group interview method to tap into the dominant, expected and approved views of a group of secondary school students. As this is an innovative method and one which might be useful to classroom teachers interested in consulting pupils, the procedures used are set out in Box 5.1.

---

### BOX 5.1

The 96 groups were asked to list, collectively and anonymously, pejorative names that they hear being used at school, while the interviewer left the room for a few minutes. Each group was given a green sheet of paper headed 'Extremely bad names to be called' and a yellow sheet headed 'Names which are bad to be called but not too bad'. The colours served as useful shorthand for referring to evaluations of severity.

Pejorative names were used as a proxy for perceived reasons for being bullied. They were coded by the researcher as targeting group or individual attributes, depending on whether they were racial or sexual epithets or insults that applied mostly to individuals. A pilot study revealed that this 'confidential' group activity was the most effective means of eliciting sensitive information regarding the pejorative names that young people hear being used between peers at school. It also revealed that abstract discussion about the relative severity of pejorative names was possible without the interviewer seeing the lists during the interview.

Discussion was prompted by the following questions:

A. What makes extremely bad ('green') names worse than not so bad ('yellow') names? Conversely, what makes not so bad ('yellow') names less severe?
B. If you were bullied, would you rather be bullied for your skin colour or for your looks?

The first question prompted general attributions, while the second forced respondents to consider what victims of different forms of bullying might feel, thereby eliciting more focused answers about protective and harming attributions pertaining to group and individual stigmas. 'Looks' and 'skin colour' were chosen because they are not necessarily distinguishable. Respondents were free to select group or individual features for either, thereby revealing their socially constructed reasons for being bullied.

*Source*: O'Brien (2007) Peer devaluation in British secondary schools, *Educational Research*, 49 (3), 297–324.

## Activity 5.4

### Preparing for an interview

If you are interested in collecting data through interviewing, then consider the following points:

### Before the interview

- What do you want to know and why?
- Have you piloted your questions?
- Make sure you are on time.
- Have you set up and checked equipment?
- How will you explain the purpose of the interview to the interviewees?
- How will you make the interviewee feel at ease?
- Have you explained the ethical guidelines?
- Have you asked the interviewee if they are happy for you to tape the interview? If they do not agree, then how will you record responses?

### During the interview

A. Procedures

- Remember that this is an interview so you need to listen more than talk.
- Avoid interrupting trains of thought and accept pauses as a natural part of reflection.
- Accept whatever is said.
- Ask for clarification if you are not sure what the respondent means.
- Prompt and probe appropriately and keep the pace moving.
- Be true to your role.
- Stop the interview when the time is right.
- Don't forget to thank the interviewee for giving up their time.

B. Questions

- How will you ease the interviewee into the interview?
- What strategic questions will you ask?
- Are you using open questions?
- Have you broken your key question into shorter questions to enable the interviewee to give you extended focused responses?
- How will you deal with responses that will take the interview off in another direction?
- Are any of your questions likely to suggest or lead the interviewee to the response you want to hear?

Recording responses can be done in a number of ways; you may need to trial a couple of recording methods in order to assess what is best for you.

**Table 5.4   Advantages and disadvantages of using interviews and focus groups**

|  | Advantages of this approach | Disadvantages of this approach |
| --- | --- | --- |
| **Interviews** | Provide rich data that paint a broad picture. | Can be difficult to get students or colleagues to participate because of time constraints. |
|  | May highlight issues not previously considered. | Interviews and large focus groups may intimidate some participants. |
|  | Can provide information to supplement quantitative data collected through other methods. | The complexities of people and the complexities of communication can create many opportunities for miscommunication and misinterpretation. |
| **Focus groups** | Small focus groups may increase the comfort level of participants. | There is a danger that you may lead participants and encourage them to agree with your own views. |
|  | Focus groups are useful for revealing beliefs, attitudes, experiences and feelings of participants. | Some participants may dominate the group and their behaviour may lead to a false sense of consensus. |
|  | Focus groups can provide an insight into multiple and different views. | You may find it difficult to distinguish between individuals in the groups. |
|  | They can also provide information about the dynamics of interaction within a group context. | It will be difficult to generalize if your group size is small or not representative of the wider population. |

- *Note-taking* – this can range from highly structured to open and interpretive.
- *Audio-recording* – audio-recording allows you to preserve raw data for review at a later date.
- *Video-taping* – video-taping offers the added bonus of being able to record visual cues, but is more intrusive, is prone to more technical difficulties, and can generate data that is hard to analyse.

# OTHER SOURCES OF EVIDENCE

## Documents

You may want to use grey literature such as government documents and other school-based data and policies.

## Secondary sources

Secondary sources are existing data that were originally collected for purposes other than your research, such as baseline data about students' performance on entry to the school, achievement data, standardized test scores, and school demographic data.

## Visual images

Visual images can be used in two ways – firstly, you may want to record events in the classroom by using photography or, secondly, photographs can be used as prompts in interviews. This second approach of a photo elicitation technique involves using photographs or film as part of the interview – in other words, you ask your research subjects to discuss the meaning of photographs, films or videos. In this case, the images can be taken specifically by the researcher with the idea of using them to elicit information and then the interviewee's comments or analysis of the visual material is itself recorded, either on audio tape or video for subsequent analysis.

## Diaries and journals

Diaries can provide a good source of data. Your own research data might be useful as a data source or you might want to ask your research participants to record their own diaries for subsequent analysis. As with interviews, the guidance given for keeping diaries may be completely open-ended and semi-structured through giving broad categories of what to consider including or by asking for regular responses to very specific questions. So it is vital, if the diaries are to be completed by the participant, that you give clear unambiguous instructions to the writer about how, when and why they should enter data. The process of writing the dairy can empower the diarist too, through encouraging reflection and through valuing their ideas. Diaries also encourage the diarist to express opinions and reflection on activities that might otherwise be difficult for a researcher to expose.

For example, Syh-Jong's paper (see Table 5.1) used teacher diaries to encourage the participants of the research programme to reflect on their teaching. The content of the journals included personal observations, impressions, feelings and analyses, and self-reflection and self-examinations concerning their team teaching performance, team meetings, and so on. The diaries proved useful as a record of the intentions of a teacher for a lesson, which could be used comparatively across the set of teachers.

Diaries do not have to be in a written form. For some students, this would present an insurmountable barrier, as well as also being a very time-consuming process. Visual diaries offer an alternative, either by asking for a set of photographs to be taken or videos to be compiled. While video capture, if by mobile camcorder, has the greatest cost implications, the advantage is that an audio record of thoughts and reflections can be included. Noyes (see Table 5.1) circumvented the need to hand out a recorder and instead set up a video diary room in 'big brother' style. Still imagery collected either digitally (whether by mobile phone or digital camera) or using traditional cameras (such as disposables) requires interviews or focus group discussion to explore the meaning associated with them.

However, Noyes's approach does present ethical dilemmas about how images of students can be used in classroom-based research.

## Visual mapping

Concept mapping and mind mapping are related techniques currently being used in educational and business settings to make explicit the connections between individuals' ideas. In a school context, these could be used to improve the planning of work, note-taking skills, the organization of thinking and the development of concepts, and in preparation and support of assessments. Many of these techniques use computer software packages both to structure data collection and to manipulate the data in analysis. There are links to these packages on the SAGE website (www.sagepub.co.uk/wilson).

These techniques can also be used for research rather than instructional purposes. As with the diary methods, these techniques allow access to the perceptions of those under study. In addition, they also allow a respondent-centred method of exposing conceptual understanding.

Other mapping or visual representation techniques involve freehand drawing of what might be termed 'spider diagrams'. It is these methods, although less straightforward to analyse, which allow the researcher to open up the scope of what is under study to the respondents. An open-ended network mapping tool developed by Fox was used to collect data for a project studying the flow of knowledge relating to the development of assessment for learning practices. This allowed members of staff to represent the personal and professional relationships relating to their school and which could act as channels for sharing practice and/or gaining new information and advice. Network mapping can be used to determine the nature and value of interrelationships relating to teachers and perhaps even be considered as a 'map' of their learning opportunities. It was not possible to guess these networks in advance of this task being used. This tool would also translate well to looking at the networks of children to consider the range of resources they have to learn from and/or to understand their social milieu. An alternative method of network mapping derived from sociological research, which can be used to examine networks of known extent, is called social network analysis. This is a tool worth considering if it would be insightful to understand the structure of a network – for example, how interconnected individuals are one with the other, and the who key individuals in a network are, in terms of their personal networks. Questions are asked systematically of all members of the network about how others relate to them and their relationship with named others. Free downloadable software is now available to handle such data.

To complement the use of imagery, referred to above with respect to diaries, freehand visual representations have also been found to be useful ways of gaining an insight into the perceptions of spaces.

## KEY IDEAS

There are numerous methods you could use to collect evidence to help answer your research question. These methods are usually identified during the research design stage. Each method has advantages and disadvantages. As a researcher, you need to be aware of what these are and do as much as you can to reduce the limitations imposed.

 *Further Reading*

Drever, E. (1995) *Using Semi-structured Interviews in Small-scale Research: A Teacher's Guide.* Edinburgh: SCRE.

Fox, A., McCormick, R., Procter, R. and Carmichael, R. (2007) 'The design and use of a mapping tool as a baseline means of identifying an organisation's active networks', *International Journal of Research and Method in Education,* 30 (2), 127–47.

Munn, P. and Drever, E. (1997) *Using Questionnaires in Small-scale Research: A Teacher's Guide.* Edinburgh: SCRE.

Simpson, M. and Tuson, J. (1997) *Using Observation in Small-scale Research: A Beginner's Guide.* Edinburgh: SCRE.

Wragg, E. (1994) *An Introduction to Classroom Observation.* Abingdon: Routledge.

# HANDLING DATA

## Elaine Wilson and Alison Fox

**Hints**

- Set up a good system for storing your data as you collect it.
- Don't let piles of unattended data accumulate.
- Allow time to read your notes, sort and store your data.
- Don't start summarizing your ideas too soon.
- Stop, think and let ideas emerge from your data.

Do not underestimate the sheer quantity of data that you will rapidly gather during your research project. It is easy to find that you have collected so much data that you are not certain how to analyse it or write it up. Somehow, gathering data seems more productive than analysing it. Guard against producing excessive unnecessary data as a bulwark against potential failure. Try to analyse your data as you go along as this will also confirm whether you are collecting the right sort and quantity of data. It will also help you to check that your original analytical intentions were correct and still appropriate to answer your questions.

Be systematic in making sense of all that you have done so far. Figure 6.1, taken from Zina O'Leary's book, *Researching Real-world Problems* (2005), sets out a methodical, organized approach to data handling which clarifies this process into five tasks.

## KEEPING YOUR EYE ON THE MAIN GAME

The danger is that you will be overwhelmed by the sheer amount of data that you have collected but don't lose sight of why you are doing the research and what you are trying to find out. Keep comparing the data that was collected earlier in the

Figure 6.1    The process of data analysis (with permission from O'Leary, 2005)

study with data collected later in the study. Create a visual representation of what you have collected and map out a summary of this. Use diagrams, sketches of things, people and happenings to show different ideas and groupings.

## SETTING UP AN ORGANIZED STORAGE SYSTEM

Data will accumulate rapidly once you start the research process so set up a recording and storage system before you start collecting data. The easiest way of doing this is to keep a research diary. Log in your data as you collect it, record information about the context and any anomalies or issues that arose while you were collecting the data.

Organize and group sources into logical categories. Start to select and focus on all the relevant important sources before you start to transform the data using presentational devices.

## PRESENTING DATA

Present your findings in ways that capture the key ideas so that it is easier to see at a glance. Using figures such as diagrams, tables, graphs, charts or maps can be a very useful way to show and emphasize information in your report. They can be used to compile data in an orderly way or to amplify a point and are a useful tool to help your readers understand complex data. Figures that are supportive rather than essential to your explanation can be placed in the appendix section so that the continuity of your writing is not broken up. Avoid including tables and figures without referring to them in the text; make sure that you do discuss the information represented in the diagrams, tables, graphs, charts and maps. Try to produce text and figures that can both stand alone, that is the text should be readable without figures, and vice versa, although a good diagram can really make your point very clearly. For example, Ivens has included a diagram of his theoretical model (Figure 6.2) being tested by his surveys.

Figure 6.2  Ivens's diagram of his theoretical model

## ANALYSING AND INTERPRETING DATA

### Working mainly with numbers

If your data is mainly numerical, then read Chapters 9 and 10 in conjunction with this section.

Determine what the most important points are and how these are related to the aims of your research project. There are various data displays that you could use to present numerical data. Tables, graphs and figures can present certain types of information, including models and sequences of events more clearly and in less space than the same information would require in sentence form. However, do not use tables, graphs and figures for small amounts of data that could be conveyed clearly and succinctly in a sentence.

### *Tables*

Summarizing your data in a clear table is a straightforward way of making your 'raw' data easily accessible. Try to make your data tables complete but not too complex. Sometimes it is helpful to break a large table into several smaller ones to allow the reader to identify important information easily.

Table 1   Percentage of gender, year and ethnic grouping interviewed ($N = 471$)

|  | Girls ($n = 253$) | Boys ($n = 218$) |
|---|---|---|
| Year 7 ($n = 159$) | 47 | 53 |
| Year 9 ($n = 156$) | 50 | 50 |
| Year 11 ($n = 156$) | 65 | 35 |
|  | East London ($n = 237$) | Cambridgeshire ($n = 234$) |
| White ($n = 311$) | 36.3 | 95.7 |
| Black ($n = 137$) | 55.7 | 2.6 |
| Mixed race ($n = 23$) | 8 | 1.7 |

*Source*: Ethnic groupings adapted from Kelly's (1988) schema.

Figure 6.3   Table used in O'Brien (2007)

For example, in Figure 6.3, O'Brien summarizes information about the size of the data sample, together with information about the gender, age and geographical location of the sample. In Figure 6.4, Ivens summarizes his correlation data and Figure 6.5 shows the pre- and post-data tables used by Hayes et al.

### *Graphs*

Graphs are one of the best ways to display data, but avoid making mistakes in how you use graphs – for example, don't connect discrete points with a continuous line. It is more

Table 2    Study 1, Correlation of SWB with adapted single-item measures

|  |  | Terrible – Delighted | Line Positive | Line Negative | Faces |
|---|---|---|---|---|---|
| Subjective Well-Being (SCHI) | Pearson Correlation | .40** | .39** | .40** | .39** |
|  | Sig. (2-tailed) | <.001 | <.001 | <.001 | <.001 |
|  | N | 77 | 77 | 77 | 75 |

**Correlation is significant at the 0.01 level (2-tailed).

Table 3.    Study 1, Correlation of SWB with multiple item measures

|  |  | Self-Esteem | Depression | Affect |
|---|---|---|---|---|
| Subject Well-Being (SCHI) | Pearson Correlation | .49** | −.55** | .71** |
|  | Sig. (2-tailed) | <.001 | <.001 | <.001 |
|  | N | 77 | 77 | 77 |

**Correlation is significant at the 0.01 level (2-tailed).

Figure 6.4    Ivens's (2007) correlation data

appropriate to use a bar graph or histograms for discrete points (see below). Hidi et al. use a graph accurately to illustrate changes in pre- and post-survey data (Figure 6.6).

A box and whisker plot is a way of summarizing a set of data measured on an interval scale. It is often used in exploratory data analysis. It is a type of graph which is used to show the shape of the distribution, its central value and variability. In other words, you can see if there are any unusual observations outside the average range. Ivens used a box plot to set out the distribution and range of the data collected from his three studies (Figure 6.7).

## Bar charts and histograms

Bar charts are pictorial representations of the distribution of values of a variable. You can use bar charts to show distributions of interval or nominal variables. Bar charts of interval variables are also called histograms.

Table 1    Pre-intervention teacher questionnaire

|  |  | % Rated 7 or more |
|---|---|---|
| 1 | On a scale of 1–10, how would you rate your confidence to manage behaviour effectively in your classes? | 50 |
| 2 | Could you rate your confidence to problem-solve situations where pupils' behaviour is particularly challenging in your classes? | 38 |
| 3 | How good are your current opportunities for discussion and planning with colleagues in relation to behaviour issues? | 38 |
| 4 | Do you find it easy to talk to colleagues about behaviour difficulties in school? | 63 |
| 5 | To what extent do you feel your personal behaviour management skills make a difference to pupils' learning in class? | 63 |
| 6 | How satisfied are you with your job overall at present? | 38 |
| 7 | How stressful would you say your job is at present? | 56 |

Table 2    Post-intervention teacher questionnaire

|  |  | % Rated 7+ |
|---|---|---|
| 1 | Please rate the value of the 5 process steps in the Staff Sharing Scheme as contributing to purposeful discussion around behaviour management. | |
| | (a) Clarifying problems situations. | 72 |
| | (b) Building up an understanding of the problem situation. | 83 |
| | (c) Generating a range of possible intervention approaches. | 84 |
| | (d) Selecting the best approach. | 89 |
| | (e) Setting up ways of measuring whether the intervention plans have actually made a difference. | 67 |
| 2 | Please rate the value of the process overall. | 83 |
| 3 | Please rate the value of the Staff Sharing Scheme in terms of outcomes for the groups as a whole. | 67 |
| 4 | Please rate the value of the Staff Sharing Scheme in terms of outcomes for your own management of behaviour. | 69 |
| 5 | How confident would you feel about facilitating another group of staff using the same/a similar process? | 45 |

Figure 6.5    Hayes et al. (2007) tables of pre- and post-data

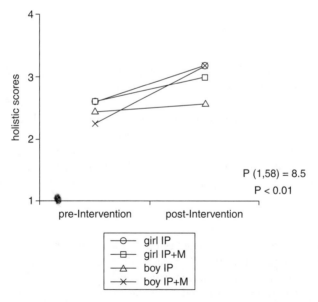

Figure 6.6    Graph used by Hidi et al. (2002)

A histogram is a graphical way of presenting a frequency distribution. It is constructed by first selecting a number of 'intervals' to be used. Most computer programmes that construct histograms will allow you to select the number of intervals, as well as their width. If you don't tell the computer how many intervals to use, it will make the decision based on the data it has. In Figure 10.1, you will find a histogram produced by SPSS.

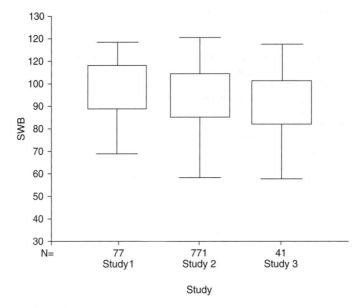

Figure 6.7    Ivens's box plot

A graph very similar to a histogram is the bar chart. Bar charts are often used for qualitative or categorical data, although they can be used quite effectively with quantitative data if the number of unique scores in the data set is not large. A bar chart plots the number of times a particular value or category occurs in a data set, with the height of the bar representing the number of observations with that score or in that category. The Y-axis could represent any measurement unit: relative frequency, raw count, per cent, or whatever else is appropriate for the situation. For example, the bar chart in Figure 6.8 plots the number of positive and negative feedback statements before and after the reported intervention.

## Pie charts

A pie chart is a way of summarizing a set of categorical data. It is a circle which is divided into segments. Each segment represents a particular category. The area of each segment is proportional to the number of cases in that category. For example, O'Brien summarizes the percentages of types of names evaluated by students as more or less severe (Figure 6.9).

## Scatter plots

A scatter plot is a useful summary of a set of two variables, usually drawn before working out a linear correlation coefficient or fitting a regression line (see Chapter 10). It gives a good visual picture of the relationship between the two variables, and aids the interpretation of the correlation coefficient or regression model.

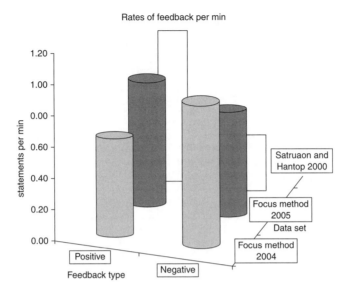

Figure 6.8    Hayes et al. (2007) bar graph

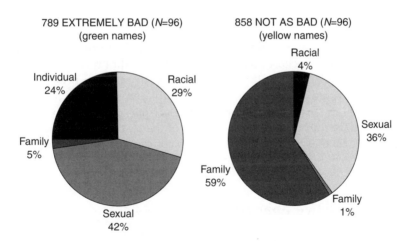

Figure 6.9    Pie chart in O'Brien (2007)

Each unit contributes one point to the scatter plot, on which points are plotted but not joined. The resulting pattern indicates the type and strength of the relationship between the two variables. Hayes et al. used a scatter plot to show the number of positive and negative comments plotted against on task behaviour (Figure 6.10).

The linked website will provide further examples.

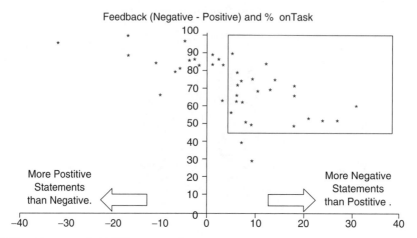

Figure 6.10 Hayes et al. (2007) scatter plot

## Working mainly with words

If your data is mainly in the form of words, then you should read Chapters 7 and 8 in conjunction with this section.

The best way of moving from raw qualitative data, such as interview transcripts or journal entries, to meaningful understanding is through becoming immersed in the data. In other words, you need to try to look for themes that run through the data and then interpret the implications of these themes for your research project. These themes can be either discovered or uncovered. For example, in Box 6.1, Nardi and Steward describe how they analysed their interview transcripts and developed headings and codes, which they used in their second reading of the text (Figure 6.11). This approach set out to discover themes inductively through a constant comparison of data, building theory by using a grounded theory approach (see Chapter 14).

---

### BOX 6.1   Inductive analysis

**Data Analysis of the Interview Data**

Immediately after each interview, an Interview Protocol, a condensed account of the interview where the interviewees' statements are reproduced from the audio-recording, not with verbatim accuracy but as faithfully and concisely as possible, was produced. The interviews were also fully transcribed and the contents of the audiotapes were digitized and

*(Continued)*

*(Continued)*

copied on compact disks. Within a spirit of seeking data-grounded theory, as proposed in Glaser and Strauss (1967), but with due attention to foundational theoretical perspectives, as indicated, for example, by Hammersley (1990), a first level of coding followed according to seven wide categories, as set out in Table I. A second-level coding of the now *Annotated* Interview Protocols led to the production of a Code System (a gradually enriched, eventually 'saturated' version of the preliminary one consisting of 36 T, 29 P, 40 C, 30 M, 14 S, 5 Sc, 2 METH categories, giving a total of 156). Numerous examples of these categories can be seen in the subsequent section of this article. Occurrences of each category in the now *27 Coded* Interview Protocols were recorded in a massive interviewee-by-category spreadsheet. The frequency of each category is available in the last row of the spreadsheet. By examining the spreadsheet horizontally, we could identify the codes in which each interviewee scored higher and thus form an impression of his/her focal points. By examining the spreadsheet vertically, we could identify the codes that featured higher frequencies across the total body of interviewees. Subsequently, each category was assigned an ordered pair $(x, y)$ as follows: $x$ corresponds to the number of times the category has been identified in the Coded Interview Protocols and $y$ to the number of students who have referred to the category. Further scrutiny based on validation of significance relating to frequency, researcher emphasis, and external theory led to the selection of the Pivotal Categories around which we clustered all the categories, across the Code System, that were tangentially relevant (covered part of the same ground, highlighted a different angle of the same issue, etc.). Out of this clustering, five major characteristics of quiet disaffection emerged. In the following, we introduce each of the characteristics using the corresponding cluster of categories and substantiate using extracts from the interviews. The evidence is supported further with references to the classroom observations, the student profiles and the relevant literature.

Nardi and Steward (2003)

Maloney and Plaut had a predetermined theory and their approach was to deductively uncover data to support this theory. For example, Maloney analysed video recordings of students' roles in lessons, using a series of codes derived from previous work carried out with teams (Figure 6.12).

Plaut constructed a conceptual model of confusion (Figure 6.13), which she then used to analyse the stimulated recall interviews with teachers.

## Other sources

### *Using focus groups in research*

If you have used focus groups, you will need to decide whether to transcribe the complete group discussions or whether to use abridged transcripts in analysis. Transcripts are useful in that they can provide more than a record of the discussion, and they also allow for a more intimate understanding of the content of the talk, the flow of discussion and

Table 1

| Name of category | Abbreviation | Content: Interviewees' statements on: |
| --- | --- | --- |
| Conceptual difficulty | C | Difficulties in various mathematica topics and ways of coping |
| Mathematics | M | Nature and significance of mathematics |
| Performance | P | Own and others' ability and performance in mathematics |
| Teaching | T | Mathematics teaching including the role of activities, teaching styles, and teacher personality |
| Social | S | The role of peers, parents and others in mathematical learning |
| School | Sc | Schooling in general |
| Methodology | METH | The impact of the researcher's presence in the classroom |

Figure 6.11    Nardi and Steward's (2003) coding schedule

the group dynamics. You could also analyse the linguistic elements such as gestures, laughter, sounds of disbelief, gaze and so on. O'Brien represents the dynamic nature of the dialogue which took place during the focus group interviews in Figure 6.14.

## Using documents for research

Your selection of a document is, in itself, part of a design process of selection so it is important to explain why you have selected the document, how it relates to your research question(s) and what you hope to discover from its analysis.

## Documentary analysis

Documentary analysis is a way of deconstructing discourse. For example, 'grey literature', such as that produced by government departments, uses official discourse related to government policy. Indeed, all written and spoken text is actually just shaped utterances. These utterances are generated within a particular circumstance and represent an overt or 'hidden' particular point of view. Documentary analysis can reveal something about the perceptions, views and values of the individuals who constructed the text. Documentary analysis can be qualitative where you would look for themes or quantitative where you could, for example, count occurrences of key words. In either case, you will need to create categories and themes to help analyse the text.

Table 5.   Characteristics of the roles

|  | Role | Code | Features |
|---|---|---|---|
| Positive Roles | Chair | Ch | Asks questions and asks others for contributions |
|  |  |  | Suggests what the group can do |
|  | Discussion Manager | DM | Starts and/or ends discussions |
|  |  |  | Makes final decision with or without consultation |
|  |  |  | Directs the groups; suggests what action to take |
|  | Information Manager | IM | Checks on the tasks to be done or validity of evidence |
|  |  |  | Refers back to the E1 evidence |
|  |  |  | Summarises evidence |
|  | Promoter of Ideas | PI | Suggests idea—may or may not be acceptable to others |
|  |  |  | Impatient when discussing ideas other than their own |
|  |  |  | Wants to get the decision made |
|  | Influential Contributor | IC | Makes claims with reference to data |
|  |  |  | Responds to others by posing questions or challenging ideas |
|  |  |  | Suggests a possible decision |
| Negative Roles | Non-influential Contributor | NIC | Responds to others' comments with agreement or confirming points made |
|  |  |  | Makes suggestions that are ignored by the others |
|  |  |  | Agrees with the decision that someone else makes |
|  | Non-responsive Contributor | NRC | Has own ideas but puts them forward only when asked |
|  |  |  | May make a different decision to the others |
|  |  |  | Does not attempt to persuade others to change their minds |
|  | Reticent Participant | RP | Makes little contribution |
|  |  |  | May read out E1 evidence but not make any comments |
|  |  |  | Makes few claims |
|  | Distracter | Di | Talks about issues not related to the task |
|  |  |  | Tells long stories that are marginally related to the discussion |
|  |  |  | Displays silly behaviour |

Figure 6.12   Maloney's codes for analysing video recordings of lessons

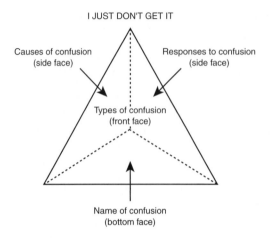

Figure 6.13    Plaut's conceptual model of confusion

### Activity 6.2

Use the following list of questions to analyse documents and other 'grey literature':

- What kind of a text is this?
- What are its distinctive features?
- Who wrote the document, and what is known about the author(s)?
- When was it written? What is the background/context?
- Where did the information come from – how was it collected/assembled?
- Who is the intended readership?
- What is it intended to do? Did the author aim to inform, persuade, express a view or preference …?
- What is being taken for granted? What is *not* being said?
- Is it complete? Has it been altered or edited? Is it an extract? If so, who selected it?
- What connections are being made with other events/arguments/ideas?
- How clearly does it communicate?
- Is the information authentic, reliable and up to date?
- Does it contain any contradictions/incoherences/understatements?
- Does it rely on facts or interpretation?
- How have the author's assumptions about the audience shaped the document?
- How might interpretations of different recipients (e.g parents/teachers/educators/policy makers) vary?
- What do readers need to know in order to make sense of the document?
- What values/ideologies or assumptions about the social/political/educational context are implicit in the text? For example, is there a sub-text? What is not seen as problematic?
- What tone does it take? How credible is it and is there a hidden agenda?

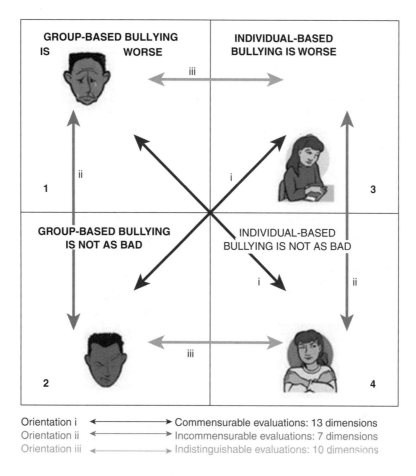

Figure 6.14   OBrien's diagram interview interactions

- What alternative discourses exist? Are these acknowledged, ignored or resisted?
- What are the potential implications/outcomes?
- Is there any external corroboration? What other forms of data would be useful?

## Content analysis

Content analysis usually takes a systematic, data reduction, linguistic approach of quantifying the number of times a particular word appears in the text. This can be done using computer software to look for themes (see Chapter 8).

## Discourse analysis

Discourse analysis explores how language changes over time rather than just focusing on what is said, so you will need to examine the texts within their historical contexts. Since texts are constructed within specific contexts, there can be no single, correct, authoritative interpretation of a document. So discourse analysis involves looking at the text from different perspectives to examine the authors' underlying assumptions, intentions and values. Since the 'meaning' of any text is constructed in the gap between the reader and the text, you need to clarify your own assumptions in creating categories.

**Activity 6.3**

- What is the focus of your analysis? How does this relate to your research question?
- Why have you selected these texts?
- How have you obtained the texts? Are there copyright conditions?
- Will you use a qualitative or quantitative approach? Why?
- What key categories and themes have you identified and why?
- What was the context in which the text was written?
- What are your own assumptions in analysing documents and generating categories?

## ANALYSING IMAGES

Photographs can provide a speedy (when using a digital camera) and clear point of reference for discussion. They can serve as an illustration to accompany transcripts. You can also print out multiple copies for learners to comment on. However, remember that viewers don't always interpret as much or indeed the same things from photographs as they would from written excerpts of conversation.

### Issues of representation

Photographs can be interpreted in two ways: firstly, you can focus on the content of any visual representation – for example, who is the person in the photograph? Secondly, you may want to look at who produced the image, and for whom. Why was this photograph taken of this particular person, and then kept by that particular person?

## Concept and network maps

You can carry out a descriptive, first-level analysis of concept maps. This could be followed by an analysis of nodes which might be grouped according to their proximity to other items, such as types of roles.

You can also extract information about the links made between words or themes. The map, and its first analysis, is a really useful basis on which to come back to people and talk about your perceptions of networks, or concept maps, the value and strength of links and how you are using them.

## KEY IDEAS

Be systematic in making sense of your data. Keep your eye on why you are doing the research in the first place. Organize your data, sort, enter and code this as you go along. Rigorously analyse your data using the conventions associated with the methodology you are using. Use a range of presentational devices to make your ideas more easily accessible.

 *Further Reading*

Altrichter, H., Posch, P. and Somekh, B. (1993) *Teachers Investigate their Work: An Introduction to the Methods of Action Research*. London: Routledge.

O'Leary, Z. (2005) *Researching Real-World Problems: A Guide to Methods of Inquiry.* London: Sage.

# RELIABILITY AND VALIDITY IN QUALITATIVE RESEARCH BY TEACHER RESEARCHERS

## Michael Evans

> ### Hints
>
> - Be honest about the process, procedures and limitations of your study. Qualitative research is as much about the process as about the outcomes of the research. Questions about reliability and validity are a good way of critically reporting on the process.
> - Think about reliability and validity issues before you start and when you have completed your data collection.
> - Don't just list the strategies you used to strengthen the reliability and validity of your study. First identify the potential threats, then talk about the strategies you devised to offset the threats.
> - Don't collect too much data or have too many research objectives. Be realistic within the time and resource constraints you're working under.

## INTRODUCTION

One of the main anxieties that someone carrying out a small-scale qualitative enquiry can have at any point in the investigation is in relation to the overhanging question: 'so what?' The research in question is only a drop in the ocean of experience and so what possible significance can the highly individual and localized findings of my experience have for anyone else? Completely different findings can emerge in different contexts so what use is my study to other people? In part, this anxiety is a reaction to the perceived weightiness of large-scale quantitative research due to the access it has to a greater volume and breadth of evidence. The more subjects, classrooms, schools, and contexts that one can draw on in an enquiry, the more one can seem to be able to make claims that will have a general relevance and applicability, especially if they are supported by statistical measurement. At the same time, worries about the reliability and validity of one's own research are a positive indication of an awareness of the limitations of educational research. What distinguishes an accomplished from a naive researcher is the former's reluctance to rush to make confident claims about findings: incontrovertible certainty is on the whole a rare commodity in educational research. At the very least, a measure of doubt is important in that it keeps us alert and open to new and at times contradictory evidence.

However, for an enquiry to stand as research, a degree of systematicity and validation is required since, despite my opening remarks, research should aim to appeal to a wider community and to represent more than an instance of personal and subjective reflection. Lincoln and Guba (1985) have argued that in the context of 'naturalistic inquiry', the quality of the study can be measured by the concept of 'trustworthiness' and by examining the procedures used as part of the process of persuasion:

> The basic issue in relation to trustworthiness is simple: How can an inquirer persuade his or her audience (including self) that the findings of an inquiry are worth paying attention to, worth taking account of? What arguments can be mounted, what criteria invoked, what questions asked, that would be persuasive on this issue? (p. 290)

It is this systematicity and wider validation that arguably makes the difference between a research study (which seeks to analyse and interpret its data) and a personal project (which merely describes the data), or between a 'case study' and 'case story' (Bassey, 1999: 62). In order to help with this, the discipline of social science has been developing two sets of concepts and strategies for strengthening the validity and reliability of research, and we shall be examining them in detail in the context of school-based research in the rest of this chapter. But before we proceed, it is worth considering what is meant by the term 'qualitative research'.

## WHAT IS QUALITATIVE RESEARCH?

Defining what qualitative research is, as opposed to what it is not, presents a challenge, as the term is used to cover a wide range of methodological and epistemological paradigms. However, in educational research, the focus of such studies is on an in-depth probing of phenomena such as people's beliefs, assumptions, understandings, opinions, actions, interactions or other potential sources of evidence of the processes of learning or teaching. Furthermore, these phenomena are often not taken as given (i.e. they are not seen as pre-existing realities waiting to be uncovered) but as complex, developing, multifaceted, intertextual and largely dependent on the process of interpretation used in the investigation. In this way, one cannot divorce a discussion of qualitative methodology from the epistemological assumptions that underpin it. The epistemological paradigm on which qualitative research is predicated rejects the positivist view of knowledge and instead sees empirical data as being the product of 'multiple constructed realities'

(Lincoln and Guba, 1985: 295). This is why it is important to distinguish between qualitative or quantitative research design and qualitative or quantitative research methods since it is quite acceptable for a qualitative study to include the use of 'quantitative instruments' such as questionnaires, or tests, but the ultimate purpose of their use is as a contribution to understanding the particular constructions, beliefs and understandings of the subjects being researched. The range of instruments most frequently used to elicit relevant qualitative data consists of interviews (of which there are several types, serving different purposes), lesson observation notes and recordings, diaries (or other forms of written narrative), as well as information captured through non-verbal means.

Despite this focus on the particular, the 'constructed' and the context-dependent, qualitative research in education also seeks to produce knowledge, hypotheses, theoretical frameworks or case studies which will contribute to the systematic understanding of aspects of the processes of education.

One can infer from my above summary that qualitative research can be grouped under two broad categories: observational and introspective. Observational perspectives within a research design involve investigating phenomena which occur under 'natural' conditions, as, for instance, in the case of a teacher examining aspects of interactional dynamics between pupils working on group tasks in lessons. Unlike the conditions of quasi-experimental research which usually involve some specially designed set up, with a control group acting as a comparison, a qualitative approach would be to examine the phenomenon as it naturally occurs in lessons. This is why the term 'qualitative research' is often used interchangeably with the term 'naturalistic research'. The emphasis of introspective research, most commonly based on the use of interviews, is an examination of how individuals or groups make sense of or conceptualize phenomena related to teaching or learning. In this case, the researcher can be dealing with two layers of evidence: the informant's verbalized introspections and the phenomena in question.

Let us look at two hypothetical examples of qualitative studies conducted by classroom practitioners at an early stage of their career: one observational study and one introspective. We should note, of course, that it is often advisable to combine observational and introspective strategies within the same enquiry as data from both sources can be complementary, but it is nevertheless important for the practitioner research to be clear which perspective is the focus of their study.

## Example A

John Smith is a PGCE student teacher who specializes in the teaching of geography at secondary school level and who has begun his main professional placement at a mixed comprehensive school. As part of his training, John is required to carry out an in-depth subject studies investigation into some aspect of his school-based experience. The guidelines for the assignment require him to engage in a study that serves three distinct purposes: pedagogical, intellectual and developmental. What this means is that the study should be useful in terms of ultimately contributing to improved teaching in the area selected; it should also explore a legitimate theme which has been discussed by others within the subject and/or educational literature; and the experience of the research should be integral to the developmental training and not just an artificial add-on. How can a qualitative study serve these purposes? Following a discussion with his faculty tutor and school mentor, John decides to conduct an enquiry into teachers' and Y7 pupils' perceptions of the Key Stage 2/3 transition with regard to the teaching and learning of geography.

Over a period of a few weeks, John carries out individual interviews with the head of department and two other teachers of geography at his school. He also interviews five Y7 pupils individually and a focus group of six other Y7 pupils. He also teaches a Y7 geography class and keeps an ongoing record of relevant data emerging from this.

## Example B

Jane Collins is in her second year of teaching at a specialist language college, teaching French and Spanish to children across the 11–18 age range. She has registered on a Masters course aimed at teacher researchers at her local university and needs to design an empirical study based on some aspect of her current practice. Again, the rationale for the choice of topic is that it should be an appropriate intellectual investigation of an issue raised in the relevant literature, and contribute to an informed development of some aspects of the teacher's professional work. So the choice of topic will normally be linked to a problem or issue which the teacher has encountered within their own classroom teaching or other sphere of work within their school. Jane has found in her experience of language teaching that target language interaction takes place predominantly in teacher–whole class mode. Group or pair work interaction has proved difficult to fit into her normal work scheme schedule, but there have been signs that the pupils would be eager to interact amongst themselves in the target language, given the right conditions and support. So with appropriate preparation and task design, Jane introduces opportunities for small group work within her lessons with a Y10 French class over several weeks. What interests her is how the pupils collaborate in learning through the group interaction, the quality of the French produced, and when and why the pupils code switch from French to English and back again. The interactions of each group are recorded and an analysis of the transcripts is based on a separate coding framework for the three areas of focus.

These two examples of qualitative studies may well provide the teachers conducting them with valuable anecdotal information and insights regardless of the quality of the study as an instance of systematic research. However, this value is largely hit-or-miss and will not normally be of much use in contributing to the body of knowledge on the subject. In order to measure the quality of the research, two criteria are available to the educational researcher: reliability and validity. It is worth noting that to some extent these are conceptual labels each enclosing a variety of different types of measurement, not all of which are applicable in the qualitative context. What follows is a description of those which are applicable in this context, and their value will be illustrated where relevant through reference to the two examples described above.

## RELIABILITY

The notion of reliability refers to the rigour, consistency and, above all, trustworthiness of the research. In this sense, reliability is 'a precondition for validity' (Lincoln and Guba, 1985: 292). If a study is unreliable, then it cannot be said to be valid, if by the latter (as we shall see in the next section) we mean the extent to which a study measures what it intends to measure. However, the reverse does not hold: a reliable study can conceivably still be invalid, as in the case of research which is rigorous and trustworthy in its procedures but ends up answering a different set of questions to the ones it claims to do.

Given the importance of the construct, how can we estimate whether a research study is reliable or not? As Denscombe (1998: 213) notes, in qualitative studies, this is commonly done by asking the following question in relation to a particular study: 'If someone else did the research would he or she have got the same results and arrived at the same conclusions?' This operation therefore consists of holding the research as a constant variable and substituting the researcher, so that if the results turn out to be the same, we can eliminate the possibility of unreliability due to researcher bias. More specifically, there are two ways in which such a reliability test can be carried out. If 'someone else' (more usefully described by Nunan (1992: 17) as 'an independent researcher', since if it were a friend or colleague then there might be a transference of the initial bias) carried out a replication study in the same or different context and reached the same conclusion, this would verify the 'external reliability' of the original study. If the independent researcher re-analysed the data from the original study and reached the same conclusions, this would be an indication of the 'internal reliability' of the research.

However, while these operations are feasible in the context of quantitative research, they are much more problematic when applied to qualitative studies. While checking internal reliability is feasible as a procedure, it is limited in the context of qualitative research. Confining one's judgement exclusively to the evidence of re-analysis is to focus solely on the data produced and to ignore everything that led to the output. As we have seen, process and product are intricately linked in qualitative research and an assessment of the latter cannot be made without also taking account of the former. Establishing external reliability is, on the other hand, totally problematic. It is obvious that the chances of a qualitative study ever being repeated in the same context using the same informants and procedures by an independent researcher are remote or even, some would say, impossible since the context-dependent conditions of qualitative research are constantly subject to change: time passes, situations change, pupils are exposed to new learning and experiences and so on. An exact repetition, which logically is what is needed for verification, thus becomes impossible. Replication based in a different context with different pupils would introduce even more new, extraneous factors potentially influencing the findings.

A further problem relates to the fact that qualitative research (particularly in the case of an ethnographic study carried out by a teacher researcher) needs to acknowledge the role of the researcher in the research: this role is not merely an instrumental or procedural one but constitutes an integral part of the findings themselves, as interaction between the researcher and the researched is seen 'as an explicit part of knowledge production' (Flick,

2002: 6). In the case of action research by teachers, it is also quite likely that the responses and behaviour of pupils (or for that matter colleagues) being researched will consciously or subconsciously be influenced by the fact that the person interviewing or observing them is their own teacher (or colleague).

So replicability as a criterion for measuring the reliability of a qualitative study is here usually confined to the realm of the virtual or the hypothetical. The importance of the criterion therefore shifts to the strategies and processes that the researcher puts in place to allow such a hypothetical replication of his or her study.

In John's case, there are three main ways in which he can be explicit about his processes so that others can (in theory) do a repeat performance:

Firstly, it is important to situate the study within the context of an existing wider, intellectual and professional debate. John needs to provide a clear account of the aims and objectives of his research. These should not merely be listed but the rationale behind them should be presented and linked to prior discussion in the literature. The latter point is important for the purpose of reliability because it allows the researcher to connect with ideas, arguments, theories and the research of others and uses aspects of this shared resource and shared understanding as a basis or starting point for the individual study. In so doing, it allows for scrutiny of the aims and objectives, at least, on a more generalized and 'objective' scale. This connection could be made in different ways, including, for instance, by alluding to the literature on relevant educational policy-making such as Ofsted's view that secondary schools fail to ensure that their 'pupils build on what they learned at primary school'. In addition, John's aims and objectives can link to prior analyses of pupils' perceptions of learning geography at KS2 and KS3.

Secondly, the reliability of a study depends on the degree of transparency of research rationale and decisions guiding the selection of the research sample. John needs to be explicit about how his research was undertaken. This information would refer to the selection of the pupil sample as well as to the educational profiles of the people involved. The rationale for the sample selection needs to be given: why were the pupils chosen from one Y7 class? Did the group include pupils who had gone to different primary schools? Why was this important as opposed to selecting pupils with the same primary school history? What was the basis for choosing to interview those teachers in particular?

Finally, reliability depends on the accessibility of data collection and analysis procedures. These will involve keeping transcripts of interviews and records of lesson observation and other fieldwork notes. Questions used at interview need to be justified in relation to the specific study aims. This is important, even though in qualitative studies, especially when interviewing children, one is likely to use semi-structured interviews which are flexible and allow individual interviewees the scope to follow their own thread of thinking rather than being constrained by closed, structured questions.

## VALIDITY

Validity too is an umbrella term which encompasses a variety of different qualities that have been applied to educational research. As with the concept of reliability, a study's validity is often identified through reference to the following binary contrast: external validity and internal validity.

External validity has been defined as the extent to which the research design succeeds in allowing one to 'generalize beyond the subjects under investigation to a wider population' (Nunan, 1992: 17). In other words, external validity is an indication of the generalizability or 'transferability' (Miles and Huberman, 1994: 279) of the study's findings. In quantitative studies, researchers use randomized samples from a given population in order to strengthen the generalizability claims of their findings. However, given that qualitative research is essentially context-bound and ethnographic, external validity is generally viewed as inappropriate since it contradicts the epistemological and methodological perspectives in this approach. However, Lincoln and Guba (1985: 301) suggest that 'thick description' should be provided 'to enable someone interested in making a transfer to reach a conclusion about whether transfer can be contemplated as a possibility'. The term 'thick description', popularized by the anthropologist Clifford Geertz who borrowed it from the philosopher Gilbert Ryle, refers to the close analytical account and interpretation of the 'structures of signification' (1973: 9) inherent in events and social behaviour.

Internal validity, on the other hand, is highly applicable to the qualitative context, and it is very important for the researcher to consider since in its most fundamental form, it refers to the extent to which a study 'actually investigates what it purports to investigate' (Nunan, 1992: 14). In other words, this quality refers to the 'authenticity' or 'credibility' of the findings (Miles and Huberman, 1994: 278). Checking internal validity involves different strategies, as we shall see, but the key element is that of evidence of a persuasive connection between the conclusions made in the outcome of the study and the procedures and methodology used in collecting and analysing the data. Maxwell (2005) usefully warns the researcher against the automatic use of strategies to offset threats to the study's validity. Masters' students sometimes describe an inventory of strategies they have used, quoting authorities from the literature but without reference to the specific threats within their own study, as if this automatically endorses the internal validity of the research. 'Validity threats are made implausible by evidence not methods' (p.105), and therefore it is important to identify the potential areas under threat in the proposed study first and then to implement appropriate strategies to counter them. The methodology chapter in the report (or thesis) should discuss that connection explicitly and should be honest about the extent to which the strategy is successful in reducing the particular threat.

What follows is a selection of strategies which are particularly applicable in the context of school-based teacher research, and illustrated through reference to the study described earlier in Example B.

## Long-term involvement

This is one strategy where the teacher researcher is at an advantage over the external researcher. The purpose of this strategy is to overcome weaknesses, errors of judgement and patchy knowledge of the field due to the researcher's status as an outsider and therefore will enhance the credibility of the study's findings. However, when teachers are researching aspects of their own practice at their own school, an ethnographic 'feel' for the context in which the data is generated, the contextual background of the research, can be more easily achieved.

## Why is it necessary?

Lincoln and Guba identify two aspects of long-term involvement (1985: 301). The first they call 'prolonged engagement' which serves the purpose of making the researcher 'more open to the multiple influences of the phenomenon being studied'. In the case of Jane Collins's study (Example B), the researcher could rightly claim that she has a good knowledge of the pupils' attitude and performance in French since she is teaching them over the academic year and may have taught some at least in her previous first year at the school. She also has access to information relating to the pupils' personalities, behaviour and general academic performance through other colleagues and extracurricular contact. This first-hand contact developed over time will help to build trust between Jane and her pupil-subjects, and will allow her to understand the 'culture' of the school and how to interpret it. It is unlikely that the validity of her research will be threatened by insufficient knowledge in this area.

The second aspect of long-term involvement which is identified by Lincoln and Guba is what they call 'persistent observation' and this does require proactive planning by Jane. The authors argue that this strategy serves the purpose of identifying 'those characteristics and elements in the situation that are most relevant to the problem' being investigated.

## How can the threat be reduced in Jane's study?

Jane's study involves the analysis of small group interaction on pupils' target language use. The purpose is to see how this kind of learning situation to which the pupils are not accustomed generates their use of spoken French. Insufficient opportunities for pupils to engage in such tasks will not lead to valid findings: two or three lessons over the term could produce results which may be invalid because insufficient time has been allowed for the pupils to overcome their lack of familiarity with the learning task and situation. Pupils who are reluctant to speak French in whole class situations may need time to adapt to group interaction. As well as its importance in allowing her pupils to adapt to their new learning situation, the strategy of 'long-term engagement' will help Jane to develop a clearer research focus through her preliminary observation of the interactions. She can do this through a pilot phase which serves the purpose of identifying what features of the pupils' interaction seem to be the most salient, what the obstacles are to her investigation and where the promising kinds of evidence in terms of her research aims seem to arise. In this way, the specific focus of Jane's observation and of her eventual analysis emerge from the research itself.

## TRIANGULATION

This is a widely endorsed strategy for strengthening the internal validity of qualitative studies in social science. It is based on the principle of confirming findings through the use of multiple perspectives. The key aspect of the strategy is threats to the validity of the conclusions, caused by the particular biases of any one source, method or agent of research, and which will be lessened by employing a variety of type.

### Why is it necessary?

Writers have argued that there is a need for several types of triangulation in relation to qualitative research, but I shall focus on three modes which can have a bearing on the type of research design discussed in this chapter: triangulation of sources, of methods and of investigators. Triangulation of different sources can mean simply the inclusion of multiple informants (i.e. interviewees or subjects under observation). However, by including different categories of informants (e.g. teachers and pupils, secondary- and primary-based informants, pupils of different gender or ability or from different classrooms), the converging perspectives will arguably make the findings more powerful. Triangulation of methods involves the use of different data-collection instruments with the same subjects. This has the merit of counterbalancing the threats inherent to any one method. For instance, the likelihood of the 'Hawthorne effect' occurring is arguably stronger in the case of individual interviews than in the case of questionnaires, particularly if the interviewer is known to the interviewee. Questionnaires, however, have their own and different weaknesses such as less freedom for the interviewee to develop their own thoughts and a reliance on the written form of expression. Finally, triangulation of investigators refers to the use of more than one person in collecting or analysing the data. One can argue that triangulation as a research device is particularly valuable in the case of introspective research, though as we shall see in our examples, it is also a useful strategy in strengthening the credibility of observational studies.

Some commentators (e.g. Silverman, 2001: 233) argue that the use of triangulation is inappropriate in qualitative research as it contravenes the ethnographic perspective in which the context of each source of evidence, of each method used and of each investigator's approach is of intrinsic value. Comparing results from different angles of enquiry therefore cannot be used to strengthen a common finding. However, a less extreme view would be that it is possible to maintain the primacy of the researcher's main source and methods of research as well as of his or her own interpretation of the results, while also drawing on the multiple sources of evidence and analysis in support of the validity of that main focus.

# How can the threat be reduced in both studies?

As an example of introspective research, John's study would benefit from all three kinds of triangulation. In particular, the type of study envisaged here calls out for the need for triangulation of sources. By interviewing teachers and pupils including, if possible, teachers from the feeder primary school, John would be able to gather together the views of a range of people on the issue of the effects of KS2/3 transfer on the learning of geography based on triangulation of sources of information. If the conclusions relied exclusively on evidence from the pupils, we would feel less confident about them since, taken alone, the pupil interview data may be skewed by the 'Hawthorne effect' or by a partial recall of geography learning in the primary school.

Despite the observational focus of Jane's study, the internal validity of the findings would be strengthened in particular by the use of triangulation of methods. In order to make general claims about how her pupils collaborate in small group interaction and what forms of target language use this generates, she needs to have some evidence that the pupils' performance is not entirely dependent on the nature of the group task or on the dynamics of particular peer interrelations. In order to do this, Jane can usefully think about different methods of eliciting group target language use by asking them to engage in different types of language tasks over her data-collection period. These could for instance include role plays, debates, problem-solving tasks or description tasks. It would be important to include a variety of task types since hidden pupil preferences may be determined by the type of language needed in the different tasks (for instance, knowledge of particular vocabulary topics), or by the possibility of different kinds of interaction (e.g. argument, collaboration) appealing to different types of personality.

Jane's interest in probing the reasons why her pupils perform linguistically in particular ways could lead to conclusions whose validity may be under threat unless she took suitable measures to strengthen her case. In order to offset exclusive reliance on her own explanation of the data, Jane could carry out individual pupil interviews as another form of methods triangulation in her study. This would be especially useful in investigating the reasons why individuals code switch at particular points in the group dialogue. Though Jane may be able to interpret some possible reasons by looking for patterns of switching in the transcripts, her analysis would benefit from asking some of the pupils to come up with their own explanations. She might also be able to use the interviews as an opportunity to test out some of her own interpretations of the code-switching patterns on the pupils themselves to see whether they confirmed her own views. Of course, even if the pupils rejected some of her conclusions, this would not necessarily invalidate them since the impulse might be operating at a subconscious level. However, having this discussion with the pupils in itself would strengthen her study by providing a thicker layering of interpreted data and by demonstrating more of an awareness of the complexities of the research process.

As far as triangulation of investigators is concerned, both John and Jane would gain some benefit from asking a colleague to examine a sample of their data relating to a particular aspect of their research, in order to see if the kind of interpretations they themselves are making of the data are reiterated in their colleagues' responses.

## LOOKING FOR NEGATIVE EVIDENCE

### Why is it necessary?

This is a way of confirming one's findings by revising hypotheses in the light of negative evidence in the data. Miles and Huberman (1994: 263) describe this tactic as part of a set of strategies for looking at 'unpatterns' that 'test a conclusion about a "pattern" by saying what it is *not* like'. Other similar strategies they list are 'checking the meaning of outliers', 'using extreme cases' and 'following up surprises'. Perhaps more explicitly than the previous two strategies I have examined in this chapter, looking for negative evidence focuses on the link between the empirical evidence collected and the theories, hypotheses or conclusions which the researcher draws once the analytical process is throwing up some insights.

### How can the threat be reduced in Jane's study?

Looking for negative evidence is one way of guarding against one's natural tendency to be over-enthusiastic about a particular interpretation or pattern of findings. Qualitative research is not about proving a point or seeking confirmation of theories, but often the excitement of discovering one or more instances in the data which support a particular interpretation of the phenomenon under scrutiny can lead the researcher to fix too quickly and too unequivocally on a particular interpretation of the data. For instance, Jane might discover that pupils are more ready to use the target language if it is in a repeat situation (i.e. where they have already encountered a need to use the expression in a similar communicative situation in a previous task). Without resorting to a quantitative count of the number of times target language use appears in a repeat situation, which would not be a very useful approach in a qualitative study, Jane could also look at cases where pupils did use French in new communicative situations or failed to do so in repeat situations. Whether this results in her revising her conclusions or not, simply by demonstrating to us (and to herself) that she has looked at negative evidence will give us and her more confidence in the hypotheses she does make and conclusions she ultimately draws.

## CONCLUSION: THINKING ABOUT RELIABILITY AND VALIDITY IN RELATION TO YOUR OWN PROJECT

As the examples discussed in this chapter have demonstrated, these two concepts are important issues to consider at different stages of your research design. At the back of your mind, you should think about how your research findings and plan will look to other practitioners in educational research. At the planning stage, think about where the weaknesses are likely to be in data collection and analysis. How effectively do they relate to your research questions and objectives? It is always useful to discuss your plan with a colleague or a supervisor before you commit to it. Look for examples in the literature to see how other people have designed similar studies. Having identified the potential weaknesses, then you can start planning strategies such as those described above which you can tailor to deal with the particular threats to the reliability and validity of your research.

Remember that there is a fundamental difference between qualitative and quantitative research: the former does not seek to reach hard factual conclusions based on some form of measurement; its aim is to generate hypotheses and arguments or to explore themes supported by trustworthy evidence from the data. Be explicit (and self-critical where relevant) about how you tried to ensure that that evidence and your analysis is trustworthy.

### Activity 7.1

#### How does pupils' use of ICT in lessons support their learning?

Imagine that you want to investigate this question in relation to the context of your subject teaching. Consider the following questions which you would need to address in the design of a qualitative study focusing on your own classroom experiences with one or more groups at your school.

- What sort of pupil use of ICT would you want to examine and why?
- Which aspects of their learning would you want to begin by looking at?
- What sort of evidence would you want to gather relating to the pupils' use of technology?
- What other forms of data collection would you carry out?
- List the procedures and types of information that would be needed for others to carry out a replication study.
- What would be the likely threats to the internal validity of your study?
- What strategies would you use to guard against these threats?

## KEY IDEAS

This chapter has sought to identify the main benefits of thinking about the *reliability* and *validity* of research carried out by teacher researchers. I have argued that the two notions are important measures for use in the assessment of both observational and introspective qualitative research. Reliability refers to the degree of rigour, consistency and trustworthiness of a study. This measurement is traditionally conceived in relation to the agent of the research. If an independent researcher carried out the same study, would they arrive at the same findings (*Internal reliability*)? If an independent researcher carried out the same research elsewhere, would they reach the same conclusions (*External reliability*)? Validity was described as the degree to which a study measures what it claims to measure. *External validity* refers to the generalizability of the findings. This was seen to be inappropriate in real terms within the epistemological framework of qualitative research. However, it can be useful if seen as a tool for hypothetical validation. *Internal validity*, on the other hand, was described as an important quality which focused on the connection between a study's findings and the data-collection and analysis procedures used to reach them. Three types of strategies for checking the internal validity of qualitative studies by teacher researchers were described and exemplified. *Long-term involvement* provides the researcher with sufficient time to develop a familiarity and understanding of the subjects, the data and research process which result in a strengthening of the validity of the findings. *Triangulation* of sources, of methods and of investigators protect the study against threats to internal validity of findings due to exposure to the biases inherent in any one source, method or individual researcher. *Looking for negative evidence* is a way of confirming particular patterns in the findings by examining contrary evidence and therefore being able to say what the patterns are not like.

## References

Bassey, M. (1999) *Case Study Research in Educational Settings*. Buckingham: Open University Press.

Denscombe, M. (1998) *The Good Research Guide*. Buckingham: Open University Press.

Flick, U. (2002) *An Introduction to Qualitative Research*. London: Sage.

Geertz, C. (1973) *The Interpretation of Cultures*. New York: Basic Books.

Lincoln, Y. S. and Guba, G. (1985) *Naturalistic Inquiry*. London: Sage.

Maxwell, J. A. (2005) *Qualitative Research Design: An Interactive Approach*. London: Sage.

Miles, M. B. and Huberman, A. M. (1994) *Qualitative Data Analysis*. London: Sage.

Nunan, D. (1992) *Research Methods in Language Learning*. Cambridge: Cambridge University Press.

Office for Standards in Education (Ofsted) (2003) Ofsted Subject Reports Series 2001/2002: *Geography in Secondary Schools*, www.ofsted.gov.uk.inspect/index.htm

Silverman, D. (2001) *Interpreting Qualitative Data*, 2nd edn. London: Sage.

# ANALYSING QUALITATIVE DATA

## Michael Evans

### Hints

- In order to analyse your data systematically, you need to have it recorded (preferably in written form). The more often you read a transcript, the more you will see in it.
- Let the transcript speak to you; don't just focus on pre-established questions and issues.
- Remember that qualitative analysis software does not do the analysing for you. You have to do that. The computer programme allows you to organize your data with ease so you can group and focus more clearly on specific bits of the data.
- Remember that qualitative research is not concerned with objective certainties. Frame your sentences with appropriate caution, e.g. 'It would seem that …'.

## THE FORM OF QUALITATIVE DATA

Most qualitative data in empirical research first appear in their raw form as oral (non-textual) data. Interviews or classroom interaction are perhaps the most common forms of oral data which are of interest to the educational researcher. In order to analyse these data, it is necessary to be able to reflect on them repeatedly and at length; to be able to fragment and manipulate them in the search for underlying patterns and meanings. For this reason, it is useful to convert the oral data into textual form through the process of transcription. However, it becomes immediately apparent that this process is usually fraught with problems related to the risk of distorting the original version. For instance, non-verbal signs (such as gestures, facial expression and pauses) which accompany verbal discourse can have an important bearing on the meanings expressed in the interaction. Efforts should be made to systematically capture such paralinguistic messages and to note them in the transcript. There are numerous differences in the systems used by researchers and it is important for you to use only those markers which are relevant to what you are looking for in your data. For instance, an extract of a transcript that focuses on pupil discourse, where the nuances of language and expression are central to the study, will look different to the transcript of an interview where the focus of interest is in the content of the informant's responses rather than on the form of their expression. So it is unnecessary, unrealistic and unwise to try to capture everything in a transcript. It *is* necessary, though, for you to think about what you do need to note and then to be systematic in the notation. The key to the coding system you are using should always be included in the report, usually in an appendix. The following is an example:

---

**BOX 8.1    Example of a transcription system (adapted from Ellis and Barkhuizen, 2005: 29)**

1. T = teacher; R = researcher; subjects are designated by their (fictional) initials, or P for pupil.
2. Each line is numbered for ease of reference (useful with long extracts).
3. Pauses are indicated in brackets:
   (.) indicates a pause of a second or shorter;
   (.3.) indicates the length of a pause beyond one second.
4. XXX is used to indicate speech that could not be deciphered.
5. … indicates an incomplete utterance.
6. Words are underlined to show overlapping speech between two speakers.
7. Words are italicized to show a very heavily stressed word.
8. A limited amount of contextual information is given in brackets.

---

## THE BLURRED LINE BETWEEN DATA COLLECTION AND ANALYSIS

Analysing qualitative data can be an exciting phase in the research process since it relies on a creative engagement by the researcher in the production, application and interpretation of ideas. To refer to it as a 'phase' is perhaps to misrepresent its nature, since in qualitative research data collection and analysis are not always separate; analysis does not always follow collection – it can sometimes precede it. It is also likely to occur at different points of the research rather than just in one block. The two are not isolated activities but interact with one another in the common pursuit of investigating the research question. This interaction between data collection and analysis is evident on different levels. At the level of research strategy, different collection and analysis activities feed off each other. For instance, in action research, the results of an analysis of one set of data will inform subsequent data collection activities. Huberman and Miles (1998) describe the process in more cyclical terms, seeing analysis as containing three interlinking sub-processes: data reduction, data display and conclusion drawing/verification:

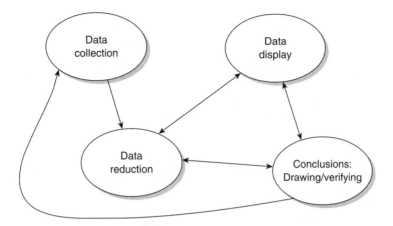

Figure 8.1    Components of data analysis: an interactive model (Huberman and Miles, 1998: 181)

These processes occur *before* data collection, during study design and planning; *during* data collection as interim and early analyses are carried out; and *after* data collection as final products are approached and completed. (p.180)

The interactive nature of their model is captured in Figure 8.1.

This interaction between data collection and data analysis is also apparent at a more local level. A semi-structured interview, for instance, allows the interviewer scope to free the interview to develop in certain directions in response to comments made by the interviewee. The following extract, for example, is from a focus group interview with Y9 pupils as part of a study I carried out on the impact of school exchange visits on pupils' proficiency in French. It illustrates how my questioning was influenced by an implicit ongoing analysis of the responses I elicited.

## Transcript Extract: Focus group interview with Y9 pupils

 1  R: Did you have a lot in common with them?
 2  P1: well, no (.) it's just that . . . I don't know, it just seemed that We didn't (.) we didn't have
 3  a lot in common. It was just that I got to know him quite quickly and I mean that we can
 4  speak together easily.
 5  R: Was it you who made the effort or him or both equally?
 6  P1: Well, he wasn't very good at English so . . . I mean, he tried to be friends, if you see
 7  what I mean. But he didn't speak that much so he just like showed me around in his room
 8  and his house and stuff like that. So that helped.
 9  R: Some of you put in your questionnaire that you got on well . . . you liked the family, or
10  the adults, but you didn't have that much in common with your partner. Was that anybody
11  from this group?

12 P2: Yes.

13 R: What did you mean by that? I'm a bit surprised by that.

14 P2: Well, the mum was really friendly to me and it was odd but because I was sharing

15 their house with Tamsin, mine seemed to offload me on to Tamsin and her French

16 exchange so I didn't really get to know my partner but I got to know the mum and

17 Tamsin's exchange, so it didn't really work that well.

18 R: And did they speak to you in French, the parents?

19 P2: Um, yes, because she didn't know any English.

20 R: And did that pose a problem?

21 P2: No.

22 R: What about the rest of you? Did you communicate in French?

23 P3: No, my parents were all like really really strong in English so we spoke in English the

24 whole time.

25 R: Did you find that a bit annoying?

26 P3: No, it was really easy!

27 R: Because that made you feel more at home?

28 P3: Yeah.

29 P4: Yeah, my one's mum got all her university English work out to show me!

30 R: Did you feel that you could say to them, 'Well, can we practise the French?' at all? I

31 know it's difficult to do that.

32 P4: No, because you've got your French person.

33 R: Right, your partner, yes. What were the sorts of situations which were difficult for you

34 in terms of language? I mean, where you had to speak in French and you thought, you

35 know, 'I don't know what to say'? Were there any particular situations where you wished

36 you could speak French?

37 P4: They had like lots of (.) kind of sayings which when they're translated into English

38 they don't like mean the same thing in English. So even if you've like translated with a

39 dictionary, it still doesn't mean anything to you.

40 P2: I would say the English. You can't explain to them like when they want to do

41 something and you don't want to do it, you can't say it politely! Because you can't say

42 'I'm sorry, I really just don't want to do this'. You have to say 'No'.

43 P5: I had loads of arguments with mine actually.

44 R: Really? With your partner?

45 P5: Yes.

46 R: What sort of thing?

47 P5: I got told to stop being rude!

48 R: Rude? Who by? By him?

49 P5: The mum.

50 R: By his mum? Right! What were the arguments about?

51 P5: About going places, because mine didn't want to go anywhere and it was my birthday

52 party and they wouldn't let me go.

53 R: Oh, right.

54 P6: I had to translate for her! Hers got really angry at *me* for saying what *she* was saying!

(Laughter)

As this extract shows, the interviewer is constantly making decisions about what to follow up from the interviewee's responses; and these decisions are made on the basis of what one might call 'online analysis', made however fleetingly and instinctively by the interviewer during the flow of the interview. For instance, Pupil 3's comments (lines 23–24) that her partner's parents spoke in English to her all the time interested me because this could potentially reveal something about how the pupil saw the relationship between language learning and personal communication. My first hypothesis-suggesting question (that the parents' use of English was 'annoying') was rejected by the pupil. But my second hypothesis-question (that communicating in English had a comforting effect) proved more acceptable and seemed to have the agreement of at least one other pupil in the group. One could therefore argue that for a brief moment what was happening here was a form of 'collaborative analysis'.

One might object at this point that we are here precariously treading the delicate line between informants' and researcher's constructions of the meanings surrounding events and experiences being researched. However, as noted earlier, qualitative research paradigms to a certain extent legitimize researcher input in the process of data elicitation, provided this input is explicitly acknowledged and critiqued. In the case of young pupil informants, the strategy is arguably particularly needed in order to draw out their analytical thinking.

## DEDUCTIVE AND INDUCTIVE ORIENTATIONS IN QUALITATIVE ANALYSIS

There are two competing tensions when embarking on qualitative analysis which are best seen as two ends of a continuum. On the one hand, qualitative researchers have an overarching idea of what it is they want to investigate in the data and some notion at least of the different areas in which this sought-after information can be grouped. This 'deductive' approach seeks to generate and examine findings in relation to pre-established themes which may not be exhaustive or totally defined at the outset, but which nevertheless provide overall direction to the development of the analysis. At the other end of the spectrum, the inductive approach, adopted, for instance, by grounded theorists, takes an entirely open mind to the data and uses themes which emerge from the data themselves as tools for the analysis. In reality, educational researchers dealing with qualitative material usually employ a mixture of the two approaches, but, as Huberman and Miles point out, the different emphases appeal to different types of studies:

> There is merit in both 'loose', inductively oriented designs, and 'tight', more deductively approached ones. The former work well when the terrain is unfamiliar and/or excessively complex, a single case is involved, and the intent is exploratory and descriptive. Tighter designs are indicated when the researcher has good prior acquaintance with the setting, has a good bank of applicable, well delineated concepts, and takes a more explanatory and/or confirmatory stance involving multiple, comparable cases. (1998: 185)

In either of the two orientations, the systematic character of the analysis is largely dependent on the use of a coding system to organize and structure the examination of the material. Coding is the process by which a text is examined thematically according to certain categories (codes) which are either predetermined or emergent from the data. The categories serve the purpose of reducing the total mass of data elicited in order to focus on what they tell us about the particular themes we are interested in. The process also allows the researcher to identify in the data evidence links to the different categories, to closely organize and inspect that evidence, and to use the process to inform and develop the themes indexed by the categories.

## Coding Framework

One of the first steps in this process is the development of a coding framework which can be applied systematically to the analysis of qualitative data. The framework should in the first instance remain fluid and develop on the basis of preliminary readings of some of the transcripts or at least of the pilot data. The following example is of a coding framework which I drew up in a study of pupils' code-switching between English and French in an online bulletin board project between pupils in England and in francophone countries. The framework was applied to the analysis of interviews I carried out with some of the English pupils involved in the project (Evans, forthcoming).

The codes, listed in the left-hand column, refer to topics which I wanted to identify and for which I wanted to collate evidence from the pupil interviews. The right-hand column provides a brief description of what each code represents. This description is useful for supporting the validity claims of your findings and therefore it is advisable to include it in your methodology chapters in your dissertation or report. The descriptions are also useful to you as a researcher in that they help you to crystallize in your mind exactly what it is that you are targeting with each code. In the above example, I grouped the codes according to different dimensions of language use identified in the sociolinguistics literature. The types of concepts referred to by my codes in this framework are fairly descriptive or factual, in that they sought to locate references to these topics either directly or indirectly in the pupils' interview responses, with minimal levels of researcher interpretation at this stage.

## Different types of coding

The second point to bear in mind is that researchers have identified the need for different kinds of coding and decisions. Although different writers define several distinct types of categories in the coding of qualitative data, it is best to focus initially on two main types: open coding and thematic coding. I shall from now on, in line with the literature, refer to categories as 'codes', defined as the names or labels that refer to concepts (synonymous with 'theme' in common parlance). The denotation of 'concept' is not trivial, however, since even at its most basic, descriptive level, coding is a process of translating raw data into conceptual references. Let us look at the example provided by

Strauss and Corbin (1998: 106–9) illustrating their coding of part of an interview with a young adult talking about teenage drug use. The following extract is taken from the beginning of the transcript presented by the authors, and the labels in square brackets are the codes the researchers applied to the text:

Interviewer: Tell me about teens and drug use.

Respondent: I think teens use drugs as a release from their parents [**"rebellious act"**]. Well, I don't know. I can only talk for myself. For me, it was an experience [**experience**] [**in-vivo code**]. You hear a lot about drugs [**"drug talk"**]. You hear they are bad for you [**"negative connotation"** to the **"drug talk"**]. There is a lot of them around [**"available supply"**]. You just get into them because they're accessible [**"easy access"**] and because it's kind of a new thing [**"novel experience"**]. It's cool! You know, it's something that is bad for you, taboo, a "no" [**"negative connotation"**]. Everyone is against it [**"adult negative stance"**]. If you are a teenager, the first thing you are going to do is try them [**"challenge the adult negative stance"**].

One can see that the codes attached by the researchers to this passage are doing more than just labelling: they are lifting the specific points made by the interviewee to a more generalized, conceptual plane. The code 'rebellious act' is an idea which has certain 'properties' and 'dimensions' which differentiate it from other related concepts, such as 'mindless act' or 'self-destructive act', and is applicable in other contexts and in relation to other people. The 'property' in this case might be that the act is directed against authority figures, and the 'dimensions' of this property might be 'parents', 'teachers', 'society in general'. Even at this initial stage of the analysis where the researchers are essentially attempting to identify and itemize the content of the data, the process involves a degree of conceptual interpretation. The above is an example of 'open coding' which Strauss and Corbin define as 'the analytic process through which concepts are identified and their properties and dimensions are discovered in data' (1998: 101).

The act of open coding has the effect of fracturing the transcript into different fragments which are labelled according to extensive lists of codes. Sometimes the same fragment can have several different codes attached to it. This process therefore results in a reduction of the material which in ethnographic studies especially can be dauntingly voluminous. These fragments can then be examined in groups, thus enabling the researcher to focus on the concepts and the related evidence from the data. The danger of such an analytical strategy is that a textual fragment (and therefore the evidence) becomes detached from its original context and might lead ultimately to a distorted or inaccurate reading. To guard against this, the analyst must attempt to preserve as far as possible a balance between the aims of categorization and contextualization.

Another feature of the process of open coding, which is illustrated by the Strauss and Corbin quote above, is the use of 'in-vivo codes'. These are words or phrases which are borrowed from the data and used as an open code. In this example, 'experience' is an in-vivo code since its use as a code is prompted by the interviewee's use of the word as part of their own explanation of their drug consumption. In-vivo codes are particularly useful in inductive analysis orientations as they help to ensure that analysis and resulting interpretations remain close to the original material and reduce the risk of extraneous ideas influencing the interpretation of the data.

Thematic (also labelled 'pattern coding' by Miles and Huberman (1994: 57–8)) coding is a form of analytical coding which involves the search for thematic patterns in the coded data, often at a higher level of abstraction than open codes. Grounded theorists like Strauss and Corbin, for whom the ultimate purpose of qualitative analysis is the construction of theory, refer to the process as 'axial coding'. As Robson has noted (2002: 494), the process is 'about linking together the categories developed through the process of open coding'. As such, it can be described as a process of analysis which is at a level which is further removed from the textual origination of the data. The focus now is on the codes themselves and their theoretical connotations. In this way, a broader theoretical argument surrounding the emergent themes begins to develop. For instance, in the example of the study referred to above, once I had gathered the relevant quotations from my data in relation to 'code choice', 'codeswitching', and 'word choice', I was able to examine them in relation to the three concepts and to compare, for instance, the pupils' explanations of their decisions in relation to the three phenomena. This allowed me to see whether different types of considerations were at play in the pupils' minds and therefore to develop an argument about the pupils' communicative priorities and the constraints on these.

**Table 8.1  A coding framework for the analysis of interview data**

| | |
|---|---|
| **Ideational Dimension** | |
| Code choice | Reasons for using French or English in posts |
| Codeswitch | Explanation of codeswitching and codemixing |
| Content | Choice of topic in post |
| Word choice | Meaning-related explanations for the choice of a particular word |
| Opinion | Opinion-related influence on the content of post |
| | |
| **Interpersonal Dimension** | |
| Borrow | Copying text from native speaker posts |
| Interact | Perceptions of interactions with other members of the group |
| Read | Comments on the experience of reading other people's posts |
| Tu/vous | Rationalization of choice between the two forms of address in posts |
| | |
| **Metalinguistic Dimension** | |
| Know | Reference to what they know |
| Learn | Reference to learning goals, outcomes and experience |
| Schoollang | Reference to the nature of their school language learning |
| SayWrite | Describing the online communicative process |

## The Practice of Coding: by hand or by computer

The first step in open coding is to go through the transcript and, line by line, label those bits of it that correspond to the codes which you have previously identified or new ones which emerge as you proceed. If you are doing this by hand, then the codes should be written in the margin with some form of highlighting of the selected text. Working on a word processor, the codes can be entered in brackets within the text, usually immediately after the relevant segment.

One of my former Masters' students gives the following vivid and honest account of how having started off by entering her data onto a computer software analysis program (namely, *NVivo*) and begun the process of coding the data, she eventually abandoned the medium in favour of the less technologically sophisticated but time-honoured tradition of pen and paper:

> Confident that the programme would help me formulate an assertion about gender and motivation, I started to form trees or families of nodes with different attribute values. It did not take me long to realize that my data was being transformed into a computer version that had very little in common with the original group interviews. So I stopped the process, printed all the units of analysis from the open coding and displayed them on a wall.

The benefit of doing the analysis manually is, as this student found, that you maintain a sense of overall control and viewing of the data globally. For some researchers, the physical ability to cut up the different quotations and to sort them according to the different code headings and to view the groupings simultaneously can provide a valuable perspective to stimulate emergent interpretations and findings. This retention of an overall view of the data is part of what helps the researcher to hold on to the original version of the events rather than, as the student above observed, transforming it into a computer version. On the other hand, there are drawbacks to the manual approach. Firstly, it is only feasible to do this with relatively small amounts of data. For studies involving several interviews with several informants or large amounts of transcripts of classroom data, the scissors-and-glue approach could quickly break down. Even with a small quantity of data, the ability to manage the data manually is very restricted: for instance, you will often want to mark the same piece of text with two or more codes. This is not easily done on paper.

Programs such as *NVivo* or *Atlas.ti* are quite costly and it may not be economic for a teacher to invest in one for personal use. However, if you are enrolled at a local university for your study, then it would normally be possible for you to make use of that facility.

It is important to recognize from the outset that computer-aided qualitative data analysis software (or CAQDAS) does not analyse the data for you: the programs are simply support platforms which facilitate the storage and management of the qualitative data and phases of analysis. You still have to do the analysis and interpretation yourself. So what are the main ways in which a program such as *NVivo* can be of use to a hard-pressed practitioner researcher?

- Software: programs such as *Nvivo* and *Atlas.ti* were developed specifically as tools for supporting the analysis of data collected in social research. They are therefore designed to incorporate a wide range of data (textual, visual or aural) which can all be subjected to the same sets of codes. This means that it is possible to link bits of visual data or taped interviews to particular open codes and therefore you can have access to an original piece of source material as well as a transcript version. More usually, the database will consist of textual data. Provided the sources are saved as txt, rtf or Microsoft Word documents, they can be uploaded and saved on to the software program and all the coding is done directly on screen. Your bank of data can include informal documents such as notes and memos as well as formal transcripts of interviews, lesson observations and so on.

- Coding: I have already mentioned some of the benefits of the computer-based coding of data, such as allowing the researcher to apply several codes to the same fragment of text, to combine different media in the same coding framework, and the general ease with which one can code (and 'uncode') a transcript. Another major facility is the ability to retrieve and print out all the quotes for particular codes, thus allowing the researcher to focus exclusively on those bits of the text that have been identified as relating to a particular theme or issue. The screen which displays the quotes will also have a hyperlink to the original source document from which each quote is taken, thus allowing the researcher to return easily and at will to the original context of the reference in order to guard against distortion through an overreliance on decontextualized fragments. *NVivo* also allows the user to incorporate their preliminary thoughts as they code by using the 'annotations' tool. This is a useful facility since it means that you can quickly jot down your thoughts, queries and interpretations of a particular instance of coding and attach it to the coded piece of text. Your fleeting preliminary thoughts are thus captured and easily retrieved whenever you call up the transcript on the program.

- Displays: these allow you to present a visual configuration of aspects of your study. This can have different objectives, including the following: to explore the interrelationship between different concepts or themes in the data; to configure the relationship between different contextual factors influencing the phenomena being investigated. A display in qualitative research can serve different purposes: it can be used as a preliminary template for organizing the analysis, or as part of a final, summative presentation of the researcher's findings. Another useful purpose to which displays can be put is that of supporting research-in-progress. By structuring and re-structuring your displays as you progress through your analysis, you can explore your research questions and experiment with your conclusions visually and in a focused way. *NVivo* refers to displays as 'models'. These are 'dynamic' in that by linking them to specific items in the source data (e.g. transcripts, notes, etc.), you can call up the evidence and examine or present its relationship to a theoretical, conceptual or other framework. In longitudinal research, a series of changing displays provides a 'snapshots' record of the development of your analysis over time and can thus make a useful component of the reflexive dimension in ethnographic research.

- Matrices: like figures and diagrams, a matrix is a particular format of an analytical display. Miles and Huberman define a matrix as 'essentially the "crossing" of two lists, set up as rows and columns' (1994: 93). The authors list the following benefits to the researcher of producing matrices during the course of the research (p. 239):

> It requires you to think about your research questions and what portions of your data are needed to answer them; it requires you to make full analyses, ignoring no relevant

information; and it focuses and organizes your information coherently. These advantages are repeated when you include displays in a final report; the reader can re-create your intellectual journey with some confidence.

The structure of a matrix is based on a comparison of two variables set out in rows and columns. For instance, the rows variable could be a set of codes focusing on a particular theme, and the columns variable might be a particular grouping of the informants. Matrices also lend themselves well to case study formats, so that the coded data might be given for individuals or other units of analysis, rather than, as in the example below, groupings made on the basis of an independent variable such as gender. The following is part of a matrix I drew up using *NVivo* for my online pupil interaction study mentioned earlier in this chapter. The organization of the data here allows me to look at gender differences in the coded responses to the themes listed: in particular, the matrix supported my analysis of the pupils' comments on how using the bulletin board led to different types of learning. The benefit of a matrix produced by a software program such as *NVivo* is that one can access the selected quotations by clicking on the number in the cells. In manually produced matrices, the cells might contain statements (instead of the numbers seen here) representing main themes expressed in the interviews. In this way, the researcher is forced to 'flesh out' the cell items by producing interim verbal summaries of the main points arising.

**Table 8.2   Example of variable-by-variable matrix: types of learning, by gender**

|  | Male Interviewees | Female Interviewees |
| --- | --- | --- |
| How others learn | 0 | 1 |
| Learning new topics | 0 | 1 |
| Learning a new language | 1 | 2 |
| Learning from others | 1 | 1 |
| Learning about culture | 3 | 2 |
| Improving writing | 2 | 1 |
| Language learning | 2 | 1 |

### Activity 8.1

- Re-read the transcript extract in this chapter and code it according to the following open codes:
    communicating in English
    communicating in French
    positive relationships
    negative relationships
    linguistic difficulties
- What other concepts emerge from the extract and how would you code them?
- What in-vivo code might a researcher find in this extract?

## KEY IDEAS

In this chapter, I have introduced some of the key features of the process of analysing qualitative data. I have also provided examples to illustrate some of the practical tools and strategies commonly used and which may be of particular relevance to the teacher researcher. I have indicated that from the outset, when conducting an interview, the researcher can be engaging in a form of *online analysis* (sometimes collaboratively with the interviewee) of the themes and issues at the centre of the study. The next step is to convert the raw data into the form of a transcript, guided by the systematic application of a *transcription system*. Transcripts need to be subsequently coded through the application of a *coding framework* which can be generated between a mixture of inductive and deductive approaches. The frameworks should include a brief description of each code listed and should be justified in the methodology section of the report. A *code* is a label that refers to a particular concept that the research is investigating. *Open coding* fractures the transcript into fragments which relate to the different concepts. *Thematic coding* results in higher level, theoretical analysis based on linkage between different open codes. The benefits of computer-aided qualitative analysis are that it facilitates the storage, management and interrogation of the data. *Displays* and *matrices* are useful tools to use on qualitative data for two main reasons: they provide a framework for structuring the analysis; and, if used repeatedly over an extended period of research, they provide a reflexive record of the progression of the analysis over time. When produced through the medium of a computer program, displays and matrices are hyperlinked to the original coded transcripts.

## *References*

Ellis, R. and Barkhuizen, G. (2005) *Analysing Learner Language*. Oxford: Oxford University Press.

Evans, M. (forthcoming) 'Using stimulated recall to investigate pupils' thinking about online bilingual communication: codeswitching and pronominal address in L2 French', *British Educational Research Journal*.

Huberman, A. and Miles, M. B. (1998) 'Data management and analysis methods', in N. Denzin and Y. Lincoln (eds) *Collecting and Interpreting Qualitative Materials*. Thousand Oaks, CA: Sage.

Miles, M. B. and Huberman, A. M. (1994) *Qualitative Data Analysis*. Thousand Oaks, CA: Sage.

Robson, C. (2002) *Real World Research*, 2nd edition. Oxford: Blackwell.

Strauss, A. and Corbin, J. (1998) *Basics of Qualitative Research: Techniques and Procedures for Developing Grounded Theory*. Thousand Oaks, CA: Sage.

# TAKING A QUANTITATIVE APPROACH

## Mark Winterbottom

> **Hints**
>
> - Read this chapter together with Chapter 10. Never collect a set of data before thinking about how to analyse it!
> - Don't be scared of numbers – even if you're not good at maths, it doesn't matter. Think of numbers as a servant to help you understand something.
> - Get someone else to check your data collection plans before you start – they'll often think of confounding variables that you've missed.
> - Collect data at the highest level of measurement possible.
> - Just because two variables are related, it doesn't mean one *causes* a change in the other.
> - Be critical of your methods and conclusions when you write up. Everyone's data have limitations – being up front about them is important.
> - Be sceptical about what the data is showing you. Be wary of blindly interpreting the data to fit your prior expectations without considering alternative explanations. Be wary of anyone else doing the same!

## INTRODUCTION

A quantitative approach means using measurements and numbers to help formulate and test ideas. It usually involves summarizing numerical data and/or using them to look for differences and associations between sets of numbers. In this chapter, I'll look at approaches to collecting and interpreting quantitative data. In the next chapter, you'll learn more about using statistics to analyse them.

If you have a natural science background, you may feel at home here, but bear in mind the complexity of human behaviour – don't ignore the depth of data available through the qualitative approaches outlined elsewhere in this book – achieving a fully natural scientific approach in a school context is almost impossible.

Before I get going, let's look at some fundamental words and ideas, which can help you to talk about, read about, evaluate and plan quantitative approaches. I'll then introduce you to two approaches for planning your own research, and look at some ways in which school performance data is used ... and misused!

## IDEAS AND DEFINITIONS

### Variables

A quantitative approach usually means measuring a property of something or someone. That property is called a variable. Variables are called variables because they are entities that can vary. You can collect quantitative data about individuals by designing questionnaires or tests. Alternatively, you can simply record data by observing the subjects 'from afar'; it all depends on the data you want. However, do bear in mind that the act of collecting data can sometimes change the data you get! Some examples of variables include:

- the number of students 'on roll'
- the test result
- the proportion of students gaining five GCSEs at A–C
- the tier (e.g. primary, secondary, etc.)
- the school governance system.

Variables described using numbers are quantitative (e.g. the proportion of students gaining five GCSEs at A–C). Those described by categories *are qualitative* or categorical (e.g. the school governance system – foundation, voluntary-aided, etc.). Although this chapter is about a quantitative approach, we usually look at qualitative variables as well.

Quantitative variables fall into two types. Continuous variables can take any value in a given range (e.g. 3.2, 4.798), whereas discrete variables have clear steps between their possible values (for example, you can't get 100.324 pupils at a school!).

Another way to think about variables is the *scale*, or level *of* measurement that we use. The scale itself determines whether they'll be qualitative/quantitative or continuous/discrete.

- Nominal scales are for qualitative variables to categorize observations. The value assigned to a group is just a label, and implies nothing about quantity. *Sex* would be a variable measured with a nominal scale: we could use '1' for boys and '2' for girls.
- Ordinal scales assess rank or order and yield discrete variables. Imagine you rank the pupils in your class according to test score; the best student has a rank of 1, etc. Rather than just being labels (as above), a '1' is better than a '2'. This type of scale gives an effective summary, but the exact value of the differences between each person's scores is unclear, and not necessarily identical.
- Interval and ratio scales provide discrete or continuous data where there are equal intervals between the units of measurement (for example, a minute is the same length however you measure

it!). In a ratio scale, a zero means zero – there are no children or they got no answers right. In an interval scale, the zero is relative – e.g. zero may describe a baseline motivation level.

## Validity and reliability

Some variables are direct measures of what we're interested in – recording a pupil's sex is a direct measure of their sex. Others are more indirect measures. For example, test scores are an indirect measure of pupils' learning. It is important that such measures provide a genuine measure of the underlying construct. Such validity is important when collecting your own data, and when interpreting other people's data and conclusions.

It's also important to consider reliability – the consistency and repeatability of data collected over time, across different samples, and across different measures of the same underlying construct. Box 9.1 suggests some ways to assess reliability using one pilot group, or using two groups that are closely matched for variables relevant to your study.

---

### BOX 9.1   Assessing reliability

- Use one questionnaire with one group on different occasions and see if their answers are significantly correlated (see Chapter 10). (Be aware that they may remember their responses though!).
- Use two different questionnaires (but whose questions examine the same ideas) on different occasions with the same group, and look at the consistency between responses to matched questions.
- Use one questionnaire with both groups, and check that their responses are not significantly different.
- Use two questionnaires (whose questions examine the same ideas) on different occasions with both groups and check that responses to matched questions are not significantly different.

---

## Samples and populations

When collecting quantitative data, distinguishing between your sample and your population is important. A sample is a sub-group of the population. Collecting data about a sample that is representative of a wider population lets you draw conclusions about the population. We often use samples because measuring all the individuals in the population is impractical.

To ensure your sample is representative, it's essential to understand who your population is – this is something it's easy to overlook. For example, if you want a study which is generalizable to the population of all the 14-year-old students in the country, then you would randomly choose your sample from all the 14 year-olds in the country – this is so-called probability sampling. You can see four types of probability sampling in Box 9.2.

## BOX 9.2    Probability sampling

- Random sampling: here there is an equal chance that each member of the population is included. Including one individual in the sample has no influence on whether another individual is included.
- Systematic sampling: sometimes practicalities may make it preferable to sample individuals in some sort of order – say every fourth subject in a line. To do so, you should randomize the list of individuals and choose your starting point randomly.
- Stratified sampling: you may suspect that other variables (e.g. sex) could affect your results. To try to eliminate the effect, you would randomly choose half your subjects from the boys and half your subjects from the girls.
- Stage sampling: you can stratify your sampling at a number of levels. For example, if you thought that the year group and tutor could affect your data, you would randomly choose year groups, then within each, randomly choose tutor groups, and then within each again, randomly choose the pupils to study.

However, your own research is likely to happen within your own school and often in your own classroom – this is so-called convenience sampling, a type of non-probability sampling (see Box 9.3). The children in your class are not representative of all the 14-year-old children across the country, and you cannot therefore make generalizations. Your pupils' characteristics may be dependent on upbringing, socioeconomic group, location, year group, on your idiosyncrasies as a teacher, and many other variables. Hence, when conducting research in your own classroom, your class is the population – there isn't a wider group to which you can generalize your findings.

## BOX 9.3    Non-Probability sampling

- Convenience sampling: you use individuals to whom you have easy access. You cannot generalize your conclusions to a wider population.
- Quota sampling: you may suspect a particular variable (e.g. sex) could affect your results. To eliminate any influence, randomly choose your subjects from boys and girls, but in proportion to the number of boys and girls in the group of pupils you are interested in (e.g. the population of pupils in Cambridgeshire). Your findings are only generalizable to this limited population of pupils.
- Dimensional sampling: if you suspect that a number of variables will influence the variable you are interested in, you can deliberately choose individuals who are subject to every combination of those variables.
- Purposive sampling: you choose which individuals will be in your sample based on how representative you think they are of the group you want to study. It is unwise to generalize beyond your sample as your choices are unlikely to be fully objective.

If you've a natural science background, you may feel this makes your research rather pointless – after all, if it's got no wider application, what's the point in doing it? There are two answers: (1) researching your own practice in your own classroom contributes strongly to your ongoing professional development, and (2) providing you make the context of your research clear when you write it up (you, the nature of the class, the lesson content, the whole school context, etc.), anyone reading your study would be able to decide the extent to which your findings may apply to them (user generalizability).

Finally, although you probably won't need to generalize to wider populations in your own research, you will read large-scale studies that do just that. Even if individuals have been sampled randomly, instinct probably tells you that a study based on two individuals is less generalizable than one based on two hundred – but why is that?

Well, if you take lots of different samples from the same population, it's unlikely that each will have the same mean (what most people would call the average) or standard deviation (how much the data is spread out around the mean) for the variable you're measuring. However, if you use a bigger sample, the mean will be closer to the population mean; hence, the bigger the sample, the better. If you do adopt a quantitative approach, a sample size of 30 or more would be good.

## QUANTITATIVE APPROACHES TO RESEARCH

So how do you actually generate some data? There are two key approaches: experimental (measuring the effect of some sort of intervention), and non-experimental (looking at what's there and trying to make sense of how different variables may affect each other). You'll learn how to analyse your data in the next chapter.

### Experimental

This approach looks at the effect of one variable on another, by making a change in one of the variables (the independent variable) and seeing how the other variable changes (the dependent variable), while keeping all other variables constant (controlling them). An experimental approach is broadly underpinned by the stages shown in Box 9.4.

---

**BOX 9.4    Planning an experiment**

1. Identify what you're trying to find out, and work out what you think will happen. Predict how you are expecting the independent variable (the treatment) to affect the dependent variable (the response).

*(Continued)*

*(Continued)*

2. A variable like 'pupils' learning' cannot be measured directly, and you'll have to use a 'proxy' or indirect measure of it, such as 'test score results'; remember to justify your choice of 'proxy' as a valid indicator of the variable you're interested in.
3. Decide who your population is, and then randomly choose a sample of individuals from the population.
4. If your experimental 'treatment' is something like 'receives new teaching approach' or 'doesn't receive new teaching approach', then randomly allocate your pupils to each group. Even if your experiment involves a more quantitative independent variable, such as the length of time spent working on computers during a lesson, randomly allocating pupils evenly across levels (one hour, two hours, etc.) is still essential.
5. Make sure that the levels of treatment are realistic within the context (usually a classroom). For example, looking at how eight hours of computer access affects pupils' learning is unrealistic in a single lesson. Also ensure that the range of treatments you provide will enable you to see trends and differences. Comparing 60 minutes of computer access with 61 minutes won't yield any startling conclusions.
6. Identify potentially confounding variables (variables that could affect your findings, such as variable C in Figure 9.2), and develop strategies to control them (keep their levels constant between individuals receiving the different levels of treatment), or eliminate them (e.g. removing a teaching assistant from the room).
7. Pilot your methods with a different sample to iron out any difficulties.
8. After the experiment, measure the dependent variable for each individual and use a statistical test to make a conclusion. Don't leave it until now though to consider which statistical tests you intend to use – it is all too common to realize that the data you've collected is not compatible with any statistical test.
9. Be careful to state the extent to which you can generalize your conclusion across a wider population.

An experimental model is a good basis for scientific research in a laboratory, but employing this approach in a classroom, with the multiplicity of variables in existence, and the constraints of school timetabling, is not always easy.

Let's imagine you're researching the effect of a six-week motivational training programme with a group of Year 9 students. Rather than being constrained by the groups already set up, you've randomly selected a group of students and you're teaching them at lunchtime. You use a questionnaire to assess their motivation beforehand. You use the same questionnaire after the six-week programme and find an increase in motivational levels. To your delight, you conclude that the training programme has had a positive impact!

Or do you? Are you certain that you've controlled all other variables that may affect your results? You may have begun your programme at the start of term, and then measured motivation again at the end of term; perhaps you could expect children to be more motivated as the end of term draws near! In fact, all sorts of other variables could be responsible for your findings. Hence, thinking about and collecting additional data to examine such confounding variables is essential to working out what's really going on. If you do want to use just one group, you may find your work sits better as one cycle of an action research approach, particularly if you were unable to sample children randomly.

## Using a control group

However, if we stick with an experimental approach, how can we get rid of the effect of these extra variables? The easiest way is to use more than one group whose members have been chosen randomly. One group gets the training programme and one group doesn't.

Because you've chosen your groups randomly, any systematic effect of the other variables should be spread across the groups, and will 'confound' your results to the same extent. You therefore look at the effect of the training programme by comparing the increase in motivation for the 'trained' group against the increase for the 'untrained' group. Even though both groups may have greater motivation at the end of term, any additional effect of the training programme should be clearer.

It's still not necessarily simple though.

- Just doing something with your experimental group (even if you gave them a free lunch for six weeks) may affect their motivation. Hence, leaving your control group with no intervention at all would not be appropriate – you'll have to consider what an appropriate control treatment would be.
- You need to be careful of the effects of other variables 'creeping in'. For example, if you taught one group on Monday lunchtime and the other on Tuesday lunchtime, you're introducing another variable which could bias your outcomes.
- Variables can interact in unpredictable ways. For example, being given a pre-test may actually influence the results of the post-test (children may think about their responses between the two tests and want to 'put the right thing'), particularly if the tests are very similar. Comparing your results with two further groups (one control and one experimental) which do not experience the pre-test would help to clarify the extent of this problem.

Identifying these problems, and collecting some supplementary data to explore them, will add weight to your study when you write it up.

## Quasi-experiments

So what happens if you cannot choose groups randomly, you cannot control variables, etc. Well, you have to do the best you can. A 'quasi-experiment' is probably as good as you're going to get.

This approach still uses an experimental and control group, but rather than being able to randomly choose the members of each, you should choose existing groups (to which you have access) which are most similar on as many relevant variables as possible. This means that if you're looking at motivation levels, you really want two groups that have very similar motivation levels in the first place, and a similar range of other variables that could be important, such as prior attainment and socioeconomic factors.

Rather than just looking at the overall differences between the two groups, comparing the effect of the experiment between pairs of pupils from the experimental and control group, matched as closely as possible on such relevant variables, is even better.

## Non-experimental

In this approach, you don't do your own experiment; you can't control any variables. You just look at what's already happened and try to understand it. This means that you take the variable showing an effect (the dependent variable) and try to find the variable(s) (the independent variable(s)) which could have a causative relationship with it.

This approach is very common in education, and is also useful when ethics preclude an experimental approach. For example, it would not be ethical to run an experiment deliberately subjecting pupils to something detrimental to their learning, but studying the outcomes of such a situation (which already exists) would be perfectly ethical. Two examples may help make things clear.

At a particular school, the governors suddenly realized that the proportion of pupils gaining five GCSEs at A–C ('5 A–C') has been dropping over the past 15 years. At their meeting, they came up with a number of variables which could be responsible. They find that as the number of teachers at the school went down each year, so did '5 A–C' (we can say that '5 A–C' correlates significantly with the number of teachers at the school – you'll learn more about correlations in Chapter 16). One of them suggests an explanation – the presence of fewer teachers leads to less variety of ideas for teaching and learning, and hence the drop in attainment.

But was the change in teacher numbers the cause of the change in '5 A–C'? Look at Figure 9.1. Actually, it may be the other way around (reverse causation). For example, the '5 A–C' may have dropped one year, and encouraged parents who are interested in academic success to send their children elsewhere. With fewer pupils, the numbers on roll go down and the same number of teachers is no longer required.

Figure 9.1   Making sense of a correlation between two variables

Let's look at a different example, which tries to explain observed differences between two groups. The head teacher at school A knows that different tutor groups have different levels of truancy. He uses a statistical test to confirm that tutor groups led by women have less truancy than those led by men. Is he justified in concluding that female form tutors are better?

Not necessarily. At this school, the extent of truancy happens to vary with age (older children truant more), the Year 9 tutor team is composed mainly of women and the Year 11 tutor team is composed mainly of men. Hence, we've a third variable – year group – which affects both truancy levels and the sex of the tutor (Figure 9.2), creating a plausibly causal, but in fact artefactual, relationship between a tutor's sex and truancy levels.

So it's important to realize that finding a relationship does not mean that it's a causal relationship, and that causation could happen in either direction. In fact, sometimes a relationship may be pure coincidence – there is a proven relationship between stork population size and human birth rate!

To some extent, you can control the effect of potentially confounding variables by how you choose your sample, and by what you measure. For example, the head teacher above could do the following:

- Randomly choose, and compare, equal numbers of male- and female-led tutor groups from each year group. This does reduce the sample size, but removes the effect of age.
- Compare multiple pairs of tutor groups, matched as closely as possible by the children's socioeconomic status and other potentially relevant variables, with the only difference being the tutors' sex.

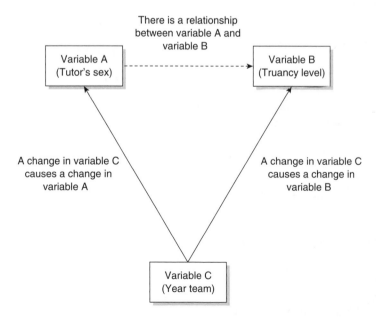

Figure 9.2   Making sense of a correlation between two variables

- Decide which variables are likely to affect truancy levels, and measure them at the same time as collecting the rest of the data. Some clever statistics (beyond the scope of this book) can remove the effect of the extra variables, and 'uncover' any effect of tutor's sex.

Even with these strategies, it is still difficult to know you've accounted for all potentially confounding variables. As such, your interpretation of the data is vulnerable to your own biases, and it's often possible to come up with contradictory explanations for the same set of data. You should discuss such explanations when you write up your research, pointing out the limitations of your derived ideas. Using other sources of data to shed more light on such alternatives would also be sensible. In an ideal world, explanations and hypotheses would be tested by experiment at a later date, but that's often not possible. The benefits and potential pitfalls of the non-experimental approach are summarized in Box 9.5 and Box 9.6.

---

### BOX 9.5   Benefits of a non-experimental approach

1. It is the 'next best thing' where an experimental approach is impossible.
2. It is good for initial exploration of a data set and for generating hypotheses, which can be experimentally tested later.
3. It avoids using an artificial intervention, examining only 'natural' variation in the data.

---

### BOX 9.6   Pitfalls of a non-experimental approach

1. It is difficult to control variables or get truly random samples.
2. It is difficult to identify all the variables (including the one(s) which actually has a causative effect) that are potentially relevant to an observed phenomenon.
3. Cause and effect are not always obvious; it is easy to assume one variable causes another if it fits in with your prior ideas.

---

## LOOKING AT OTHER PEOPLE'S DATA

Looking at data with a healthily sceptical eye is always a good idea! In the rest of the chapter, I'll help you to examine the story of pupil and school performance data.

### League tables

When league tables were first introduced in 1992, exam results were used to decide if a school was effective – on the assumption that better results means better schooling. Ofsted based their assessment of school performance on raw exam results, and teachers were (and are) expected to use pupils' attainment data to support their own promotion applications. So what's the problem?

**Activity 9.1**

Many commentators have criticized 'exam results' as not being a valid measure of school effectiveness, and suggested that they should not be used to compare schools. Think about the following questions.

- Why do 'exam results' only give a limited picture of school 'effectiveness'?
- What other variables could affect exam results, which are unrelated to the school itself?
- Suggest reasons why it is not valid to reward secondary science teachers on the basis of their classes' exam results.

Hopefully, you've realized that there's an enormous number of variables which could affect exam results. Research suggests that 76 per cent of variation in GCSE scores is determined by pupils' prior attainment (which itself is related to their own prior education and socioeconomic characteristics). This means that the influence of a secondary school on GCSE scores is pretty limited, and the best way for schools to improve their league table position is to select pupils according to prior attainment!

## Value-added

In 2004, the Department for Education and Skills published a *value-added* measure; it was billed as a more valid measure of the 'value' that a school 'adds', taking into account prior attainment. The aim was to help parents make valid comparisons between schools.

**Activity 9.2**

Explain why this ought to be a more valid measure of school effectiveness, and what you think it still lacks.

Let's look at how they worked out value-added between key stage 2 and key stage 3, using SATs results as a measure of attainment in each case, but comparing pupils with similar levels of prior attainment. Here's a simplified explanation of it:

- All the pupils in the country who performed very similarly (e.g. within half a level) at Key Stage 2 are put in order of numerical result for their Key Stage 3 results.
- For each set of pupils, the median result (the middle one) is found, and every pupil is given a value-added score relative to that result. If someone does better than the median pupil, they get a positive score. If someone does worse, they get a negative score.

- Hence, for schools with a low-attaining intake, it should be easier to see the 'value' they are 'adding', even if their Key Stage 3 results are much lower than, for example, another school which selects on prior attainment.

To assess the whole school's performance, you average the results of all the pupils in the school and add the result to 100. Hence, a score of 100 reflects 'average' value-added, 98 reflects 'below average' value-added and 102 reflects 'above average' value-added.

### Activity 9.3

A local journalist is looking at the value-added scores for the schools in her county. She realizes that half of the schools have value-added scores below 100 and publishes the story with the following headline: 'Scandal! Letting down our children – half of Smedshire's schools are below average'. What is wrong with this headline?

But how do you interpret these scores? If the average (mean) value-added score for a school is a long way below the mean value (100) for all the schools, then you may be pretty confident that there's a problem. If it's really way above the mean, then you know something is going right. But how far apart do schools' scores need to be to know they're really significantly different?

Statisticians work this out by calculating something called confidence limits above and below the mean for each school. This is often not quoted in the media, but without it, you can't interpret league tables properly.

- You can only say that two schools really have significantly different value-added scores if the confidence intervals (between the upper and lower limit) do not overlap.
- You can only say that a school is above the national average if the school mean is above the national mean, and if the school confidence interval does not include the national mean.

### Activity 9.4

Look at Figure 9.3. For each school, it shows the mean and confidence intervals. Which two of the following is it possible to say with 95 per cent confidence?

- School A is significantly better than school B.
- School D is significantly worse than school B.
- School C is significantly better than the national average.
- There is a significant difference between school A and school C.
- Schools A and B are the only ones significantly better than the national average.

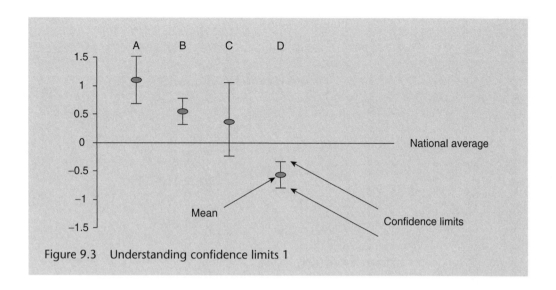

Figure 9.3    Understanding confidence limits 1

However, it gets even more complicated. The way in which confidence limits are calculated means that:

- if you calculate the mean and confidence interval for a small school with few pupils, the limits are likely to be relatively far apart
- if you calculate the mean and confidence interval for a school with a lot of pupils, the limits are likely to be relatively close together.

These differences make it difficult to validly compare schools of different sizes, and even more difficult when comparing particular subjects or classes with even fewer pupils.

**Activity 9.5**

Look at Figure 9.4. It shows mean and confidence intervals for three schools. School A has 2000 pupils, school B has 500 pupils, and school C has 2000 pupils. Which of the following can you say with 95 per cent confidence?

- School A is significantly below the national average.
- School B is significantly above the national average.
- School C is significantly above the national average.
- There is no significant difference between school A and school B.
- There is no significant difference between school B and school C.
- There is no significant difference between school A and school C.

Figure 9.4    Understanding confidence limits 2

## Contextual value-added

Using value-added scores still assumes that all changes in pupil performance are determined by what happens in the school. But what about the other variables that could affect performance? Is it possible to tease apart their effects from the effects of the school?

Initial attempts to do this adjusted for the number of pupils on free school meals as an index of socioeconomic status. More recently, the government has developed a complicated statistical model. They have tried to identify relevant variables, and remove the effect of each, one by one, using clever statistics, to provide a way of predicting 'expected' attainment for each pupil. The deviation from that 'expected' attainment then provides a *contextual-value-added* score (CVA). The variables included in calculating the 2007 scores include the following:

- pupil prior attainment
- gender
- Special Educational Needs
- first language
- measures of pupil mobility
- age
- an indicator of whether the pupil is 'in care'
- ethnicity
- free School Meals
- Income Deprivation Affecting Children Index (IDACI)
- the average and range of prior attainment within the school (KS2–3, KS2–4 and KS3–4 only).

But is this the end of the story? Not yet ...

- We can't be certain that there aren't other relevant variables which need controlling for.
- The CVA calculation does not include the possibility that such variables could interact. For example, income deprivation may affect the attainment of younger pupils more than that of older pupils (i.e. you have age and income deprivation interacting to affect CVA).
- Schools may have different effects on the performance of different types of pupil, and schools' 'value-added' for different subjects may differ significantly. Obscuring such differences in single CVA values loses useful information.

There are two more fundamental problems:

- Recent research suggests that value-added scores are very tightly aligned (correlated) with raw performance scores anyway (because of the way in which they're calculated), and do not provide a valid reflection of the 'value-added'.
- Recent research also suggests that assumptions about the data, which are required for the valid calculation of CVA scores, are usually unfulfilled.

Of course, even if CVA data were statistically valid, given the data are collected from pupils who've been in the school for, for example, the last three years, they may not actually provide insights into *current* school effectiveness, given there will certainly have been staff and financial changes in that time.

Finally, parents and others instinctively base their judgements on figures they understand, and continuing to publish raw data about school performance is therefore misleading. That said, the authority associated with statistically derived data could also mislead parents into trusting such data unquestioningly.

## Other pupil performance measures

You may know about other systems used by schools to predict pupil performance and to work out value-added. Let's look at ALIS, the oldest of these. This enables schools to predict A-level scores from GCSE scores. It involves plotting GCSE scores against A-level scores and drawing a line through the middle of the points (this is called a regression line and uses a little maths to get it in the right place). You can see such a graph in Figure 9.5.

This line represents average performance. Hence, you can use it to predict a student's performance (see Figure 9.6) prior to their A-level exams, and to look at the value-added by examining the extent to which each individual is above or below the line (see Figure 9.7).

First warning! Remember that the line predicts *average* performance across a huge data set. By definition, 50 per cent of students are below average, so don't be surprised if half of your students do not meet their Advanced Level Information System (ALIS) predictions.

Second warning! The deviation from the line is caused not just by the school's impact but also other contextual factors, as indicated earlier on.

Figure 9.5    Regression between GCSE score and A-level score

Figure 9.6    Using a regression to predict A-level score from GCSE score

Figure 9.7    Residuals from the regression between GCSE score and A-level score

Hence, if your pupils don't meet their ALIS predictions, you can explain to the head teacher that you'd expect half of them to be below their predicted Uniform Mark Scale (UMS) scores (score before translation into a grade) anyway, and that there's an awful lot of things which can affect the results that are not under your control!

## KEY IDEAS

- You can use a quantitative approach to describe and analyse your own data.
- Experimental research involves changing a variable (the independent variable) in order to examine its effect on another variable (the dependent variable) while controlling for any other confounding variables that could affect the dependent variable.
- Non-experimental research involves looking for explanations for phenomena by seeking out potentially causal relationships between variables, while accounting for the effect of other variables.
- An association between variables A and B does not necessarily mean that an increase in A causes an increase in B. It could be the other way around, or both may be affected by a third variable, C.
- Understanding the derivation of data (such as performance data) is essential to make informed conclusions about it.

## *Further Reading*

For a useful text on designing your data collection, have a look at:

Cohen, L., Manion, L. and Morrison, K. (2000) *Research Methods in Education.* London: RoutledgeFalmer.

Other useful texts include:

Brace, N., Kemp, R. and Snelgar, R. (2006) *SPSS for Psychologists,* 3rd edn. Basingstoke: Palgrave Macmillan.

Coolican, H. (2004) *Research Methods and Statistics in Psychology*, 4th edn. London: Hodder & Stoughton.

Sani, F. and Todman, J. (2006) *Experimental Design and Statistics for Psychology*. Oxford: Blackwell Publishing.

For the DfES contextual-value-added ready reckoners, see: www.standards.dfes.gov.uk/performance/1316367/CVAinPAT2005/?version=1

For the Curriculum, Evaluation and Management Centre at the University of Durham (for ALIS, YELLIS, etc.), visit: www.cemcentre.org

# ANALYSING QUANTITATIVE DATA

## Ros McLellan

**Hints**

- Don't be scared of statistical analysis – even if maths was a mystery at school, you *can* do this – anyone can – you just need to know some basics.
- *Don't* think of analysis as something you do after you've collected the data. Plan this before you collect the data so you can be sure that the data you gather can answer the questions you want to ask.
- You can create discrete categories (such as low, average and high) for a variable such as ability, from data that has been assessed on a continuous scale (such as scores on NFER Cognitive Ability Tests) but you can't do the reverse. So, if in doubt, collect data at the highest level of measurement possible.
- Don't forget that *you* tell the computer program what to do. It just follows your instructions. So if you put rubbish in, you'll get rubbish out!

## INTRODUCTION

This chapter is about how to use some statistical techniques to start to analyse and interpret quantitative data. I am not claiming that you will be an expert by the end of the chapter but I hope you will have the confidence to get started. Those of you who want to pursue this type of approach will need to consult more specialist texts, and some appropriate references are listed at the back of the chapter that you'll need to move on to.

Let's start by debunking a myth. You do not have to be brilliant at mathematics to do quantitative analysis. Many people are put off statistics by the complicated-looking equations they see but computers can do the number crunching for you, and at one level you don't need to understand any of the hieroglyphics you might see in advanced statistical texts. What is important is that you understand some basic concepts and what sorts of analysis are appropriate to apply to answer particular questions. An appropriate analogy is that of driving a car: you need to know to put fuel in (the basic concept of fuel provides the driving force) and how to drive (the right technique for the situation – for instance, not to brake too sharply on a frosty morning), but you don't need to understand the underlying mechanical and electrical engineering principles which make it operate, if you just want to drive it. Similarly, with statistics; you need to know the statistical entities you might calculate and what would be appropriate to the situation in hand, but you don't need to have a detailed understanding of how the computer processes data to calculate these entities. This chapter therefore aims to give you a sense of these basic entities and processes and to introduce you to a particular statistical package, SPSS, which is widely used to do such number crunching.

The other important point I would like to make before we get down to business is that analysis is *not* something you start thinking about once you have collected all your data. This is a common error made by newcomers to research. If you don't think about analysis before you collect your data, it is quite likely that your data won't be able to answer the questions you wanted to ask. For instance, if you wanted to examine the relationship between ability and motivation, it would not be enough to use ability band/stream as a measure of ability if you wanted to know whether the motivation of the most able students in the top band/stream was different to those who had just scraped into that band/stream. A finer graded scale or instrument for measuring ability, such as the NFER Cognitive Ability Tests, would need to be used. Hence, you need to think ahead and pre-empt the type of questions you want to ask, in order to plan data collection accordingly. As a rule of thumb, collect data at the highest level of measurement you can sensibly manage because you can create discrete categories from data measured on a continuous scale (such as the ability categories 'low', 'average' and 'high' by deciding cut-off points on an ability scale), while you cannot create a continuous scale from discrete categories.

It should now be clear that it is essential to consider what analysis you want to do during the initial design stages of the research so that appropriate data, as far as possible, is collected in the first place. For this reason, if you have not yet read Chapter 9, I strongly urge you to at least skim through it before going any further.

Now we can turn to the matter in hand: the analysis of quantitative data. Assuming you are planning to use a computer to assist you in this process, the first step is to set up a database using the appropriate software program. In this chapter, I will be referring to the SPSS package, as this is the most widely used program of this type in the social sciences and most higher education institutions subscribe to it. Once the data is entered, analysis, which has two distinct phases, can be conducted. The first phase is to describe the data that has been gathered, which involves the calculation of descriptive statistics and the graphical presentation of the data. The second phase is to interrogate the data to answer the research questions posed, which entails calculating inferential statistics. The rest of the chapter, therefore, gives an overview of each of these steps. As it is easier to understand such processes if they are discussed with reference to a specific example, data gathered during my PhD research will be used for illustrative purposes. I start therefore with a brief description of my PhD research in order to contextualize the examples given in the rest of the chapter.

## THE EXAMPLE DATABASE

Cognitive Acceleration through Science Education (CASE) is an intervention programme consisting of thirty science activity lessons for students in Years 7 and 8, which aims to promote cognitive development. It is widely used by secondary schools, despite the fact that some students make very limited progress and it has been suggested that student motivation might account for this, but this had not been investigated. Consequently, my main research question was: 'Do differences in motivation account for the differential gains made by students doing CASE?'. I was also interested in whether there was any difference in the progress made by boys and girls, as the literature suggests that girls are more motivated than boys; and in school generally, girls get better exam results than boys. Employing a longitudinal quasi-experimental design so that I could compare students following the CASE programme with similar students that were not (to allow for normal cognitive development), I followed a cohort (over 1700 students) through the first two years of secondary school in nine schools (five doing the CASE programme and four that were not). This is probably a lot more students than you might be considering including in your study, as in all likelihood you are studying students in your own school. However, the process of analysis is the same whether your sample size is 1700, one year cohort, or one class.

I assessed the cognitive development and motivation at the start of Y7 (before starting CASE – the pre-test) and at the end of Y8 (after completing the programme – the post-test) so that changes in cognitive development could be measured. I could also see whether any changes in motivation had occurred. Here, we will only focus on some of the data gathered at pre-test.

I used a commercially available test to measure cognitive development (a Science Reasoning Task). This is conducted as a series of teacher-led demonstrations, which students then have to answer questions about on an answer sheet. Answers are marked using the mark scheme provided and then the total score is converted to a level of cognitive development (a numerical score which is an interval level measurement).

**Table 10.1   Example items in motivation questionnaire**

| Scale | Underlying Motivation | Example Item[1] |
|---|---|---|
| Task | To develop competence | … I finally understand a really complicated idea |
| Ego | To demonstrate competence | … I do better work than other students |
| Work Avoidance | To avoid demonstrating incompetence (passive avoidance) | … I don't have to do any homework |
| Alienation | To avoid demonstrating incompetence (active disruption) | … I mess around and get away with it |

*Note:* [1]The common stem is 'I feel successful when'

Motivation can be measured in many ways, according to which theory of motivation you subscribe to. I chose a framework that suggested there were four dimensions to motivation. Each dimension can be assessed using a scale comprising a number of items, which students are asked to respond to. I used a questionnaire that had been used in previous research. There is a common stem for each item – 'I feel successful when' – and students indicate their level of agreement on a five-point Likert scale (from 'strongly disagree', scoring 1 to 'strongly agree', scoring 5). The overall score for each dimension is the total score of the individual items for each scale. An example item from each of the four scales is shown in Table 10.1, to give a sense of what the four dimensions relate to.

I asked students to give their opinion about science, English and school in general, as these were different areas I was interested in. Hence, the database contained three answers to each question, and separate total scores for each dimension for the different subject areas.

Now that you have a sense of the data I gathered, we can consider how I set up the SPSS database to do the analysis.

## CREATING A DATABASE IN SPSS

In this section, I will take you through some of the issues you need to consider when setting up an SPSS database, illustrating these with reference to my own database. If you go to the website, you will find a tutorial that takes you through the process of setting up a database using SPSS, which you will probably find helpful to look at in conjunction with this section. At the end of the section, you will find an activity to allow you to check that you have understood how to set up a database.

Blank databases in SPSS look quite like Excel spreadsheets when you open them initially, however, unlike Excel, there are two ways of looking at the same database: 'data view' and 'variable view'.

'Data view' (the default shown on opening a database) shows you the actual data in your database. Each row represents one 'case'. I collected data from over 1700 students, hence I have over 1700 rows in my database. Cases do not need to be individual people. If, for instance, you have collected data about schools rather than individual students, then the rows would represent each school. The columns represent each variable you have collected data on. In my study, this includes demographic data (such as gender), level of cognitive development score, and answers for each of the questions on the questionnaire. There are also a number of variables I created in the database from existing variables. For instance, there are variables for the total scores for each motivation dimension.

'Variable view' provides information about each of your variables. This is one of the ways SPSS differs from a spreadsheet – because it is a database, it can hold all sorts of useful information about your variables that Excel isn't capable of and this information is needed for conducting statistical analyses. Before entering data, you set up your variables in variable view. Here, each row relates to one variable and the columns represent specific characteristics of the variable. To avoid much later grief, it is well worth defining your variables fully before entering data, as SPSS has default settings which may not be appropriate for all your variables.

Regardless of whatever else you have data for, it is sensible to define your first variable as a unique identifier for each case, so that you have a way of going back to the original data you collected later if you need to. For data protection and ethical reasons, you should create a code rather than type in an identifiable name. I therefore called my first variable 'ID'. You are limited to eight characters for variable names and if you attempt to type in more, SPSS will truncate it. However, you can list a name in full, such as 'unique identifier' under 'label' and when you later do analysis, SPSS will use what is listed under the label rather than the variable name in its output of results.

SPSS will generate default information for the remaining headings. Although most of these are appropriate, you do need to consider 'type', 'values', 'missing' and 'measure'. SPSS has different options for these already stored. For instance, for 'type', you can select from many options, including numerical and string. I decided that the easiest way to give a unique identifier to every student's response would be to give each student a number and to write this number on their questionnaires/cognitive development test sheets. Thus, I selected 'numerical' under 'type' for variable 'ID'. It is possible that you might want to give non-numerical codes, for instance pseudonyms (but note that if you have a large number of cases, this can quickly get confusing so it is often better to stick to numbers). In this case, you would select 'string' as the type, and in both cases, the 'measure' is 'nominal'.

In order to understand how to use 'values' and 'missing', we need to turn to a different variable. I wanted to record some background demographic information, and it is quite likely that you would want to do the same. For instance, I wanted to record whether each student was male or female. Thinking ahead, I knew I wanted to compare boys and girls on a number of dimensions (for instance, scores on the 'task' motivation scale). To do this sort of analysis, you have to create a numerical rather than string variable so I chose 'numerical' under type and 'nominal' under 'measure'. I used the code 1 to represent boys and 2 to represent girls and recorded this information under 'values'. As with variable labels, SPSS shows value labels rather than numerical codes in analyses, which is handy as you don't have to remember whether '1' represents 'boys' or 'girls' (although of course you can look this up at any time in variable view).

It is important to set up missing data values for variables where missing data is very likely to occur. For instance, although students were asked to indicate their gender on the front of their questionnaires, a number did not and as gender is not always obvious from a name (for instance, Sam can be a girl or a boy), in these cases, it needed to be recorded as missing. Setting up a special numerical code for missing data enables SPSS to recognize cases where data is missing and omit them from specific analyses. You define one or more values to represent missing values under 'missing'. Usually, you would define one value and this can be whatever you like, as long as it is not a value you have already used in your coding (so I couldn't use 1 or 2 for gender), but traditionally researchers tend to use '9' or '99' so that missing data stands out. You can use different values for different variables but I would caution against this, as it will get confusing. You might define more than one missing value to represent different reasons for the data being missing – for instance, 'the student was away on the day of the test' compared to 'the student missed one question on a test', but again keep it simple to start with.

Once you have set up all the variables you want to include, you can then start to enter your data. You do this in 'data view', where you will find that the column headings now refer to the variables you have defined. Entering data is a simple case of typing in the relevant values for each variable for each case. Usually, you would enter all the data on your first case before moving on to your second, but of course you can go back at any time to add in any missing data gathered at a later point in time. So in my database, I started with the first student I had data for, and typed '1001' under 'ID', '2' under 'gender' because she was a girl, and so forth. If you forget any of your codes, you can always check under value labels in variable view. Don't forget to save periodically.

You will probably come across some problems with data entry, for instance students who have ringed two answers on a questionnaire. There are various ways of dealing with this. You can either go back to the student and get them to clarify their response (which is time-consuming), you can code it as a missing response (this is probably the best approach but you may then be losing a lot of data), or you can decide to code new values to allow midpoints on scales (but this can distort later analysis). Whatever approach you choose, make sure you apply it consistently.

You should now be in a position to set up your own SPSS database.

**Activity 10.1**

1. Go to the SAGE website (www.sagepub.co.uk/wilson) and access the example student questionnaire. This comes from the database discussed above. Set up a database to record the data on the questionnaire (including demographic information) and then enter the data for that student. You can check you did this correctly by looking at the database used in Activity 10.3 at student 1002.
2. Set up a database for an investigation you have in mind.

## DATA ANALYSIS – GENERATING DESCRIPTIVE STATISTICS

### 1. Checking the accuracy of data entry

The very first thing you should check is that you have entered your data correctly, as no matter how careful you are, mistakes can be made. This 'cleaning' of the data also starts the process of examining the data. One of the most common errors is entering the wrong code for a particular response, for instance '11' instead of '1' (i.e. the value entered doesn't match a code you've set up), and the quickest way of checking for this is to look at the frequency distribution (or summary of response) for each variable.

In SPSS, descriptive statistics, such as frequency distribution information, are accessed from the 'analyse' drop-down menu. There are various descriptive statistics options but frequency distribution tables are generated using 'frequencies'. By selecting

Table 10.2   Frequency distribution for gender

|         |       | Frequency | Per cent | Valid per cent | Cumulative per cent |
|---------|-------|-----------|----------|----------------|---------------------|
| Valid   | Boys  | 710       | 41.2     | 43.0           | 43.0                |
|         | Girls | 942       | 54.7     | 57.0           | 100.0               |
|         | Total | 1652      | 95.9     | 100.0          |                     |
| Missing | 9.00  | 71        | 4.1      |                |                     |
| Total   |       | 1723      | 100.0    |                |                     |

this option, SPSS produces a dialogue box asking you which variables in your database you want frequency information about. You need to select the variable(s) of interest and ask for the relevant information. SPSS then generates the frequency distribution table(s) requested, which is produced in an SPSS output file that appears on the screen. For each variable requested, you will be able to see the different response categories listed in the first column of the table and the number of responses for that category in the second column. A quick glance down the first column will reveal whether there are any illegal responses. Tables 10.2 and 10.3 show frequency distributions for two of my variables, 'gender' and 'task motivation (science)' scale scores.

If you don't have any illegal responses, as there aren't here, you can move on to other descriptive analyses. If you want to save the frequency distribution data (which you might if you planned to copy and paste the table into a report), you can save the output file in the same way you would save any other file. If you have some rogue responses, you will need to go back to your data to find them. This can be done using 'find' in 'data view' (much as you would find and replace in Word or other packages). By looking at the identifier for the case identified, you can go back to the original data (for instance, the original questionnaire) to amend the response.

## 2. Producing variable summaries

While the frequency distribution provides information about all the responses for a particular variable, quite often we want to give a more succinct summary, especially for variables measured at an interval level. For instance, knowing that the task motivation (science) scale scores in my study varied from 8 to 30 does not really help paint a picture of the overall response to this scale. If I told you a particular student scored 18, you wouldn't know without looking carefully at Table 10.2 whether this seemed typical or not. We really need to know two things to make judgements about individual scores. Firstly: what is a typical response? For this, we would normally calculate the mean score (obtained by adding up every individual score and dividing the sum by the number of scores included). Secondly: how much variation is there in the responses? If there is a small amount of variation, then most people are recording the same responses. A larger variation implies that scores that markedly differ from the average (lower and higher) are not that unusual. The commonly used measure for this is the standard deviation, which is one measure of the average deviation from the mean score.

**Table 10.3   Frequency distribution for task motivation (science)**

|  |  | Frequency | Per cent | Valid per cent | Cumulative per cent |
|---|---|---|---|---|---|
| Valid | 8.00 | 1 | .1 | .1 | .1 |
|  | 9.00 | 1 | .1 | .1 | .1 |
|  | 10.00 | 3 | .2 | .2 | .4 |
|  | 11.00 | 1 | .1 | .1 | .4 |
|  | 13.00 | 4 | .2 | .3 | .7 |
|  | 14.00 | 6 | .3 | .4 | 1.1 |
|  | 15.00 | 9 | .5 | .6 | 1.8 |
|  | 16.00 | 8 | .5 | .6 | 2.3 |
|  | 17.00 | 14 | .8 | 1.0 | 3.3 |
|  | 18.00 | 31 | 1.8 | 2.2 | 5.5 |
|  | 19.00 | 32 | 1.9 | 2.2 | 7.7 |
|  | 20.00 | 52 | 3.0 | 3.6 | 11.3 |
|  | 21.00 | 66 | 3.8 | 4.6 | 16.0 |
|  | 22.00 | 88 | 5.1 | 6.2 | 22.1 |
|  | 23.00 | 111 | 6.4 | 7.8 | 29.9 |
|  | 24.00 | 131 | 7.6 | 9.2 | 39.1 |
|  | 25.00 | 144 | 8.4 | 10.1 | 49.2 |
|  | 26.00 | 167 | 9.7 | 11.7 | 60.9 |
|  | 27.00 | 159 | 9.2 | 11.1 | 72.0 |
|  | 28.00 | 167 | 9.7 | 11.7 | 83.7 |
|  | 29.00 | 126 | 7.3 | 8.8 | 92.5 |
|  | 30.00 | 107 | 6.2 | 7.5 | 100.0 |
|  | Total | 1428 | 82.9 | 100.0 |  |
| Missing System[1] |  | 295 | 17.1 |  |  |
| Total |  | 1723 | 100.0 |  |  |

*Note:* [1]System missing responses appear because students had not supplied answers for one or more of the questionnaire items that make up the task motivation (science) scale.

Summary statistics including the mean and standard deviation (usually referred to in textbooks as descriptive statistics) are obtained using the 'descriptives' option of descriptive statistics. Summary statistics for 'gender', 'task motivation (science)' and 'level of cognitive development' are shown in Table 10.4.

Returning to the question of whether 18 is a low score on the task motivation (science) scale, knowing that the mean score for this scale is 25.0 (rounded off) and that the standard deviation is 3.6 suggests that a score of 18 is unusually low, as most people are scoring between 21.4 (3.6 below the mean of 25) and 28.6.

Table 10.4 also illustrates an important point to bear in mind when using a computer program. As gender is a nominal-level variable, it makes no sense to talk about the average or mean gender, as clearly my participants were either boys or girls. Yet SPSS will calculate this value if asked. You always need to ask yourself the question, is what I'm asking the computer to calculate sensible? In simple terms, if you put rubbish in, you will get rubbish out!

**Table 10.4** Descriptive statistics for gender, task motivation (science) and level of cognitive development

|  | N | Minimum | Maximum | Mean | Std Deviation |
|---|---|---|---|---|---|
| Gender | 1652 | 1.00 | 2.00 | 1.5702 | .49519 |
| Task motivation (science) | 1428 | 8.00 | 30.00 | 24.9965 | 3.60574 |
| Level of cognitive development | 1723 | 2.00 | 9.00 | 6.1977 | 2.18647 |

**Activity 10.2**

Go to the SAGE website (www.sagepub.co.uk/wilson) and access the example 'SPSS database for motivation'. Obtain descriptive statistics for the remaining motivation scales. What conclusions do you reach about student 1001's motivation (you will need to look at her scores in the database)?

## 3. Producing graphs

It is often easier to get a sense of how frequency distributions look by plotting graphs rather than looking at tables or summary statistics. For instance, you have seen the frequency distribution table and know that the mean score on the task motivation (science) scale was 25.0, while scores ranged from 8 to 30 and there was a relatively small amount of variation as the standard deviation was 3.6. If you think about these figures carefully, they suggest that scores were bunched up at the higher end of the scale. This can be seen much more clearly by plotting a histogram, which is a graph of the frequency distribution.

In SPSS, graphs can be produced through the 'graph' drop-down menu, which gives you the option of producing a histogram. The histogram for the task motivation (science) scale is shown in Figure 10.1 and, as expected, students' scores are bunched up towards the top of the scale. This scale is about learning things so it is hardly surprising that most students say they are motivated by this, given that they know their answers are going to be scrutinized by someone else.

A second type of graph that is useful when conducting a descriptive analysis of data, which is also an option from the graph menu, is a scatter diagram. This shows the relationship between two interval-level variables. For instance, I was very interested in knowing whether there was a relationship between students' cognitive development scores and their task motivation scores. I expected students who said they were motivated to try hard to learn new things to develop cognitively. A scatter diagram would help me decide whether I was right about this relationship and this is shown in Figure 10.2.

Each circle represents one or more students' scores on the variables in question. For instance, the circle at the bottom right of the graph represents students that scored 30

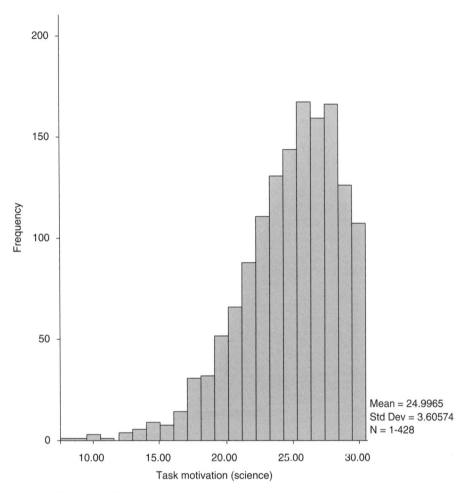

Figure 10.1    Histogram showing the distribution of response to the task motivation (science) scale

(the maximum value) on the task motivation (science) scale (so are highly motivated to learn new things) but at the same time got the lowest score of 2 on the level of cognitive development test. So, for these students, being very keen to learn new things does not appear to be associated with helping them to develop cognitively. In general, if there was a positive association, which statisticians call a positive correlation, between task motivation and level of cognitive development, the graph would show a series of circles falling around an imaginary line sloping from the bottom left to the top right of the graph (i.e. sloping upwards). Here, we have a general swirl of dots filling most of the graph, suggesting no relationship (or no correlation) between task motivation and level of cognitive development. This is not what I expected. Note that it is also possible to have a negative correlation between two variables. For instance, you would expect a negative

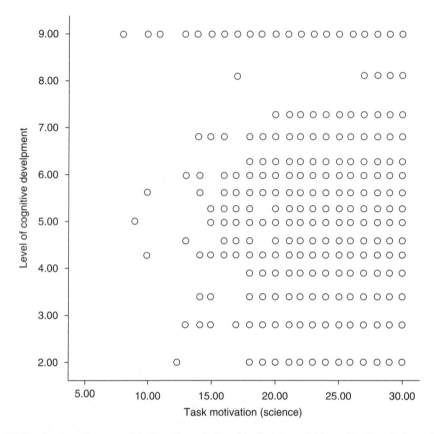

Figure 10.2   Scatter diagram showing the relationship between task motivation (science) and
level of cognitive development

correlation between alienation and cognitive development, which would appear as a
band of circles following an imaginary line from the top left to the bottom right (i.e.
sloping downwards).

**Activity 10.3**

1. Using the example database on the SAGE website (www.sagepub.co.uk/wilson) produce
   a histogram for the work avoidance (science) scale. What conclusions would you draw
   about this distribution?
2. Examine the relationship between work avoidance and the level of cognitive development scores. What would you expect this relationship to be? Is your hypothesis correct?

# DATA ANALYSIS – INFERENTIAL STATISTICS

Having explored the data and gained a sense of the relationships between different variables, it is now time to get to the crux of the matter and answer the original research questions. I was interested in the relationship between motivation and level of cognitive development. I predicted that students scoring highly on the task motivation scale (the desire to learn and master new things) would have overall higher scores on the test of cognitive development than students with low scores on the task motivation scale. Similarly, I would expect that students with high scores on the alienation scale (actively disrupting learning) would have overall lower scores on the test of cognitive development than students who have low scores on the alienation scale. I also thought that girls would have higher scores on the task motivation scale and lower scores on the alienation scale than boys, and that girls' level of cognitive development would be higher.

In order to assess whether these hypotheses are correct, we need to run a number of statistical tests. Essentially, I am asking two different types of question:

1. Is there a relationship between two variables (for instance, between task motivation and level of cognitive development)?
2. Is there a difference between two groups on a given variable (for instance, between boys and girls on task motivation)?

Each type of question requires a specific statistical test, and these are outlined below.

## 1. Tests of correlation

The first type of question relates to relationships or correlations between variables, therefore the appropriate statistical test in this case is a test of correlation. The logic behind this type of test is that we look at the actual relationships found (so we need to calculate a particular entity to assess this) and then make a judgement as to how likely this result would be, if in fact there wasn't a relationship between the variables of interest. In essence, we are judging the likelihood that the results we found were a fluke, i.e. in reality, motivation and cognitive development aren't related in any way; it just happened in this sample of schools that there was some type of relationship. The reason we have to take this approach is because we simply don't know whether there is in fact a relationship or not, and we have to make the best judgement we can based on the data we have on the balance of probabilities. These probabilities can only be calculated by starting from a position that the variables are not related. A slightly different starting point is taken when we are looking at differences between groups, which is described below. However, it is the case that the calculations conducted in any statistical test involve calculating probabilities to enable the person running the test to make a judgement call. This is why the outcomes of the calculations made are referred to as inferential statistics and the tests themselves are often called significance tests.

The entity calculated in a test of correlation to quantify the relationship between the two variables of interest is a correlation coefficient. The statistical test enables me to judge whether this is significant (i.e. the balance of probabilities is that there is a relationship between motivation and cognitive development). At this point, I have several choices of correlation coefficients to calculate dependent on the measurement level and distribution of my variables. If you intend to use inferential statistics, you will need to read up on this in more detail, as all I am doing here is giving an introduction to this area. Specifically, you can choose to do either a parametric or non-parametric test. The former is generally preferred because it is more powerful and sensitive to your data, however it also makes certain assumptions about your data. For reasons there isn't the space here to explain, my data are acceptable for a parametric test, hence I need to calculate the appropriate correlation coefficient, a Pearson correlation coefficient, and then look at the significance test results. In SPSS, this procedure is conducted in the 'correlate' option of the analyse menu. The results for the test of correlation between level of cognitive development and task motivation (science) scores are shown in Table 10.5.

Initially, this may look a little confusing because the same information is repeated in the table. What we are interested in is the relationship between the level of cognitive development and task motivation (science). If you look in the relevant quadrant (top right or bottom left), you can see the correlation coefficient, significance figure and number of students whose data contributed to calculating the statistic (1428). The correlation coefficient -0.043 is practically zero. As correlation coefficients range from -1 (strong negative correlation) through zero (no correlation) to +1 (strong positive correlation), this indicates that there is no relationship between the level of cognitive development and task motivation, which is contrary to initial predictions (but perhaps not that surprising having seen the scatter diagram previously). The significance figure tells you the probability that you would have obtained the correlation coefficient of -0.043 if cognitive development and task motivation were not related in real life beyond my study. Hence, there is a probability of

**Table 10.5** Significance test for correlation between task motivation (science) and level of cognitive development

|  |  | Level of cognitive development | Task motivation (science) |
|---|---|---|---|
| **Level of Cognitive development** | Pearson Correlation | 1 | −.043 |
|  | Sig. (two-tailed) |  | .104 |
|  | N | 1723 | 1428 |
| **Task motivation (science)** | Pearson Correlation | −.043 | 1 |
|  | Sig. (two-tailed) | .104 |  |
|  | N | 1428 | 1428 |

0.104 (which you can transform into a percentage by multiplying by 100 – so 10.4%) that my correlation coefficient of -0.043 would have arisen by chance when there is no relationship between these two variables. Although 10% chance might sound quite low to a newcomer to this approach, in fact that is still reasonably likely. Consequently, we conclude that there is no evidence to deviate from the status quo that cognitive development and task motivation are not related. In fact, a rule of thumb is that in this type of test (a two-tailed test – again, I won't say more but you can look this up), you would have to have a probability of less than 2.5% before you would make a judgement call that the two variables might be related. Even then we don't know for sure one way or the other, so you are never able to couch your conclusions in definitive terms.

### Activity 10.4

Using the example database on the SAGE website (www.sagepub.co.uk/wilson) conduct tests of association between level of cognitive development and each of the other three motivation scales for science. What is your overall conclusion about the relationship between motivation and level of cognitive development?

## 2. Tests of difference

As with tests of correlation, there are different types of tests of difference available to suit the characteristics of the data you have (relating to the measurement level and distribution of the variable under consideration). If we conduct a parametric test of difference (because the data are appropriate, as noted in the previous section), then we compare the mean score of each group on the variable of interest. So, for instance, if we want to know whether girls and boys differ in their scores on the task motivation scale, we compare the mean scores of girls and boys on this scale. The entity calculated in the comparison process is called the $t$ statistic and the test itself is referred to as a $t$-test. Here, the assumption underlying the calculations of the $t$ statistic is that there is no difference between the two groups under consideration (i.e. boys and girls).

In SPSS, $t$-tests are accessed via the 'compare means' option in the analyse menu. Although we are conducting a parametric test, there are different ways of comparing means and this is reflected in the choice in the 'compare means' procedure. Because we are comparing two different groups (boys and girls) on a particular variable (task motivation), this is an independent samples test. This is in contrast to a situation where you might be comparing the same people on two different variables (for instance, in my study, I compared students' scores on each of the motivation scales at the start and end of the two-year study to see whether they had changed), which would require the use of a repeated measures test. You also need to specify which groups you are comparing (under 'define groups'), which you do by inserting the codes you created for the groups you want to compare (in my case, 1 and 2, representing boys and girls respectively). The reason you need to specify groups is because it may be that you have more than two groups for a particular variable in the database (for instance, I might want to compare task motivation scores from two of my nine schools). The results of the test are shown in Table 10.6.

The top part of the table shows descriptive statistics, which is handy because we hadn't found out in advance what the mean scores for boys and girls are on the task motivation scale (although normally in this sort of analysis you would start by looking at the descriptive statistics before conducting statistical tests). As might be expected, the mean scores for boys and girls are not exactly the same. In fact, boys (with a mean score of 25.02) overall record slightly higher scores than girls (with a mean score of 24.98), which is not what was expected. To see whether these small differences are statistically different, we need to look at the lower part of the table.

Although there is a lot of information given, for the purpose of this introduction, you only need to focus on two figures: the $t$ value and the second 'sig' (significance) value. There are two variants for each and the one that is appropriate to interpret again depends on the characteristics of the data (in this case, whether the amount of variation in the girls' scores is as great as that in the boys', which for these data is a fair assumption – again, you would need to read up more on this). Hence, assuming equal variances, we need to focus on the top figure in each case. The calculated $t$ value is 0.239. Unlike the correlation coefficient, this in itself doesn't tell you much about the difference between boys' and girls' scores, except to say that the larger this value, the bigger the difference between the groups. The significance value (0.811), however, tells us how likely it is that we would have got a $t$ value of 0.239 if there was no difference between boys and girls. Therefore, in this case, the probability of getting a $t$ value of 0.239 if there was no difference between boys and girls is 81.1%, i.e. very likely. Using the same benchmark as before (i.e. we would have to have a probability of less than 2.5% for a two-tailed test), there is clearly no evidence to depart from the status quo of no difference. So our conclusion would be that there is insufficient evidence from these data to suggest that boys and girls differ in their task motivation.

**Activity 10.5**

Using the example database on the SAGE website (www.sagepub.co.uk/wilson) conduct tests of difference to see whether boys and girls differ in their scores on the other three motivation scales for science. What is your overall conclusion about boys' motivation compared to girls'?

## CONCLUDING COMMENTS

The purpose of this chapter has been to introduce some statistical techniques and to show you how to use a widely available statistical program to do this. Inevitably, this has been a real rattle through some quite complicated ideas and some details have been glossed over. However, hopefully, you feel you've grasped some of the basics and have the confidence to follow these ideas up by consulting one or more of the texts listed under Further Reading. If so, the chapter has served its purpose.

**Table 10.6  Significance test for the difference between boys and girls on the task motivation (science) scale**

**Group Statistics**

| Task motivation (science) | Gender | N | Mean | Std Deviation | Std Error Mean |
|---|---|---|---|---|---|
| | Boys | 625 | 25.0224 | 3.65273 | .14611 |
| | Girls | 803 | 24.9763 | 3.57090 | .12601 |

**Independent Samples Test**

| | | Levene's Test for Equality of Variances | | t-test for Equality of Means | | | | | 95% Confidence Interval of the Difference | |
|---|---|---|---|---|---|---|---|---|---|---|
| | | F | Sig. | t | df | Sig. (two-tailed) | Mean Difference | Std. Error Difference | Lower | Upper |
| Task motivation | Equal variances assumed | .101 | .750 | .239 | 1426 | .811 | .04606 | .19240 | -.33136 | .42348 |
| | Equal variances not assumed | | | .239 | 1326.515 | .811 | .04606 | .19294 | -.33245 | .42457 |

## KEY IDEAS

- Note that use of a specialist program, such as SPSS, means you do not need to be a specialist at number crunching, however you still need to understand what is going on to ensure you conduct the most appropriate analysis to answer your research questions.
- Spend time setting up your database properly by allocating an identifier and relevant demographic variables and defining characteristics of your variables and allocating values for missing data, and always deal with ambiguous data consistently.
- Always clean your data before starting on statistical analysis to ensure any input errors are removed.
- Start your analysis by examining the frequency distributions through producing frequency distribution tables and, where appropriate, histograms. Look at the relationships between variables measured on scales by plotting scatter diagrams.
- Calculate descriptive statistics to summarize and describe the frequency distributions.
- Only then, use inferential statistics to test whether:

  - there is a relationship between two variables, or
  - there is a difference between two groups on a particular variable.

- Test relationships between variables using a test of correlation, by calculating a correlation coefficient.
- Test differences between groups on a variable using a test of difference, by calculating a $t$ value.
- Remember that you can only conclude that you have evidence to reject the default position (of no relationship/no difference) if your significance figure is less than 2.5% for a two-tailed test.

## *Further Reading*

For a good introduction to quantitative analysis, see:

Cohen, L., Manion, L. and Morrison, K. (2000) *Research Methods in Education*. London: RoutledgeFalmer.

For a clear and detailed exposition, see:

Coolican, H. (2004) *Research Methods and Statistics in Psychology,* 4th edn. London: Hodder & Stoughton Educational.

For more details on using SPSS, see:

Brace, N., Kemp, R. and Snelgar, R. (2006) *SPSS for Psychologists,* 3rd edn. Basingstoke: Palgrave Macmillan.

Other useful texts are:

Howitt, D. and Cramer, D. (2005) *Introduction to Statistics in Psychology,* 3rd edn. Harlow: Pearson Education Limited.

Sani, F. and Todman, J. (2006) *Experimental Design and Statistics for Psychology.* Oxford: Blackwell Publishing.

# WRITING ABOUT YOUR RESEARCH

## Elaine Wilson

---

**Hints**

- Don't procrastinate.
- Discipline yourself to write about your work as you go along.
- Keep a notebook readily available at all times in which to write down your ideas.
- Write in regular short bursts.
- Avoid writing frantically just before a deadline.
- Draft, restructure, redraft and edit your work.

---

## INTRODUCTION

Writing research reports and dissertations is a daunting process for the novice researcher and this can cause extreme anxiety which can lead to writer's block. There are number of ways of reducing the complexity of the task and, more importantly, of minimizing the stress on yourself when you start to write in earnest. This chapter will provide advice on strategies and structures to help you write about research projects. The intended audience here is novice researchers about to write an extended essay for a post-graduate certificate course and Masters students who need to write a fairly lengthy thesis.

## GETTING STARTED

Essay and thesis writing is a difficult task, so the temptation will be to put off starting to write and to get side-tracked by deflecting activities such as sharpening your pencils and ordering your desk! Discipline yourself to write something each time you sit down. Don't be too much of a perfectionist at the early stages and don't discard your early ideas even if they are far from final draft material. Also, don't worry about handing in draft work to your supervisor – nobody produces perfect work at the first attempt, and that is what your supervisor is there to help you with. Don't be put off either, if there are a lot of corrections when you get your draft back – keep in mind that your draft work is not being evaluated; only the final product will receive a grade.

## Planning is crucial

Set yourself targets and discuss a reasonable schedule for producing chapters and, ultimately, finishing your thesis with your supervisor. Draw up a schedule that is broken down into chapters with indicators of when certain chapters are due and take these dates seriously. Successfully completing each section will also boost your confidence.

## *Be disciplined and write up as you go along*

Set aside some time each week to write a little and don't put off writing tricky sections – write down your ideas even if this is in the form of rough notes. Leave enough time to step away and think about your ideas. You will have a fresh perspective on things when you return.

## *Organize your draft sections using electronic folders*

Make a folder for your whole thesis or essay, a subfolder for each section or chapter, an additional folder for your references, and a final folder just for general notes. As you proceed with writing your thesis, include notes and reminders in each folder as well as your general notes folder. Try putting notes and text in different colours. Don't forget to save your work and make back-up copies of each change.

## *Know what you want to write*

Plan time for reading because if you start to write too soon, you won't have anything to say so you will tend to 'freeze' at the sight of a blank screen. Above all, do not suffer in silence or put the process off – ask your tutor for help!

**Activity 11.1 – Generating ideas**

1. Imagine that you are being interviewed by someone. What questions would the other person ask you about your work? What would they want to find out about your project? Why did you do it? When did you do it? Where did you do it? How did you do it? What did you find out and so what?

*Or*

2. Map out and organize your ideas visually to explore relationships between the processes.

Then write freely or brainstorm ideas and don't worry about revising or proofreading at this stage.

## COMPOSING YOUR ESSAY OR THESIS

### Planning the structure of the work

Composing your essay or thesis involves making major decisions about what you need to include and how to organize the work. This is probably the most difficult part of the writing process. The next paragraph written by Peter Lipton, the late Professor of History and Philosophy of Science at the University of Cambridge, sums up this process of essay writing succinctly:

> 'An essay is not a list of sentences: it has *structure*. The structure should be obvious to the reader. Write informative introductions and conclusions. The introduction should not only introduce the topic, it should introduce your argument. That means that you should tell the reader what you are going to prove and how you are going to prove it. Unless the introduction gives the reader a clear *map* of the essay, she is likely to get lost. Be direct and specific. Replace sentences like 'Throughout the centuries, the greatest minds have pondered the intractable problem of free will' with 'In this essay, I will show that free will is impossible'. The conclusion of the essay should tell the reader what has been accomplished and why the struggle was worthwhile. It should remind the reader how the different moves in the body of the essay fit together to form a coherent argument.'

Before you start, organize your essay in the form of an outline to help you to visualize the flow of ideas and ensure coherence throughout the work (see Figure 11.1).

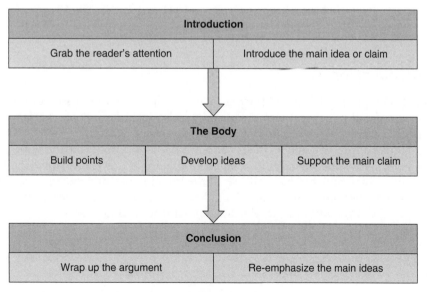

Figure 11.1    The structure of an extended essay or thesis

## *The title*

Although you will probably be asked early on to submit an essay or thesis title, it is highly likely that you will refine this and even rewrite the title after you have finished writing up your project. A title ought to provide a succinct summary of the whole essay or thesis.

---

### BOX 11.1

Examples of PGCE essay titles:

- Does the use of active teaching approaches to encourage independent learning increase students' understanding in Year 12 chemistry lessons?
- How effective are the use of analogies in teaching electricity to a Year 11 class in a 11–18 mixed comprehensive school?

Examples of thesis titles:

- Developing the role of written feedback in promoting students' engagement in early secondary mathematics: An action research study.
- 'Ebbing the tide' of teaching to the test in secondary science classrooms.

Some unusual academic paper titles:

- McIntyre, D., Pedder, D. and Rudduck, J. (2005) 'Pupil voice: comfortable and uncomfortable learnings for teachers', *Research Papers in Education,* 20 (2): 149–68.
- Warrington, M. and Younger, M. (2003) '"We decided to give it a Twirl": Single-sex teaching in English comprehensive schools', *Gender and Education*, 15 (4): 339–50.

---

## *The Introduction*

The introduction is a statement of purpose which will contribute to answering a central question expressed in general terms. This might also include, firstly, a summary of the more specific aims of your research and, secondly, a justification of the significance of the substantive topic you have chosen and why this is important for your practice. Explain your own value position in relation to this topic that has shaped the focus of your enquiry. Then you should clarify what the broad issues or problems are, linked to the specific aims of your research and include a brief description of the context of your enquiry. Table 11.1 illustrates how Martin (2007) introduced her work.

## THE MAIN BODY OF THE WORK

The main body of the work is likely to include the following sections:

**Table 11.1    Introduction**

| | |
|---|---|
| A *justification* of the significance of the substantive topic | In accordance with national and local priorities, the school prioritizes raising achievement in literacy. |
| A *statement* of the broad issues | The Big Book approach was already an established reading strategy in the early stages, up to Primary 3 (aged 7). As a class teacher, my intention was to investigate the potential of interactive talking books and an interactive whiteboard as a teaching and learning resource, to develop writing with Primary 6 children. |
| A *description* of the context of your enquiry | This research was carried out in the school where I teach, as part of the new Scottish qualification of MSc. in Chartered Teacher Studies, for which students are required to plan, implement and evaluate small-scale research and development work that has professional relevance to the student and to the school. |
| An *outline* of the rest of the study | Through this medium, I wanted to find out how helping children to interact with and reflect on the writing of professional authors might motivate them, develop their understanding and influence their own writing. |

*Source*: Martin (2007)

## A review of the literature

The literature review sets out what is already known in your area of study (see Chapter 3) and should start by signposting what will be covered. Firstly, you should set out a critical and focused review of the literature, guided by review questions relating to your substantive and theoretical issues or problems in turn. Start with your substantive knowledge area and then the theoretical ideas informing your study. Secondly, include a brief summary of your position concerning your ideas about the substantive and theoretical issues or problems in the light of your review. Finally, end this section with an indication of how the research design you plan to use will take forward your work in relation to the substantive and theoretical areas and your research questions (see Table 11.2).

## Details of your research design

This section will set out your research questions and the theoretical framework you are using to help you understand and analyse the substantive topic relating to the central question. If you are writing a thesis, this section will be substantial and will also include a brief critical and focused review of the literature relating to your methodological

**Table 11.2    Literature Review Section**

| | |
|---|---|
| A *critical and focused* review of the literature guided by review questions | Martin's review considered literature about: The Big Book approach Whole-class interactive teaching Interactive whiteboards |
| A *brief summary of your position* concerning your substantive and theoretical issues or problems in the light of your review | The conclusion made is that there is a strong relationship between the ways in which ICT has been used and the resulting attainment outcomes. This suggests that the crucial component in the use of ICT within education is the teachers and their pedagogical approaches. |
| An *indication of how the research design will take forward* your work in relation to the substantive and theoretical areas and your research questions | For the reasons set out above, in order to improve children's writing, I therefore decided to explore the use of interactive electronic Big Books that have graphics and sound to support the text. In addition, an interactive whiteboard would allow children to make use of writing tools such as highlighter pens, speech and thought bubbles while composing, using the touch screen facility. |

*Source*: Martin (2007)

issues or problems, indicating how other researchers have approached them and have investigated similar substantive topics. Finally, include a brief summary of your position about your methodological approach and any issues which arise in the light of what your have read and found out so far.

## Your methodology and methods

In the methodology section, justify the methodological approach you have taken and explain the methods of data collection you are using and your justification for using them (see Chapters 7–14).

Table 11.3 shows Martin's research methods section from her paper in *Literacy* (2007). This section is an a bridged version of Martin's final thesis which would also have included a summary description of her data collection instruments, indicating how her research questions are addressed and her rationale for the instruments chosen. In her thesis, she will have also presented a summary of her pilot data collection stage and included details of how data were analysed. The thesis would also have included an extended ethics section, outlining how Martin ensured that her research followed all the necessary school and research ethical guidelines. Finally, Martin would also have discussed the strengths and limitations of her design and told us how she had overcome the threats to the reliability and internal and external validity of her methods (see Chapter 7).

## Your presentation of the findings

This findings section will set out a summary of all the findings broken down into topics relating to the research questions. It is a good idea to support this in the form

**Table 11.3   Research Methods Section**

As a class teacher investigating my own classroom, I felt an action research model was most appropriate as this would allow me to reformulate ideas in response to my findings, and feed these back into teaching in a continuous process. It would also allow me to include qualitative as well as quantitative approaches.

| Research Questions | Data Collected |
|---|---|
| 1. To what extent has using interactive whiteboard technology (IWB) to support whole-class teaching of reading and writing improved children's writing? | A random sample of six boys and four girls (every third child on the class register) provided samples of character description and persuasive argument before and after the project, producing four pieces per pupil. (It is recognized that this was a very small sample and no generalizations can be made from the results.) It was agreed beforehand that two colleagues would assess the writing pieces. However, because of constraints of time and workload, four colleagues were eventually involved. 'Taking a Closer Look at Learning to Write' (SCRE, 1995) was used as the assessment tool and the writing samples (with pupils' names and dates removed) were graded on a scale of one to six, where one represented limited understanding, and six represented sound understanding. |
| 1. To what extent has using interactive whiteboard technology (IWB) to support whole-class teaching of reading and writing improved children's writing? | The second question set out to monitor the effect of interactive whiteboard technology on the learning of two boys in class labelled pupil X and pupil Y, both with additional support needs. I created a scaled observation schedule that measured aspects of behaviour before and during the project, and in each of four writing sessions. My support assistant observed one boy and various colleagues shared in observations of the other, leaving me free to teach the rest of the class. To address issues of reliability, an inter-observer agreement (Simpson and Tuson, 2003) was drawn up and discussed with colleagues beforehand. |
| 3. What benefits/disadvantages for the teaching and learning of writing are offered by using IWB? | The third question looked at the advantages and disadvantages of using the technology in teaching and learning. Two questionnaires were designed to assess children's understanding about their learning and their views on using the technology in writing lessons. As the project developed I took the decision to investigate patterns in pupil behaviour during interactive whiteboard lessons and a further observation schedule was designed and administered by my support assistant. |

*Source*: Martin (2007)

of tables, matrices, diagrams and quotations from participants and informants, where appropriate, and end the section with a concluding summary of key findings and emerging issues which you have identified.

## Your discussion of the findings

The purpose of the discussion section is to explain the meaning of the results you have obtained. Although the discussion comes at the end of your thesis or essay, constantly keep in mind why your study is important and how your study relates to previous studies while you are doing the research. Your final discussion should include the following five points:

### State the major findings of the study

The discussion should begin with a statement of the major findings of the study which will be the very first paragraph in the discussion in the form of a direct statement. Don't include data or reference to the study design at this stage.

### Explain the meaning of the findings and why the findings are important

By this stage in the research process, you will be so close to the design and data collection process that the meaning of the results and their importance will seem obvious to you. However, your reader might not be so familiar with all that is in your head, so you need to explain everything really clearly and not assume that the reader can interpret the tables and data for themselves.

### Relate your findings to other similar studies

The discussion section should relate your study findings to those of other studies. You can tell the reader about the prompts and questions raised by previous studies which motivated you to do your study. These other studies may support your findings and this will serve to strengthen the importance of your work.

### Consider alternative explanations for the findings

The purpose of research is to *discover* and not to *prove*. It is easy to fall into the trap of designing the study to prove your strongly held bias rather than to challenge and test this out by looking at the evidence. Consequently, when you write the discussion section, carefully consider all possible explanations for the study results, rather than just those that fit your biases.

## *Make suggestions for further research*

Although a study may answer important questions, other questions related to the subject may remain unanswered. Moreover, some unanswered questions may become more focused because of your study. You should make suggestions for further study in the discussion section too.

Table 11.4 shows how Pedder (2006) has done all of this very succinctly in the discussion from his paper about class size.

**Table 11.4   Structure of the discussion section**

| | |
|---|---|
| State the study's major findings | The secondary school study developed no evidence of simple one-way relationships between class size and optimum conditions for all kinds of teaching and learning. This is a key finding. |
| Explain the meaning and importance of the findings | Different teachers recognized increased opportunities for promoting and supporting learning in large as well as in small classes; they also recognized constraints in small as well as in large classes. Politicians therefore need to be receptive to the possibility that benefits to pupils' learning arise in large as well as in small classes and thus need to promote frameworks within which schools can adopt more flexible approaches to allocating pupils to learning groups of different size for different teaching and learning purposes. |
| Relate the findings to those of similar studies | The American large-scale class size reduction experiments mentioned the beginning of this article appear to be motivated by a concern with political and economic decision-making at government level more than with decision-making at school or classroom level. |
| Consider alternative explanations of the findings | At a glance it might seem, therefore, that the focus on class size as an isolated variable is not only understandable but also justifiable. However, research approaches that combine, within the same design, observation of patterns of classroom behaviour with fine grained analysis of practitioners' perspectives stand the best chance of developing evidence that is relevant to, and useful for, thinking and decision-making at the global policy level. The challenge is for politicians to face up to the complexities involved and to be open to more flexible approaches to the organization of teaching and learning in schools. |
| Make suggestions for further research | McIntyre argues for flexible reform that includes increased non-contact time for teachers and pupils and more flexible arrangements for conducting face-to-face contact between teachers and pupils individually as well as in classes and groups of different size on a fitness for purpose basis. Should politicians and policy makers begin to construe the development of class size policy within this kind of inclusive framework of change, then it may be possible to gain the potential benefits from small classes but also the benefits from large classes without a net increase in expenditure in the long run. |

*Source*: Pedder (2006)

> **Activity 11.2**
>
> **Use the checklist below to assess your own discussion section:**
>
> 1. Have you included all the points set out in the discussion of findings section (see Table 11.4)?
> 2. Are you confident that your interpretation of the results does not go beyond what is supported by the data and that you are not being speculative?
> 3. Are there any tangential points included which run the risk of diluting and confounding your message?

## Conclusion and recommendations

Finally, Table 11.5 illustrates what a good conclusion should look like. Pedder (2006) has included: *recommendations* for different audiences – in this case, policy makers; suggestions for further research; an evaluation of his research design, including flagging up his uncertainty about answers to research questions; and a final clear take-away message. Wyse (2006) has provided guidance on the approximate length and word count for each section and this is included in Table 11.6.

Now that you have got all your ideas down on paper, it is a good idea to leave the draft for a few days before you come back to revise it. Writing is a process of progressive refining so don't underestimate the time it takes. Visit the library and look at examples of previous students' work in readiness for the next reviewing stage.

## REVIEWING WHAT YOU HAVE DONE

Reviewing your work involves revising the essay at the ideas level. It is literally seeing the argument of the paper through revising the organization to make the essay coherent and clear.

Peter Lipton explained this reviewing stage very eloquently as:

> Think(ing) of your essay as composed of a series of descriptive and argumentative moves. Each major move deserves a paragraph. Generally speaking, a paragraph should start with a transition sentence or a topic sentence. A transition sentence indicates how the paragraph follows from the previous one; a topic sentence says what the paragraph is about. Both types of sentences are really miniature *maps*. In the middle of a paragraph you may want to give another map, explaining how the move you are making here is connected to others you have made or will make. The order of your paragraphs is crucial. The reader should have a clear sense of *development* and *progress* as she reads. Later paragraphs should build on what has come before, and the readers should have a feeling of steady formation. To achieve this effect you make sure your sentences hang together. Think about glue. You can get glue from maps from transition sentences and words and especially from the logic of your argument.

## Table 11.5  Conclusion

| | |
|---|---|
| *Recommendations* for different audiences – in this case, policy makers | Politicians can be helped in their decision-making by research that uses multiple methods of inquiry into effects of class size variation in both primary *and* secondary school contexts. |
| Suggestions for further research | Further research is needed to help us develop much better understanding of the kinds of strategies and knowledge teachers can adapt for effectively promoting high quality learning opportunities for all pupils in different contexts of class size variation. Such research should aim to generate useful insights into how, in large and small classes, learning for a range of different purposes can best be promoted. Class size research needs to attend to the contexts within which class size variation occurs by investigating the different ways class size interacts with other key variables. Teachers bring different strengths and expertise to the classroom. They teach different subjects and work in contexts of varying levels of resourcing and space. |
| | The pupils they teach come to class with different personalities, behavioural and ability characteristics. Taking all these facets of classroom life into account, it is unsurprising if we find teachers maximizing opportunities for pupils to learn in classes of different size in different ways. We need further research to find out how teachers manage to do this in classes of different size in different primary and secondary school contexts. |
| Evaluation of research design and degree of certainty about answers to research questions | Blatchford and colleagues have made important headway through their CSPAR study in developing research that investigates the impact of class size as one among many important factors influencing classroom processes. Greater sophistication of qualitative design is still needed, though, if we are to adequately understand and represent the kinds of teacher and pupil expertise involved in promoting and maximizing opportunities for high quality learning in different large and small class contexts. Here, class size research can learn a great deal from a growing tradition of classroom-based research that is making exciting progress in gaining access to pupils' perspectives and experiences of classroom learning as a means to improving what we know about effective classroom processes (e.g. Cooper & McIntyre, 1996; Pollard, 1996; Rudduck et al., 1996; Pollard & Triggs, 2000; Rudduck & Flutter, 2000, 2004). By contrast, class size research has neglected  pupils' voices as key sources of insight. |
| Final take-away message | Embracing their perspectives, as well as their teachers', provides the best opportunity for improving our theoretical and practical understandings of class size effects on classroom teaching and learning processes and outcomes. |

*Source*: Pedder (2006)

**Table 11.6** Recommended lengths for different sections of a 6000-word research report

| | Percentage of the overall report | Number of words | |
| --- | --- | --- | --- |
| | | 6000-word essay | 20,000-word thesis |
| Abstract | 2.5 | 150 | 500 |
| Literature review | 30 | 1800 | 6,000 |
| Methodology | 17.5 | 1050 | 3,500 |
| Results | 30 | 1800 | 6,000 |
| Discussion/Conclusion | 20 | 1200 | 4,000 |

Adapted from Wyse, 2006

## The structure of argument

An academic essay is about persuasion, and the structure of your argument plays a vital rôle in this. To persuade a reader, you must explain why you are undertaking your research, provide a context, and then explain your evidence, so don't just list findings without a discernible logic.

## Constructing an argument

Don't assume that the reader is as familiar as you are with the subject. Are your points really clear? Try them out on a non-expert – in other words, you need to make the familiar unfamiliar. Put yourself in the reader's position so that you can convince them that your argument is sound.

### Have a clear point to argue

Start by making some sort of claim. By that I mean you will need to agree or disagree with the statement in the title you have chosen, then use evidence to support your argument. In other words, you need to stake out a position and use evidence to argue your case.

Begin by asking yourself, 'What is my point?' If your essay does not have a main point, then you cannot argue for anything. Having a point will help you avoid your essay being simply a list of findings.

It is likely that the person who is assessing your essay knows a lot more than you do about the subject matter. So don't simply provide them with material they already know; instead demonstrate to them that you understand the issues fully. In your essay, you can do this by engaging critically with the material you have read and applying it to your own school situation.

### Back up your point with evidence

You must back up your point with evidence by demonstrating that you can collect reliable and valid data to test out your ideas and that your claims are warranted by the evidence you are presenting. The strength of your evidence, and how you use it, can make or break your argument. Be consistent with your evidence but make sure that within each section you are providing the reader with evidence appropriate to each claim. Getting the structure of your essay tidy and ordered will be important because you can't convince a confused reader.

## Include a counter argument

Be up front about the limitations of your research design and the possible threats to the validity of your claims and point out what you have done to minimize these threats. You can test out counter arguments by asking your tutor or peers to challenge your claims.

## REVISING YOUR WORK

### Revising the organization

Start by revising the organization and check for clarity and coherence. If your writing is ungrammatical or difficult to follow, it will be awkward to read. This may be because you are not using your own words and are relying on too many phrases and quotations. Even if you are using somebody else's ideas, try to use your own words to paraphrase this. And acknowledge this by adding a reference. Try reading your work aloud to see if it flows.

### Proofreading your work

Leave enough time to sort out the mechanics of writing, that is, checking spelling, punctuation, sentence structure and referencing. You have spent a long time on the organization so don't skimp on the time spent on this stage, as a poorly presented study will detract from the overall work.

Finally, use the checklist in Activity 11.3 before you submit your work.

**Activity 11.3    Questions to ask yourself regarding the presentation of your study**

**Coherence**

- Is the main argument clearly stated and logical?
- Are there clear headings and sub-headings so that the reader can follow your thinking throughout the essay or thesis?

## Content

- Is the content connected within and among sections of your essay?
- Is the work coherent?
- Does the abstract provide an overall representation of your thesis?

## *Clarity of information*

- Have you used a range of presentational devices, such as tables, figures and graphs?
- Do you explain any technical language introduced?

## *Clarity of Data*

- Have you presented data in an understandable layout and explained findings clearly to support your argument?

## *Format*

- Does the format of your manuscript conform to the style recommended in your course handbook or used by the journal (e.g. Harvard)?
- Have you avoided sexist language?
- Have you used current terminology (e.g. participants rather than subjects)?
- Have you explained abbreviations or acronyms, demystified jargon and avoided the overuse of metaphors?
- Have you used the correct mechanics (e.g. grammar, punctuation)?

## KEY IDEAS

1. Check out the criteria which will be used to judge your work.
2. Structure your essay clearly and include an introduction which sets out a clear 'map' of your ideas.
3. Link paragraphs explicitly.
4. Include a final succinct conclusion that summarizes your key ideas.
5. Demonstrate that you fully understand the key ideas, supported by the choice of references you use.
6. Only include information relevant to the point you are trying to make.
7. Substantiate all the claims you are making.
8. Ensure adequate depth to the points to show the value of the idea.
9. Ensure adequate breadth to the work to enable you to discuss your ideas in the wider context.
10. Write the essay in your own words.
11. Use clear, concise language.
12. Take an original, insightful and imaginative approach.
13. Cite all the ideas you use in the text.
14. Use the recommended referencing system consistently.
15. Proofread your work and give ample attention to spelling, grammar and punctuation.
16. Include an accurate reference list.

*Further Reading*

BERA (2000) Good practice in educational research writing, www.bera.ac.uk/publications/pdfs/GOODPR1.PDF (Accessed March 2008)

*References*

Lipton, P. (2007) *Writing philosophy*. Department of History & Philosophy of Science. http://www.hps.cam.ac.uk/research/wp.html (Accessed July 14 2008)

Martin, S. (2007) 'Interactive whiteboards and talking books', *Literacy*, 41 (1): 26–34.

Pedder, (2006) 'Are small classes better? Understanding relationships between class size, classroom processes of pupils' learning', *Oxford Review*, 32 (2): 213–34.

Wyse, D. (2006) *The Good Writing Guide for Education Students*. London: Sage.

# SECTION 3

## METHODOLOGIES

# ACTION RESEARCH

## Elaine Wilson

This chapter will introduce the principles and processes of action research and will draw on published examples of expert researchers' work to illustrate how you might carry out your own action research. The chapter will conclude with criteria you could use to judge the validity of your own action research outcomes.

## WHAT IS ACTION RESEARCH?

Teachers are often concerned with issues in their classrooms and actively try to address these. When a teacher intervenes to make changes to their practice and at the same time systematically collects evidence of the effects of these changes, then they are engaging in action research.

There are many interpretations of action research because the approach is used in a wide range of education and other settings. However, in all cases there is a common intention, which is to change practice in response to a problem identified by the practitioner researcher.

Another important feature of action-research inquiry is that it is always done *by* or *with* insiders within an organization or community and not by an external team of researchers who usually study teachers or students in action.

School-based action research is about investigating human actions and social situations that are experienced by teachers. The impetus for the research might stem from a situation being considered as unacceptable in some respects, susceptible to change or requiring a practical response. Accordingly, action research is concerned with the everyday practical problems experienced by teachers and as such is a flexible research approach, where methodology is defined as an orientation towards research, rather than a particular set of research methods.

## HOW TO DO ACTION RESEARCH IN YOUR CLASSROOM

In essence, when a classroom teacher undertakes action research, he/she tries a new approach, studies what happens, shares findings with others, reads what experts say and then in light of their research findings, reformulates the problem and repeats the process again. Figure 12.1 presents an example to illustrate the stages involved. In this example, a secondary science teacher carried out action research in her classroom.

## REFINING THE PROBLEM

The example given in Figure 12.1 was initiated by a secondary science teacher who was unhappy with a new curriculum development and wanted to improve her teaching of the new approach called 'How science works'. However, this was much too general so the teacher first narrowed her focus to that of helping her students to structure an argument.

The next stage involved further reconnaissance in the classroom to establish exactly what was currently being done by her colleagues to help students understand the different ways of thinking about complex controversial issues in the science curriculum. The teacher also asked a colleague to observe her approach and she consulted the students in her class. At this stage, the teacher also found it useful to broaden her thinking about teaching controversial issues through reading published accounts in the literature and by discussing this with other colleagues beyond the science department. As a result, the teacher refined her area of interest to argumentation in science lessons and decided that the students' problem may be aggravated by not knowing how to analyse the issues surrounding the complex contexts she was teaching. The literature search and discussion with colleagues outside her immediate environment had been crucial in helping her to restate the original problem.

## PLANNING THE ACTION RESEARCH

Having narrowed her focus, the teacher arrived at a manageable research question for her pilot intervention. This was: 'Will my students be able to structure an argument if I teach them explicitly how to analyse the issues?'. The next stage involved not only planning how she would change her practice to help the students to analyse complex issues, but

**Research question:**
'Will my students be able
to structure an argument
better if I teach them explicitly
how to analyse the issues?'

**Reflect:**
Analyse the evidence. Has the
problem been solved? If not,
decide on the next step. Has
this raised new questions?

Reflect    Plan

ACT and Observe

**Plan:**
(a) how to teach students to
analyse complex issues
(b) how to collect data to
monitor effect
(c) how to analyse data

**Act and observe:**
Carry out new teaching
approach and data-
collection process

Re-Plan

Reflect

ACT and Observe

**Re-plan:**
The revised plan to answer
the new question that has
arisen from the first cycle

Figure 12.1    Action-research cycles

also how she would collect reliable evidence to monitor the effect of her new approach
and how she would analyse the data collected.

## ACTING OUT AND OBSERVING THE INTERVENTION

The teacher subdivided her research question into two parts. She looked first for evidence of the students' ability to analyse issues, and secondly at how her students were constructing arguments. The data collected included audio recordings of small-group dialogue, lesson observation notes carried out by a colleague and, following the intervention, the use of a diagnostic probe to find out about students' views of the concepts and the teaching approach. The teacher also analysed the students' written work and interviewed a small representative sample of students (see Table 12.1).

## REFLECTING AND RE-PLANNING

Subsequent analysis of the data and reflection on the issues arising from the intervention prompted the teacher to modify her approach and to undertake a second revised action-research cycle with the same data-collection methods.

Table 12.1    Action-research data-collection plan

| Research Question | Will my students be able to structure an argument better if I teach them explicitly how to analyse the issues? | | | |
| --- | --- | --- | --- | --- |
| Sub-question | Data source | Data source | Data source | Data source |
| 1. Can students analyse complex issues? | Audio recording of small-group dialogue | Diagnostic probe | Semi-structured interviews with students | Colleagues' observation  notes |
| 2. Can students structure an argument? | Students' written work | Diagnostic probe | Semi-structured interviews with students | |

To be transformative, action research needs to be carried out over a sustained period of inquiry and involve reframing the problem in light of new sets of questions. It is this ongoing reframing of the problem that leads to the transformative *action* that characterizes action research.

## Going further than simply reflecting in action

In the example given in Figure 12.1 the teacher's aim was to be more reflective and to develop a deeper understanding of this practice. The teacher researched her own classroom through close observation and reflection as well as undertaking informed action. This intervention did not involve the teacher in taking undue risks or making dramatic changes.

Other forms of action research are associated with social transformation through research efforts. Such situations may require that teachers or other researchers make high-risk changes that are driven by a deep commitment to equality, human well-being, deeper understanding, and respect for others. In these circumstances, classroom-based action researchers need to have a strong personal interest in the proposed action and also have the authority to act for themselves in the research setting. Consequently action research involving social changes will mean taking calculated risks and making prudent practical judgements about how to act in specific, often unique, classroom situations.

For other action researchers, the primary goal will be to generate knowledge or theoretical frameworks that other practitioners can draw on and adapt to improve practice within their own context.

Accordingly, because of these broad aims, action research has struggled to establish itself as a serious form of academic research. Many questions continue to be raised, such as: do practitioners draw on theoretical foundations when investigating and reflecting on their practices and, if so, how? Do practitioners generate new knowledge as a result of their action research? If so, what type of knowledge is this? Can this knowledge be considered valid? These questions will be considered in this chapter.

## LEARNING HOW TO DO ACTION RESEARCH BY READING EXPERTS' WORK

Although action research is a reflective process, it is also a deliberate and systematic undertaking which generally requires that some form of evidence be presented to support the research findings, and it is the nature of this evidence that is hotly debated by professional educational researchers. Indeed, like all forms of inquiry, action research is value-laden, so it is crucial that teachers interrogate received notions of improvement or solutions in terms of who will ultimately benefit from the actions undertaken.

### Positioning, values and beliefs

Action research, like all other social-based research work, will be underpinned by values and beliefs. The language or discourse used when describing action-research goals will give you an indication of the values informing the action research. For example, some groups talk about improving practice or of developing individuals; this could be interpreted as assuming that existing practice is somehow deficient and in need of development. By contrast, other researchers consider action research as a process of transforming practice.

Consequently, when reading other people's work and embarking on your own research, you need to remember that knowledge production is never neutral, but rather is always pursued with some interest in mind. The knowledge you will generate in your classroom as a teacher will be very different from the knowledge created by a team of research scientists in the tightly controlled world of scientific research. Scientific enquiry centres on practical improvements; for example, in the case of medical research, the focus may be on producing new clinical treatments or in engineering to develop new techniques that are 'validated' by whether they 'work' in practice. Such enquiry reduces and isolates parts of what is a very complicated natural world into component parts that can be tested, experimented with and have patterns extracted from. The social situations you will encounter in your school and classroom are complex, and therefore it will be more difficult for you to make absolute claims or draw generalizable theories.

## ACTION-RESEARCH TRADITIONS

There are three different action-research traditions represented in the literature. Each tradition places different emphasis on the role, nature and purpose of practitioner research although there is quite a lot of overlap. Table 12.2 sets out the expert proponents from each tradition. These names will become familiar to you as you read more of the published literature (see Table 12.2).

The first tradition based on teachers' classroom intervention is attributed to Stenhouse and developed further by Elliott, Rudduck and Somekh in the UK. Lawrence

**Table 12.2** Action-research traditions: principles and purposes

| Approach | Key Proponents | Principles | Purposes |
|---|---|---|---|
| Practitioners conducting research about their own practice to better understand and improve practice | Lewin, Corey, Zeichner, Noffkee (USA) Stenhouse, Elliott, Rudduck, Somekh (UK) | Changing practice is educative and linked to practitioner personal growth | To test out ideas To change and improve practice and evaluate these changes To enable professional growth of the practitioner |
| Collective self-enquiry undertaken by participants in social situations which contribute to greater equity and democracy in schools and society | *Critical Emancipatory.* Carr and Kemmis (Australia) Freire (S. America) Elliott (UK) | Undertaking action research is an emancipatory process | To close the gaps between problems and theoretical ideas |
| | *Living theories through self-study and auto ethnography.* Whitehead (UK) McNiff (Ireland) | | To examine personal values and beliefs, and to uncover hidden dispositions to guide actions and choices |
| Practitioners producing knowledge which can be shared with other educators | McTaggart (Australia) Argyris and Schön (USA) | Knowledge produced in action by insider practitioners is useful and should be shared | To build up knowledge to support professional practice |

Stenhouse was the first researcher in the UK to advocate and work towards enabling teachers to take an active role in teacher research. This tradition perceives that action research is about testing ideas in real classrooms, so that changes can be made to improve practice through the systematic evaluation of these changes and that in the process the practitioner also develops.

The second tradition is linked with Carr and Kemmis' emancipatory notions of action research and of living theories expounded by Whitehead and McNiff in the UK and Ireland. This group perceives that action research is about closing the gaps between problems and theoretical ideas through examining personal values and beliefs and uncovering hidden dispositions to guide actions and choices.

The third tradition, based on Schön's reflective practitioner idea, proposes that action research is about building knowledge to support professional practice.

## ACTION-RESEARCH METHODOLOGY

Action research is a methodology that is intended to have both action outcomes and research outcomes. Although in teacher-based research the action is primary, there are some forms of action research where research is the main emphasis and the action is almost a fringe benefit.

A strength of the methodology lies in being able to be responsive through developing hypotheses from the data as the process develops and understanding unfolds. Equally, action-research methodology is not confined to one philosophical tradition. Indeed, it is this very flexibility and unwillingness to be positioned in one theoretical camp or follow one methodological approach that leaves action research open to criticism.

Nonetheless, there are many examples of action research published in reputable international journals, although it seems to be the case that there are rather more examples of researchers studying action researchers in action than straightforward accounts of practitioner, school-based research.

**Activity 12.1**

Activity 12.1 is a study of four recent examples of published action research.

As an action researcher, you must be able to defend and follow the rules of the particular tradition you have chosen to work from and appreciate the differences between these different theoretical stances. In the first part of the activity, you will use the description of two theoretical categories to judge the work of expert action researchers (see Box 12.1).

### Box 12.1

1. *Technical rationale or positivist/post-positivist research* (see Chapter 15)

   Researchers who are situated within a positivist/post-positivist theoretical perspective try to:

   - be objective through distancing him/herself from the focus of the research
   - look for evidence of a linear causal relationship between the action being taken and what happens
   - find patterns that might be generalizable and applicable to other similar situations.

2. *Interpretive rationale* (see Chapter 16)

   Researchers who adopt an intrepretivist theoretical perspective try to gain understanding through:

   - observing people or practice in natural settings
   - reflecting on, describing and interpreting what people are doing
   - negotiating and explaining what people are doing.

*(Continued)*

*(Continued)*

**What you have to do**

1. Read the abstracts and study design from each paper referred to in Table 12.3 and assign them to one of the categories. The role of the researcher is different and consequently this will be reflected in how the action-research methodology is used. In these four examples, all the researchers have used action-research methodology although they have collected a wide variety of data.
2. What are the research questions being asked in each paper? What data-collecting methods has each researcher used to answer the questions?
   Use the headings in Table 12.3 to collate your data.

**Table 12.3   Analysing action research**

| Action Research Paper | Theoretical Perspective | Research Question | Methods Used by the Researcher |
|---|---|---|---|
| Torrance, H. and Pryor, J. (2001) Developing formative assessment in the classroom: using action research to explore and modify theory. *British Educational Research Journal*, 27 (5): 615–31. | | | |
| Trent, A. (2003) Decentering the teacher: a practitioner's account. *Teachers and Teaching, Theory and Practice*, 9 (4): 295–307. | | | |
| Nixon, D. and Ackerson, V. (2004) Building bridges: using science as a tool to teach reading and writing. *Educational Action Research*, 12 (2): 197–218. | | | |
| Ferguson-Patrick, K. (2007) Writers develop skills through collaboration: an action-research approach. *Educational Action Research*, 15 (2): 159–80. | | | |

## RESEARCH TRADITIONS

Technical rationality suggests that there are general solutions to practical problems and that these solutions can be developed outside the practical situations in research or administrative centres that can be translated into teachers' actions by means of publications, training and strategies, whereas interpretive rationality suggests that complex practical problems demand specific solutions and these solutions can only be developed inside the context in which the problem arises and in which the practitioner is a crucial and determining element. Therefore, it is difficult for such solutions to be directly applied to other contexts, but they can be made accessible to other practitioners as hypotheses to be tested.

## CHALLENGING YOUR INTERPRETATIONS

You will always bring a number of assumptions to any process, so you need to be clear about your own values and challenge your existing ideas. It is difficult to reflect on your assumptions until you are aware of them and even more difficult to engage in discourse about something you have not identified. This is why it is essential for you to work with a critical friend or group of people and to constantly ask yourself, 'What is happening in my class?' 'What is important here?' and 'How can I understand what is happening?'. Questions such as these can lead to inquiring, testing out and reflecting upon practical, personal or political issues within educational situations.

**Activity 12.2**

Read the following extract of a classroom teacher's analysis of data she collected from the first cycle of an action-research process and then discuss the questions that follow this with your peers or your critical friend.

The picture that emerges from our various data sources is complex. By certain standards, our class could be considered an accepting and inclusive environment for all children.

Every student received compliments from his or her peers, most children felt that they were liked by their classmates, and all children were eventually selected as someone's 'favourite' friend. However, upon closer investigation, a disturbing fact emerges: the children who look and sound different are not as popular as their classmates. In fact, they form their own, separate social grouping. This may be due to several factors.

First, the majority of our students with special needs suffer from expressive and receptive language delays, which may impede their ability to engage in conversation, share stories, and play with their schoolmates. Children of average development became more linguistically adept across the year, and despite explicit social instruction, the special education students were not acquiring verbal skills at the same rate, and therefore did not learn to be able to negotiate challenging social situations. As a result, they often relied on less language-based play, such as fantasy games, or less rule-oriented physical games such as swinging on the monkey bars in the playground.

Second, because they do not live in the immediate neighbourhood, and because of their parents' busy work schedules, our children with special needs had difficulty participating

*(Continued)*

*(Continued)*

in out-of-school activities, and missed out on key opportunities for shared social experiences and non-academic interactions. As one parent reached out to these children and made efforts to integrate them into her son's after-school life, they brightened up, and seemed to feel ever more accepted and excited by the prospect of a play date. It was astounding what a play date could do for these children's self-esteem, engagement in the community, and social status.

Finally, when in school, the Inclusion students spent much of their time together, away from the classroom. Jennifer and I tried to schedule group activities when we knew we would have our full enrolment, but students' individual schedules were complex and often unpredictable, and it was impossible to keep all students involved in every activity. In giving them special support, the instruction itself was setting them apart from the mainstream.
In some sense, a caste system has been set up in my classroom. While the children in the class have been open-minded, flexible, and accepting towards one another, some obstacles seem to be insurmountable in creating a truly 'inclusive' classroom. (Zindler, 2003)

1. What assumptions underlie this teacher's interpretation of the data?
2. Is there another perspective or way of interpreting this situation?
3. What further questions does this analysis raise?
4. What sort of strategies would you suggest that this teacher might use to try to transform the situation?

See the SAGE website (www.sagepub.co.uk/wilson) for further information.

## WHY SHOULD TEACHERS DO ACTION RESEARCH?

It seems to be the case that when teachers engage in enquiry in their classrooms, they gain a better understanding of their practice and ways to improve it. This not only involves a high level of reflexivity and sensitivity to the role of the self in mediating the whole research process, but also encourages exploratory engagement with a wide range of existing knowledge drawn from psychology, philosophy, sociology and other fields of social science. As a consequence, powerful learning takes place for participants through combining research with reflection on practice. Indeed, many teachers who undertake higher-degree work as part of their action-research programme also speak of experiencing a renewed sense of purpose and of feeling more autonomous, linked to an enhanced sense of professionalism.

Teachers can also come to understand their students' perspectives better, which results in the development of knowledge and understanding of a unique type that, although limited in wider application, will nonetheless be of great value to the classroom teacher. However, in some cases, it is possible to also make a significant contribution to public knowledge about teaching and learning. For example, the Raising Boys' Achievement project was a ten-term government project which sought to address issues of under-achievement and raising achievement of boys and girls in primary, secondary and special schools. The intervention stage of the project worked with a number of schools where the gender gap in public examination performance had narrowed, and where promising inter-vention strategies had seemed to have some effect upon the achievement profile of boys (and girls) within the school. Working with schools, the research team tried to identify the essential characteristics of such strategies, and developed these further in partnership with the schools (see www-rba.educ.cam.ac.uk/proj.html).

## ASSESSING THE QUALITY OF ACTION RESEARCH

Action research, particularly classroom-based teacher work, is not universally accepted as a public knowledge-generating process, and this might go some way to explaining why there are few published examples of teachers' own work. Nevertheless, experts in educational research are beginning to argue that existing criteria for judging practitioner research are inadequate. John Elliott, a well-respected and active proponent of practi-tioner research, argues that simply using existing tests of theoretical and methodologi-cal robustness as the only way of judging practitioner research fails to recognize the value such work has for classroom teachers and the importance such work has for build-ing capacity among teachers as potential agents of educationally worthwhile change.

Elliott has recently published criteria drawing on his own experiences of teacher research to help make such judgements. See the SAGE website for an extended list of cri-teria recommended for judging externally mediated action-research work, experimental teaching, and networked learning communities' forms of practitioner-focused research.

The final section of this chapter will consider how you as a classroom-based action researcher might ensure that you undertake your work in a rigorous way while also rec-ognizing the value of such work for you as a teacher researcher.

## ENSURING THAT YOUR OWN WORK IS RIGOROUS AND VALID

At the end of your action-research project, and particularly if you are intending to dissem-inate your findings to the wider world through the publication of a thesis or at a conference, it is important that you address how well you have met the aims of your research project.

For most classroom-focused action-research projects, the aim is to bring about a change in your classroom practice so that you and your students grow as a result of your inter-vention. In the process, you will generate new knowledge which is relevant to your own classroom. This knowledge will have been validated through the systematic collection of evidence by using appropriate methods. In other words, it will be possible to judge the process, outcome, and catalytic and democratic validity of your own work (see Table 12.4).

**Table 12.4   Linking action-research goals with quality criteria**

| Goals of Action Research | Quality/Validity Criteria |
| --- | --- |
| 1.  The generation of new knowledge | Process validity |
| 2.  The achievement of action-oriented outcomes | Outcome validity |
| 3.  The education of both researcher and participants | Catalytic validity |
| 4.  Results that are relevant to the local setting | Democratic validity |
| 5.  A sound and appropriate research methodology | Process validity |

*Source*: Herr and Anderson (2005)

**Activity 12.3**

In the final activity, you will use these categories and Elliott's criteria (set out in Table 12.5) to help you to make judgements about the value of published action-research work so that you can ensure that your own work is equally rigorous.

Use Table 12.5 to help you judge the three recent examples of teacher-led action research, all of which are linked on the SAGE website. These are as follows:

1.  How can we encourage pupil dialogue in collaborative group work?
    www.standards.dfes.gov.uk/ntrp/lib/pdf/seal.pdf
2.  Using the 'Thinking Frames' approach to improve pupil engagement and attainment in science, Cams Hill Science Consortium: www.standards. dfes.gov.uk/ntrp/lib/pdf/camshill.pdf
3.  Bencze, L. and Hodson, D. (1998) 'Coping with uncertainty in elementary school science: A case study in collaborative action research', *Teachers and Teaching, Theory and Practice*, 4 (1): 77–94.

Finally, you will find that being able to work collaboratively with colleagues or having a critical friend who can catalyse the process of critical thinking will support you during the action-research process and ensure that you are always reflexive about the process.

It is also important to have the support of your department and the autonomy to explore the complexity of your classroom and to take risks to make changes to your practice.

You must remember that your classroom is unique and that the dynamics will change daily so try to avoid being despondent when things do not follow your plan exactly. However, you need to persevere with your idea and modify your approach in light of your increased understanding. Above all, recognize and value your own skill as a class-room practitioner, especially when you first start to learn about the methods of education research. If possible, seek out expert help from a more experienced researcher or undertake formal research-methods training. Finally, and probably most importantly, set aside sufficient dedicated time to think, reflect and talk so that you can really engage fully with this professionally liberating process.

**Table 12.5   Assessing the validity of action research**

*Process Validity*

Are appropriate methods used to answer the question?

(a) Does the research focus on a problem that is of practical concern to the teachers involved?
(b) Does the research involve gathering data from the different points of view, for example, the teacher, an observer, and students (triangulation)?
(c) Does the research enable the teacher researcher to call their existing stock of professional knowledge (tacit theories) into question, and to test it against evidence gathered in their practical situation?
(d) Does the research extend teachers' understanding of their situation in a way that opens up new possibilities for action?

*Democratic Validity*

Are the researchers and researched engaged and included in the inquiry?
Is the research a rigorous conversational process in which the teacher opens up his/her practice to the rational scrutiny of students and peers, 'in-voices' their views of the action situation, and in the process demonstrates a disposition to subordinate his/her own prejudices to the search for an overlapping and un-coerced consensus?

*Catalytic Validity*

Is the research transformative?

(a) Is the research a deliberative and self-reflexive process in which the teacher calls into question both his/her teaching strategies (means) and the aims (ends) to which they are directed, and then modifies each by reflecting on the other?
(b) Is the research a process in which the teacher displays:

 • integrity in the pursuit of his/her educational aims and values
 • curiosity about other people's interpretations of the action situation
 • objectivity and honesty about his/her own motives and reasons for action
 • open-mindedness towards the views of others and respect for their freedom of thought and action?

*Outcome Validity*

Has the process led to a resolution and/or a reframing of the problem?

(a) Does the research enlarge the teacher's sphere of personal agency in the practical situation through the realization of his/her educational aims in a sustainable form?
(b) Does the research enable a teacher to generate a description of the complexities of the case in sufficient detail to be of universal significance to other teachers?

## KEY IDEAS

Action research is an educative process carried out in social situations that usually involves posing and solving problems resulting in a change intervention. This cyclic process of improvement and involvement is common to the research traditions discussed: technical, positivist/post-positivist, interpretive and also to critical inquiry, although each tradition approaches the methodology in different ways. Quality criteria recently developed to help judge the rigour of action-research projects have also been presented here.

## Further Reading

Altrichter, H., Feldman, A., Posch, P. and Somekh, B. (1993) *Teachers Investigate Their Work: An introduction to action research across the professions.* London: Routledge.

Baumfield, V., Hall, E. and Wall, K. (2008) *Action Research in the Classroom.* London: Sage.

Elliott, J. (2006) *Reflecting Where the Action Is.* London: Routledge.

Kemmis, S. and McTaggart, R. (2005) 'Participatory action research: Communicative action and the public sphere', in N. Denzin and Y. Lincoln (eds) *Handbook of Qualitative Research* (3rd edn). Beverly Hills, CA: Sage.

Kemmis, S. and McTaggart, R. (eds) (1988) *The Action Research Planner,* (3rd edn). Geelong: Deakin University Press.

McNiff, J. and Whitehead, J. (2005) *All You Need To Know About Action Research.* London: Sage.

McTaggart, R. (1991). 'Principles for participatory action research'. *Adult Education Quarterly,* 41 (3): 168–87.

Stenhouse, L. (1985) *Research as a Basis for Teaching: Reading from the work of Lawrence Stenhouse.* London: Heinemann.

Zuber-Skerritt, O. (1996) (ed.) *New Directions in Action Research.* London: Falmer.

## References

Carr, W. and Kemmis, S. (1986) *Becoming Critical. Education, knowledge and action research.* Lewes: Falmer.

Elliott, J. (1991) *Action Research for Educational Change.* Buckingham: Open University Press.

Herr, K. and Anderson, G. L. (2005) *The Action Research Dissertation: A guide for students and faculty.* Thousand Oaks, CA: Sage.

Schön, D. A. (1991) *The Reflective Turn: Case Studies In and On Educational Practice.* New York: Teachers Press, Columbia University.

Somekh, B. (2005) *Action Research: A Methodology for Change and Development: Doing Qualitative Research in Educational Settings.* Buckingham: Open University Press.

Zindler, R. (2003) *Trouble in Paradise: A study of who is included in an inclusion classroom.* Teacher's Network Policy Institute. www.teachersnetwork.org/tnli/research/achieve/zindler.htm (Accessed July 14 2008).

# THE CASE STUDY
## Helen Demetriou

---

**Hints**

- Define your case boundary.
- Use a wide range of data-collection methods.
- Organize your data handling carefully and keep accurate records of when data is collected.

---

The case study is a versatile, qualitative approach to research which enables the researcher to understand a complex issue or object and brings with it a familiarity to the case that no other research approach is able to do.

It is an attractive research method because it has 'face-value credibility', which means that it can provide evidence or illustrations with which readers can readily identify.

The case study approach is now more popular than ever, mostly because it is seen as a convenient and meaningful technique that captures a time-framed picture of an individual or another focus of enquiry.

This chapter will focus on the case study. Its aim is to enlighten and entice you to play detective and thereby use this powerful approach to research. This will be illustrated with examples of research that incorporate the case study in their design, followed by two case study-related activities that aim to consolidate your knowledge of this important area of research.

Let's begin by looking more closely at what a case study is, and learning a bit about its history, criticisms and design.

## WHAT IS A CASE STUDY?

### Some definitions

Fry, Ketteridge and Marshall (1999) described case studies as complex examples that give an insight into the context of a problem as well as illustrating the main point.

Lamnek (2005) defined the case study as '… a research approach, situated between concrete data taking techniques and methodologic paradigms'.

Yin (1984: 23) defined the case study as a research strategy with an empirical enquiry that investigates a contemporary phenomenon within its real-life context, when the boundaries between phenomenon and context are not clearly evident, and in which multiple sources of evidence are used.

Case study research is a traditional, systematic approach to looking at events, collecting data, analysing information and reporting the results, with the end goal of describing the case under investigation as fully and accurately as possible. It is a research strategy that investigates a phenomenon within its real-life context. Rather than using large samples and following a rigid protocol to examine a limited number of variables, case study methods involve an in-depth, longitudinal examination of a single instance or event – the case. This approach gives you, the researcher, a sharpened understanding of why the instance happened as it did, and what might require greater scrutiny in future research. This approach to research is purely qualitative as only a few instances are normally studied, thereby limiting the use of multivariate statistics. However, case study research can include single and multiple case studies and quantitative evidence, thereby relying on multiple sources of evidence. Case studies should not be confused therefore with qualitative research as they can be based on any mix of quantitative and qualitative evidence. This is often considered to be a strength of case study research, as it has the capability of uncovering causal paths and mechanisms and interaction effects. It can be used either on its own or alongside other methods. Recent years have seen the case study being used increasingly as the sole means of investigation, although it is more often recommended as part of a multi-method approach of triangulation, in which the same dependent variable is investigated using multiple procedures. The flexibility of the case study approach therefore is that it can involve single and multiple case studies, can include quantitative evidence, relies on multiple sources of evidence and benefits from the prior development of theoretical propositions.

## A SHORT HISTORY OF THE CASE STUDY

As a distinct approach to research, use of the case study originated only in the early 20th century. Dictionary definitions trace the phrase *case study* back as far as 1934, after the establishment of the concept of a *case history* in medicine and the earliest examples are to be found in the fields of Law and Medicine. Despite being used for many years across a variety of disciplines, the case study research method has not always been at the forefront of research. In the early to middle part of the 20th century, case studies were sometimes used to visualize whole organizations or communities; to describe phenomena, for example, findings about mental health in the longitudinal case studies conducted by Vaillant; or to describe individuals, for example, as the basis of a developmental model in Levinson's examination of male adults. The preference for quantitative methods resulted in the decline of the case study. However, in the 1960s, researchers were becoming concerned about the limitations of quantitative methods and, as a result, there was a renewed interest in case studies. Glaser and Strauss (1967) developed the concept of 'grounded theory' and this, along with some well-regarded studies, accelerated the renewed use of the methodology. This trend of continuous, albeit somewhat infrequent, usage continued through most of the 1980s, and more recently, the popularity and frequency of case studies have increased.

## CRITICISMS OF THE CASE STUDY

Despite the many advantages of the case study procedure, it has had a somewhat bumpy ride from its critics. However, as you will see, the various negative comments targeted at the case study approach are often turned on their head and viewed as advantageous and necessary for this particular approach to research. Moreover, where limitations to the approach exist, researchers have attempted to remedy these.

The case study has been criticized for limitations in validity and construct validity in particular, the result of which is potential subjectivity by the researcher. Yin (1994) proposed three remedies to counteract this: using multiple sources of evidence, establishing a chain of evidence, and having a draft case study report reviewed by key informants. Internal validity is a concern only in causal (explanatory) cases. This is usually a problem of inferences in case studies, and can be dealt with using pattern-matching. External validity deals with knowing whether the results are generalizable beyond the immediate case. This criticism of case study methodology is that its dependence on a single case limits its generalizability. Unlike random sample surveys, case studies are not representative of entire populations, although they do not claim to be. Critics of the case study method believe that the study of a small number of cases is limited when aiming to establish reliability or generality of findings. Others feel that the intense exposure to the study of the case biases the findings. Some dismiss case study research as useful only as an exploratory tool. Giddens (1984) considered case methodology 'microscopic' because it 'lacked a sufficient number' of cases. However, provided the researcher refrains from over-generalization, case study research is not methodologically invalid simply because selected cases cannot be presumed to be representative of entire populations. Therefore, whereas statistical analysis involves the generalization to a population based on a sample that is representative of that population, in case studies, one is generalizing to a theory based on cases selected to represent dimensions of that theory.

In support of case studies, Hamel (1993) and Yin (1994) have argued that the relative size of the sample – whether 2, 10 or 100 cases – does not transform a multiple case into a macroscopic study. The goal of the study should establish the parameters, and then should be applied to all research. In this way, even a single case could be considered acceptable, provided it meets the established objective. A subsequent researcher using case methods will naturally be studying a different case, and therefore may come to different conclusions. Similarly, in experimental and quasi-experimental research, the subjects will differ, meaning relationships may differ. What makes research replicable in either case study or experimental research is not the units of analysis but whether the research has been theory-driven. If the case researcher has developed and tested a model of hypothesized relationships, then a future case researcher can replicate the initial case study simply by selecting cases on the basis of the same theories, then testing the theories through pattern-matching.

## DESIGNING A CASE STUDY

## Different Methodological Approaches to the Case Study

The approach that you take with your case study can take one of three forms. As proposed by Yin (1993) case studies can be *exploratory, explanatory* or *descriptive*.

In *exploratory* case studies, fieldwork and data collection may be undertaken before you define your research questions and hypotheses, although the framework of the study must be created at the outset. Pilot projects are very useful in determining the final protocols that will be used and this will enable you to drop or add survey questions based on the outcome of the pilot study.

*Explanatory* cases are suitable for doing causal studies. In very complex and multivariate cases, the analysis can make use of pattern-matching techniques. Yin and Moore (1988) conducted a study to examine the reason why some research findings get into practical use. They used a funded research project as the unit of analysis, where the topic was constant but the project varied. The utilization outcomes were explained by three rival theories: a knowledge-driven theory, a problem-solving theory and a social-interaction theory.

*Descriptive* cases require a descriptive theory as a starting point. Pyecha (1988) used this methodology to study special education, using a pattern-matching procedure. Several states were studied and the data about each state's activities were compared with idealized theoretic patterns. This type of study therefore advocates the formation of hypotheses of cause–effect relationships. Hence, the descriptive theory must cover the depth and scope of the case under study.

## TYPES OF CASE STUDY

A general approach to designing case studies was propounded by Jensen and Rodgers (2001) who classified case studies as follows:

- **Snapshot case studies** – the detailed, objective study of one research entity at one point in time. It includes hypothesis-testing by comparing patterns across sub-entities.
- **Longitudinal case studies** – the quantitative and/or qualitative study of one research entity at multiple time points.
- **Pre-post case studies** – the study of one research entity at two time points separated by a critical event. A critical event is one that – on the basis of a theory under study – would be expected to impact case observations significantly.

- **Patchwork case studies** – a set of multiple case studies of the same research entity, using snapshot, longitudinal, and/or pre-post designs. This multi-design approach is intended to provide a more holistic view of the dynamics of the research subject.
- **Comparative case studies** – a set of multiple case studies of multiple research entities for the purpose of cross-unit comparison. Both qualitative and quantitative comparisons are generally made.

## CONDUCTING CASE STUDY RESEARCH: TIPS FOR THE CASE STUDY RESEARCHER

In order to organize and conduct case study research successfully, you should employ the following techniques and procedures:

1. Determine and define the research questions.
2. Select the cases and determine the data gathering and analysis techniques.
3. Prepare to collect the data.
4. Collect data in the field.
5. Evaluate and analyse the data.
6. Prepare the report.

## Step 1. Determine and define the research questions

The first step in case study research is to establish a firm research focus to which you as the researcher can refer over the course of study of a complex phenomenon or object. You should have one or more hypotheses and establish the focus of the study by forming questions about the situation or problem to be studied and determining a purpose for the study. The research object in a case study is often a programme, an entity, a person or a group of people. Each object is likely to be intricately connected to political, social, historical and personal issues, providing wide-ranging possibilities for questions and adding complexity to the case study. You should investigate the object of the case study in depth, using a variety of data-gathering methods to produce evidence that leads to understanding of the case and addresses the research questions.

## Step 2. Select the cases and determine the data-gathering and analysis techniques

During the design phase of case study research, you should determine what approaches to use in selecting single or multiple real-life cases to examine in depth and which instruments and data-gathering approaches to use. When using multiple cases, each case is treated as a single case. Each case's conclusions can then be used as information contributing to the whole study, but each case remains a single case. Exemplary case studies carefully select cases and critically examine the choices available from among many research tools available in order to increase the validity of the study. Careful discrimination at the point of selection also helps to form boundaries around the case.

You must determine whether to study cases which are unique in some way or cases which are considered typical, and may also select cases to represent a variety of geographic regions, a variety of size parameters or other parameters. A useful step in the selection process is to repeatedly refer back to the purpose of the study, in order to focus attention on where to look for cases and evidence that will satisfy the purpose of the study and answer the research questions posed. Selecting multiple or single cases is a key element, but a case study can include more than one unit of embedded analysis. A key strength of the case study method involves using multiple sources and techniques in the data-gathering process. You should determine in advance what evidence to gather and what analysis techniques to use with the data to answer the research questions. Data gathered are normally qualitative, but may also be quantitative. Tools to collect data can include surveys, interviews, documentation review, observation, and even the collection of physical artifacts and archival records.

Throughout the design phase, ensure that the study is well constructed in order to achieve construct validity, internal validity, external validity and reliability. Construct validity requires you to use the correct measures for the concepts being studied. Internal validity (especially important with explanatory or causal studies) demonstrates that certain conditions lead to other conditions and requires the use of multiple pieces of evidence from multiple sources to uncover convergent lines of enquiry. External validity reflects whether or not findings are generalizable beyond the immediate case or cases; the more variations in places, people and procedures a case study can withstand and still yield the same findings, the more external validity. Reliability refers to the stability, accuracy and precision of measurement. If your case study design is robust, then the procedures used will be well documented and can be repeated with the same results.

## Step 3. Prepare to collect the data

Because case study research generates a large amount of data from multiple sources, the systematic organization of the data is important to prevent you from becoming overwhelmed by the amount of data and to prevent you from losing sight of the original research purpose and questions. Advance preparation assists in handling large amounts of data in a documented and systematic fashion. Researchers prepare databases to assist with categorizing, sorting, storing and retrieving data for analysis.

Exemplary case studies prepare good training programmes for investigators, establish clear protocols and procedures in advance of investigator field work, and conduct a pilot study in advance of moving into the field in order to remove obvious barriers and problems. You need to be able to ask effective questions, be a good listener – listening carefully to the exact words during an interview, and be able to interpret the answers fully. You should review documents looking for facts, but also read between the lines and pursue collaborative evidence elsewhere when that seems appropriate.

You need to understand the purpose of the study and grasp the issues and must be open to contrary findings, as well as being aware that you are going into the world of real human beings who may be threatened or unsure of what the case study will bring.

## Step 4. Collect data in the field

You must collect and store multiple sources of evidence comprehensively and systematically, in formats that can be referenced and classified so that converging lines of enquiry and patterns can be uncovered. You should carefully observe the object of the case study and identify causal factors associated with the observed phenomenon. Renegotiation of arrangements with the objects of the study or the addition of questions to interviews may be necessary as the study progresses. Case study research is flexible, but when changes are made, they are documented systematically.

Effective case studies use field notes and databases to categorize and reference data in order to be readily available for subsequent reinterpretation. Field notes record feelings and intuitions, pose questions and document the work in progress. They record testimonies, stories and illustrations that can be used in later reports. They may warn of impending bias because of the detailed exposure of the client to special attention, or give an early signal that a pattern is emerging. They assist in determining whether or not the inquiry needs to be reformulated or redefined based on what is being observed. Field notes should be kept separate from the data being collected and stored for analysis. Maintaining the relationship between the issue and the evidence is mandatory. You may enter some data into a database and physically store other data, but you should document, classify and cross-reference all evidence so that it can be efficiently recalled for sorting and examination over the course of the study.

## Step 5. Evaluate and analyse the data

You can examine raw data using many interpretations in order to find links between the research object and the outcomes with reference to the original research questions. Throughout the evaluation and analysis process, you should remain open to new opportunities and insights. The case study method, with its use of multiple data-collection methods and analysis techniques, provides researchers with opportunities to triangulate data in order to strengthen the research findings and conclusions.

A good case study will deliberately sort the data in many different ways to expose or create new insights and will deliberately look for conflicting data to disconfirm the analysis. You should categorize, tabulate and recombine data to address the initial propositions or purpose of the study and conduct cross-checks of facts and discrepancies in accounts. Focused, short, repeat interviews may be necessary to gather additional data to verify key observations or check a fact.

Specific techniques include placing information into arrays, creating matrices of categories, creating flow charts or other displays, and tabulating the frequency of events. You should use the quantitative data that have been collected to corroborate and support the qualitative data, which is most useful for understanding the rationale or theory underlying relationships. Another technique is to use multiple investigators to gain the advantage provided when a variety of perspectives and insights examine the data and the patterns. When the multiple observations converge, confidence in the findings increases.

Pattern-matching compares an empirical pattern with a predicted one. Internal validity is enhanced when the patterns coincide. If the case study is an explanatory one, the patterns may be related to the dependent or independent variables. If it is a descriptive study, the predicted pattern must be defined prior to data collection. Yin (1994) recommended using rival explanations as pattern-matching when there are independent variables involved. This requires the development of rival theoretical propositions, but the overall concern remains the degree to which a pattern matches the predicted one.

## Step 6. Prepare the report

A good case study reports the data in a way that transforms a complex issue into one that can be easily understood, allowing the reader to question and examine the study and reach an understanding independent of the researcher. Case studies present data in very publicly accessible ways and may lead the reader to apply the experience in his or her own real-life situation. You should pay particular attention to displaying sufficient evidence to gain the reader's confidence that all avenues have been explored, clearly communicating the boundaries of the case, and giving special attention to conflicting propositions.

Techniques for composing the report can include handling each case as a separate chapter or treating the case as a chronological recounting. Alternatively, you could relate the findings from the case study as a story. During the report preparation process, you should critically examine the document, looking for ways to perfect the report and rewrite and make revisions accordingly.

## THE USE OF CASE STUDIES IN EDUCATION

One of the areas in which case studies have been gaining popularity is education and in particular educational evaluation and instructional use in order to develop critical thinking, skills and knowledge (Stake, 1995). Teaching and learning styles are, by their very nature, changing, and in recent years, there has been a noticeable move from lecture-based activities towards more student-centred activities. Students can learn more effectively when actively involved in the learning process, and the case study approach is one way in which such active learning strategies can be implemented. Such student-centred activities are typically based on topics that demonstrate theoretical concepts in an applied setting. This definition of a case study covers the variety of different teaching structures we use, ranging from short, individual case studies to longer, group-based activities.

In order to illustrate the implementation of case studies in the field of education, there follow some examples of research that have incorporated this methodology.

## Example 1

*A critical evaluation of visual teaching and learning methods with special reference to animation and modelling for their conceptual and motivational value in teaching environmental chemistry (research completed for a Masters degree in Education)*

The study examined the use and effectiveness of animation and modelling for both their conceptual and motivational value in the teaching of environmental chemistry.

To investigate the role of animation in facilitating students' learning and improving motivation in science, a mixed-gender, high-ability, Year 9 set was chosen as the study group. Flash animation was used to teach the concept of acid rain formation and Stop–Start animation was used to teach the concept of global warming. Students' views on the usefulness of using animation to promote learning and motivation were obtained by talking to the students individually during lessons. Students also completed a questionnaire, which requested information about the students' favourite subjects and their views of science. In addition, students were asked about their feelings on the animations over the course of the sequence of the lessons. Although there is no measurable indication that animations increased students' learning in science, the majority of the students did report that they felt the animations helped them understand and remember the dynamic concepts. It must therefore not be disregarded as a possible teaching tool for aiding the understanding of concepts in science.

## Example 2

*Gifted and talented: policy and implementation in schools (research completed for a Masters degree in Education)*

A study was conducted into the provision made for Gifted and Talented (G&T) pupils at a whole school and departmental level at two high-achieving mixed comprehensive schools. Data were collected via G&T documentation provided by schools, observation of lessons, and via interviews with G&T coordinators, science teachers and G&T pupils. The interview with the GATCO was used in conjunction with the schools' documentation (policy, advice to parents, etc.) to identify how the school had interpreted and implemented the national G&T initiative. The data collected in this project suggest that in order to maintain the motivation and enthusiasm of G&T pupils in our schools, we neither have to differentiate the work for them in every lesson nor overload them with extra work. Rather, by ensuring that they are challenged and stimulated in some areas of their school life (be these curriculum related extension activities, sport, in-school responsibilities, or other extra-curricular activities), G&T pupils can be provided with a healthy balance between challenge and success.

## Example 3

*What effect does group work have on the learning and motivation of a Year 7 science class? (research completed for a Masters degree in Education)*

This research was conducted as a result of the wider demand for effective groupwork, both from an academic perspective – Beyond 2000 stated that 'young people need some understanding of the social processes internal to science' (Millar and Osborne, 1998: 20) – and from a national outlook – it has been posited that schools needed to '… use more flexible and successful approaches to the grouping of pupils …' (DfEE, 1997: 39). A sequence of Year 7 lessons on forces was taught, each containing a groupwork task. To address the motivation strand, pre- and post-groupwork motivation questionnaires were given. To assess the students' learning, their levelled test results were compared to a previous test on cells, a topic that was taught with no groupwork. During the teaching period, there were weekly discussions with a small group of students to probe their thoughts on the groupwork. It was found that students responded positively to the work initially and overall there were favourable impacts on learning. With time, social factors began to dominate the effective functioning of the groups and the progression slowed. Motivation styles altered as a result of the sequence, with polarized responses. The use of groupwork is advocated, but with an emphasis on careful planning and preparation of the students' social skills in order that they gain fully from collaboration.

## Example 4

*Disavowed: The stories of two novice teachers*
*By Lisa Scherff,* Teaching and Teacher Education (2008)
   This case study used narrative inquiry to explore two novice English teachers' experiences in the classroom and factors that caused them to leave the profession. Participants were one male and one female located in two south-eastern states in the USA. Data include transcripts of emails spanning a 17-month period between the participants and researcher as well as individual audio-taped interviews conducted by the researcher. The teachers' narratives of disavowal reinforce the need for strengthening induction and mentoring programmes, as well as the fostering of caring, healthy work environments.

## Example 5

*The transfer of pupils from primary to secondary school: A case study of a foundation subject –*
*physical education*
*By Susan Capel, Paula Zwozdiak-Myers and Julia Lawrence,* Research in Education (2007)
   Results of research to date (e.g. Galton, Gray and Rudduck, 1999; Schagen and Kerr, 1999) suggest that, although continuity and progression are promoted in National Curriculum documents in England, they are not promoted consistently by schools during the transfer from primary to secondary school. Fourteen secondary school PE heads of department (ten male and four female) in five local education authorities (LEAs) were selected for this research. These fourteen heads of department had been identified as being involved in a range of activities to support the transfer of pupils from primary to secondary school in relation to physical education in an earlier part of this study. Interviews were semi-structured and lasted between forty minutes and one hour. To

ensure a consistency of approach, one researcher interviewed all fourteen heads of department. This interviewer had taught physical education in secondary schools in England. The interview comprised questions about the perceived importance of transfer of pupils from primary to secondary schools in physical education; the activities undertaken to support the transfer of pupils from primary to secondary school in physical education and reasons for these; and the factors constraining support for transfer and potential ways to develop and maintain this support. Follow-up questions were asked specific to responses from each head of department. The interviews were recorded on audio-cassette tape and then transcribed. The transcripts were then read in full by two people and the responses were coded. The results of this small-scale qualitative study showed that these fourteen heads of department identified that transfer from primary to secondary school was important in physical education. However, results suggested that this was not consistently translated into practice. This was demonstrated by the majority of these heads of department reporting that they had neither formalized nor written their practice into departmental policy. Rather, transfer seemed to be something that they were trying to do, but rather informally.

## Example 6

*From 'consulting pupils' to 'pupils as researchers': a situated case narrative*
*By Pat Thomson and Helen Gunter,* British Educational Research Journal (2006)
   Schools in England are now being encouraged to 'personalize' the curriculum and to consult students about teaching and learning. This article reports on an evaluation of one secondary school which is working hard to increase student subject choice, introduce integrated curriculum in the middle years and to improve teaching and learning while maintaining a commitment to inclusive and equitable comprehensive education. The authors worked with a small group of students as consultants to develop a 'student's-eye' set of evaluative categories in a school-wide student survey. They also conducted teacher, student and governor interviews, lesson and meeting observations, and student 'mind-mapping' exercises. The research has highlighted the importance of the processes that the authors used to work jointly with the student research team, and how they moved from pupils-as-consultants to pupils-as-researchers, a potentially more transformative/disruptive practice. Also queried is the notion of 'authentic student voice' as discursive and heterogeneous.

### Activity 13.1

1. Categorize each research study above into the different types of case study as outlined in this chapter and thoroughly examine each project for the ways in which the research was conducted.
2. Devise your own case study, using a topic for exploration that interests you and employing the optimal case study procedure for it.

## KEY IDEAS

Case study research is a traditional approach to the study of topics and its goal is to describe the case under investigation as fully and accurately as possible. Researchers have used the case study research method for many years across a variety of disciplines. Rather than using large samples and following a rigid protocol to examine a limited number of variables, case study methods involve an in-depth, longitudinal examination of a single instance or event – the case. Case studies therefore emphasize detailed contextual analysis of a limited number of events or conditions and their relationships. Case study research excels at bringing us to an understanding of a complex issue or object and can extend experience or add strength to what is already known through previous research. It can be exploratory, explanatory or descriptive in nature. A typical protocol for a case study is to: determine and define the research questions, select the cases and determine the data-gathering and analysis techniques, prepare to collect the data, collect data in the field, evaluate and analyse the data and prepare the report. A frequent criticism of case study methodology is that its dependence on a single case limits its generalizability. Unlike random sample surveys, case studies are not representative of entire populations, although they do not claim to be. Case studies have been increasingly used in education. In particular, education has embraced the case method for educational evaluation and instructional use in order to develop critical thinking, skills and knowledge.

 *Further Reading*

Eisenhardt, K. M. (1989) 'Building theories from case study research', *The Academy of Management Review*, 14, 532–50.

Flyvbjerg, B. (2006) 'Five misunderstandings about case study research', *Qualitative Inquiry*, 12, 219–45.

Hamel, J. (1993) *Case Study Method*. Beverly Hills, CA: Sage.

Ragin, C. C. and Becker, H. S. (1992) *What is a Case?: Exploring the Foundations of Social Inquiry*. Cambridge: Cambridge University Press

Scholz, R. W. and Tietje, O. (2002) Embedded case study methods. *Integrating Quantitative and Qualitative Knowledge*. Thousand Oaks, CA: Sage.

Singleton, R. A. and Straits, B. C. (1988) *Approaches to Social Research*. Oxford: Oxford University Press.

Stake, R. E. (1995) *The Art of Case Study Research*. Thousand Oaks, CA: Sage.

Yin, R. K. (2002) *Case Study Research: Design and Methods,* 3rd edn. Newbury Park, CA: Sage.

# *References*

Capel, S., Zwozdiak-Myers, P. and Lawrence, J. (2007) 'The transfer of pupils from primary to secondary school: A case study of a foundation subject – physical education', *Research in Education*, 77: 14–30.

DfEE (1997) *Excellence in Schools*. London: The Stationery Office.

Fry, H., Ketteridge S. and Marshall, S. (1999) *A Handbook for Teaching and Learning in Higher Education*. Glasgow: Kogan Page.

Galton, M., Gray, J. and Rudduck, J. (1999) 'The impact of school transitions and transfers on pupils' progress and attainment.' Research report for the DfEE.

Giddens, A. (1984) *The Constitution of Society: Outline of the theory of Structuration*. Cambridge: Polity Press.

Glaser, B. G. and Strauss, A. L. (1967). *The Discovery of Grounded Theory: Strategies for Qualitative Research*. New York: Aldine de Gruyter.

Hamel, J. (1993) *Case Study Method*. Beverly Hills, CA: Sage.

Jensen, J. and Rodgers, R. (2001) 'Cumulating the intellectual gold of case study technique', *PAR*, March/April, pp. 235–46.

Lamnek, S. (2005) *Qualitative Sozialforschung*. Basel: Beltz PVU.

Levinson, D. (1978). *The Seasons of a Man's Life*. New York: Ballantine.

Millar, R. and Osborne, J. (eds) (1998) 'Beyond 2000: Science education for the future'.The report of a seminar series funded by the Nuffield Foundation. Published by King's College London, School of Education.

Pyecha, J. (1988). *A Case Study of the Application of Noncategorical Special Education in Two States*. Chapel Hill, NC: Research Triangle Institute.

Schagen, S. and Kerr, D. (1999) *Bridging the Gap? The National Curriculum and Progression from Primary to Secondary School*. Slough: NFER.

Scherff, L. (in press). 'Disavowed: The stories of two novice teachers.' Manuscript accepted for publication in *Teaching and Teacher Education*.

Stake, R. E. (1995) *The Art of Case Study Research*. Thousand Oaks, CA: Sage.

Thomson, P. and Gunter, H. (2006) 'From 'consulting pupils' to 'pupils as researchers': a situated case narrative, *British Educational Research Journal*, 32: 839–56.

Vaillant, G. (2002) *Aging Well*. Boston: Little, Brown & Co.

Yin, R. (1984). *Case Study Research: Design and Methods*, 1st edn. Beverly Hills, CA: Sage.

Yin, R. (1993) *Applications of Case Study Research*. Beverly Hills, CA: Sage.

Yin, R. (1994). *Case Study Research: Design and Methods*, 2nd edn. Beverly Hills, CA: Sage.

Yin, R. and Moore, G. (1988) 'Lessons on the utilization of research from nine case experiences in the natural hazards field, *Knowledge, Technology and Policy* (1) 25–44.

# BUILDING THEORY FROM DATA: GROUNDED THEORY

## Keith S. Taber

This chapter discusses the value and difficulties of an approach to educational enquiry called 'grounded theory' (GT). This chapter considers the purpose and advantages of this approach, but also why GT is *seldom a sensible option for any student needing to complete a project in a short timescale*. Despite this, there are aspects of the GT approach that can be useful in studies that do not adopt the approach wholesale. It is also important to understand the GT approach when critically evaluating other studies, as many research reports claim to report GT or to use methods drawn from the GT approach.

## WHAT IS 'GROUNDED' THEORY?

Grounded theory is an approach to building up theories about educational or other social phenomena. When the complete set of processes is applied, it is a very demanding way of doing research. However, it does offer a system that is designed to develop rigorous theory in contexts where little reliable theory already exists.

> Grounded theory methodology ... is a specific, highly developed, rigorous set of procedures for producing formal, substantive theory of social phenomena ... Experience with data generates insights, hypotheses, and generative questions that are pursued through further data

generation. As tentative answers to questions are developed and concepts are constructed, these constructions are verified through further data collection. (Schwandt, 2001: 110)

GT has been applied to understanding a range of educational phenomena. It is also name-checked in many studies where it may be less clear that the full set of procedures is being applied. As Juliet Corbin has noted:

a lot of people claim to be doing Grounded Theory studies. But whether or not they are building theory is quite another matter ... There is ... a lot of work being done all over the world ... that claims to be theory that bears no resemblance to theory, Grounded Theory or otherwise. (quoted in Cisneros-Puebla, 2004: 52)

In practice, then, in education, there are probably many more studies 'informed by' GT than actually reporting fully grounded educational theories.

## EXAMPLES OF EDUCATIONAL STUDIES DRAWING UPON GT

In this chapter, three educational studies drawing upon GT will be used as examples.

### Example 1: learning to play the violin

Calissendorff (2006) reports a study into five-year-olds learning to play the violin, where she used a GT approach to data analysis. She reports her aim as 'to acquire a deeper understanding of how small children learn an instrument in the presence of their parents'. She observed six young children when they attended their music lessons, visited the children's homes, and interviewed parents and the violin teacher.

### Example 2: learning advanced chemistry

In my own doctoral research, I was concerned with why (my) 16–18-year-old students studying chemistry found the topic of chemical bonding so difficult. I wanted to understand their developing thinking about the topic, to see if I could identify any 'learning impediments' that explained why students commonly misunderstood this topic. This study was primarily based around sequences of interviews with about a dozen students.

### Example 3: the overrepresentation of minorities referred to special education provision

Harry, Sturges and Klingner (2005: 3) report a study of 'the referral and placement of Black (various ethnicities, such as African-American and Haitian) and Hispanic (various ethnicities, such as Cuban and Nicaraguan) students in special education programmes in a large urban school district' in the USA. The project had three identifiable stages of field research, in a sample of 12 schools that varied in (a) terms of patterns of ethnicities of the students, and (b) rates of referring students for special educational needs provision.

## DATA AND THEORY

As the name suggests, the outcomes of GT studies are considered to be 'theory'. This means that GT attempts to go beyond the description of events to produce models that can explain what is going on.

> Theory: A set of well-developed concepts related through statements of relationship, which together constitute an integrated framework that can be used to explain or predict phenomena. (Strauss and Corbin, 1998: 15)

Ultimately, 'grounded theorists' look to produce models that are general – that have widespread value beyond the specific research contexts visited in the study. The 'grounded' part of the name refers to the claim that the theories of GT are 'grounded' in the data – that is, they derive from an analysis of empirical evidence collected in the research. Now, we might expect that in educational studies, all research findings should derive from an analysis of data (rather than perhaps guesswork or some magical divination process). Therefore, this reference to grounding theory in data is claiming more than simply that GT is the outcome of empirical research.

The key point is that not just the findings, but also the concepts used in a GT, are said to derive from the analysis of the data, rather than being drawn from previous literature. In a GT context, a concept is 'a pattern that is carefully discovered' by a process defined as 'constant comparing of theoretically sampled data until conceptual saturation' (Glaser, 2002a: 4). This particular meaning (explained below) provides the basis of both the strength and some of the challenges of GT research.

## CONFIRMATORY VERSUS EXPLORATORY STUDIES

There are different ways of characterizing types of research, but one common distinction is between those studies that are intended to be open-ended and those that are testing a pre-specified question (Taber, 2007: 36–42). Confirmatory studies set out with an existing hypothesis to be tested (even if it is not always described as a hypothesis). In these studies, existing theory would seem to potentially apply in a new context, and the research tests out the ideas in this context.

For example, the government may produce the guidance that an effective lesson is commonly divided into three parts. (Whether we should consider such a bland statement as 'theory' in any meaningful sense is questionable – but it is an idea most teachers will have been exposed to!) However, no one has ever undertaken any research to evaluate the effectiveness of this lesson structure in your particular Y9 class, in the school where you are teaching. Rather than just accept and adopt this recommendation, you could decide to read up on the reasoning behind it, and then set out to test whether it is a useful approach in your own lessons with this class.

There are lots of well-developed and argued ideas in the educational literature that might lead you to ask 'does that apply here?' or 'will that work here?'

- Should you increase the wait time between asking a question and selecting a respondent?
- Is it useful to identify profiles of learning styles for the students in this class?
- Does organizing students in mixed-ability teams for group work support the weakest and stretch the highest achievers?

The advantage of this type of approach for a student is that there is suitable literature to provide the background reading, and so support the conceptualization of the project (Taber, 2007: 57–61), and – as there is a single, clear, principle research question – there is a firm basis for designing the study.

However, such approaches are also limiting, as they rely upon the available ideas in the literature. They can provide the basis of a very useful exercise in educational enquiry for a student looking for a project. However, they may not always be as useful for a practitioner with a genuine issue deriving from their teaching practice. If you are concerned about the behaviour, or achievement, or engagement of your class, then you will find plenty of suggestions in the research literature for why there might be problems and how you might address them. However, it is always possible that in your particular class there is a specific factor that is fundamental to the problem you have identified, but which may not relate to the findings from previous research. This is where more exploratory ('discovery') approaches are useful. In an exploratory approach, the researcher has identified an issue or context that is worth researching, but does not have a pre-formed hypothesis. The research question is more 'what is going on here?' rather than 'is this an example of X?'; or 'what might be a good way forward here?', rather than, 'will Y work in this context?'.

So, in reporting their study, Harry et al. (2005: 3) take the 'disproportionate placement of minorities in special education' as well established, but explain that 'what continues to be missing from this body of research is an understanding of the motives and pressures that drive decision-making in this area; in other words, the "hows" and "whys" of the process'. GT is the ultimate approach to exploratory research, as it takes the open-ended nature of the study very seriously.

### Activity 14.1

Which of the following questions are more suitable starting points for (a) confirmatory studies, and (b) exploratory (discovery) research? Try to explain your reasoning:

1. Does setting homework increase test scores?
2. What metacognitive knowledge and skills do students use when studying in my GCSE class?
3. Is this textbook suitable for my class?
4. Do students find groupwork helpful in my classes?
5. Can peer assessment increase student metacogntion?
6. Would 'brain-gym' be a useful way of beginning my lessons with less motivated groups?

*(Continued)*

*(Continued)*

7. How does the setting of homework influence student perceptions of the subject?
8. What types of starters will be most useful in engaging my students?
9. What kind of interactions occur during group activities in my class?
10. Is the reading age of this text too high for Year 9 students?

(Hint: can you readily rewrite the question as a specific hypothesis to be tested?)

## CHARACTERISTICS OF GROUNDED THEORY

GT studies are characterized by a number of features, which include:

- a delayed literature review
- an emergent design
- flexible and responsive ('theoretical') sampling
- an iterative approach to analysis ('constant comparison')
- an open timeline for the research ('theoretical saturation').

Each of these features is important in a full GT study, in order to lead to theory that can be considered to be a valid model. However, as will become clear, these features also make a full GT approach potentially inappropriate for any student (or other researcher) who needs to produce a project report or thesis within a limited time-span!

**Activity 14.2**

Consider the expectations on a practitioner researcher when charged with a research project by the department/school, or setting out on research to support a higher-degree dissertation. Why might it be difficult to persuade a head of department/head teacher/university supervisor that a GT approach should be adopted?

## WHAT ARE GROUNDED THEORY 'METHODS'?

GT is not an approach that defines a specific set of methods that must be used (Glaser, 1978, 2002a; Glaser and Holton, 2004). GT studies tend to produce data sets that are largely (but not always exclusively) qualitative, but may involve various types of interviews, observations, questionnaires and so forth. So it is not the data-collection techniques that define a GT study, but rather the way they are selected and organized 'for collecting and analysing qualitative data to construct theories "grounded" in the data themselves' (Charmaz, 2006: 4).

# INDUCTION: THE CONTEXT OF DISCOVERY

To understand the logic of a GT approach, we need to consider 'the problem of induction' (discussed in Chapter 15). In a confirmatory approach, we start our research with existing concepts to apply to our data: concepts that have operational definitions. In other words, if we are testing a hypothesis about learning styles, we will have developed a conceptualization of the topic before designing our study (Taber, 2007: 57), and our data-collection instrumentation and analytical frameworks will then be designed around an understanding of what we are taking learning styles to be, and how we will recognize and identify them.

However, a GT study that explored the question of *whether* learners in a class exhibited 'learning styles' would not apply pre-existing definitions of how learning styles can be identified, or start with assumptions about which potential 'styles' might be uncovered. Rather, the GT approach would attempt to build up a model from the data collected, starting from a very open question (e.g. 'do these students have preferred ways of learning, and – if so – can I characterize them?').

Answering such questions means being able to spot the patterns in data, without filtering that data through the biases of our existing knowledge and understanding. Yet, if all our perceptions are 'theory-laden' (we cannot help but see the world through our existing conceptual frameworks), then this is an impossible task! There is no logical solution to this problem, although one idea that has been found useful is to attempt to separate the context of discovery from the context of justification.

The context of discovery refers to how we came by an idea. As much of our thinking is subconscious and not open to introspection, we cannot ever be sure how we came up with an idea.

> Grounded theory arrives at relevance, because it allows core problems and processes to emerge. (Glaser, 1978: 5)

When we examine data, and spot a pattern, we can never be sure how much of that pattern derives from us rather than the data. Human brains are exceptionally good at finding patterns that have no basis in the external world: as when children see intruders in the shadows at night, or when a cloud is said to be the shape of a weasel (Hamlet) or of Ireland (Kate Bush).

# POST-INDUCTIVE RESONANCE?

When I was undertaking my own research into student thinking about chemistry, I experienced some 'aha' moments where suddenly I had insight into patterns in my data. After 'immersing' myself in data (listening to interviews, transcribing, reading, coding), I would find I could suddenly interpret what a student was telling me. I moved instantly from recognizing that a student was 'misunderstanding' what they had been taught to understanding how they understood differently. This process of making sense of how another understands was largely a subconscious process, leading to the abrupt change in my conscious thinking (Koestler, 1982). Although I was grateful for the insights, I was concerned with how I would justify them in my thesis – a report where I had to argue a case for my findings.

However, it was not the process of insight I had to justify. Rather, those insights had to be tested further against data, to see whether they 'resonated' (or 'fitted'). This would mean revisiting the data sets to see if the new interpretations made sense of other comments the student had made in related contexts. The new interpretation was also used during subsequent interviews, where it was possible to check my own interpretation more directly by asking the student whether I had grasped their way of thinking.

As we cannot control the subconscious aspects of pattern recognition, we have to justify our findings not in terms of how we came up with an idea, but rather how we then tested it to ensure it had a good match with the data (Medawar, 1990). This is sometimes referred to as the 'context of justification'. We can have our good ideas in the bath, in dreams, or perhaps even inspired by the patterns we see in tea leaves: what matters is how we rigorously test their relevance to the data.

GT research therefore uses an approach to encourage the 'induction' process (of having the ideas), followed by rigorous testing of those ideas to ensure a good fit with the data – this has been called 'post-inductive resonance' (Taber, 1997).

## AN OVERVIEW OF THE GROUNDED THEORY APPROACH

### Washing the mind clean

The characteristics of GT research are intended to support the induction and testing of ideas that best fit the data that can be collected. As 'it is critical in GT methodology to avoid unduly influencing the pre-conceptualization of the research through extensive reading in the substantive area' (Glaser and Holton, 2004: 46), the literature review is often delayed (rather than being carried out before the research starts). This is to avoid findings from previous related research 'contaminating' the researcher's thinking about their data, so they can 'enter the research setting with as few predetermined ideas as possible' (Glaser, 1978: 2–3). This is said to allow the researcher to retain 'theoretical sensitivity' to their data.

In practice, researchers normally bring a wide range of potentially relevant ideas from their previous training, reading and experience – so delaying the literature search is seen as necessary but not sufficient. Researchers are advised to try to 'wash their minds clean' before entering the research context (Measor and Woods, 1991). However, there is a limit to how viable this is, and clearly concepts and ideas from other related research could prove very useful – providing 'points of departure for developing, rather than limiting, our ideas' (Charmaz, 2006: 30). GT experts disagree among themselves on how strict one should be about this point – and on the extent to which it is acceptable to adopt and adapt concepts from previous work when they seem to fit our current context.

Calissendorff (2006: 90) reports that in her study, 'the formation of the core category owed a great deal to [a previously published] learning style model'. Although she drew upon an existing model to organize her findings, she *adapted* the existing idea so that although the final version 'owes a debt' (p. 92) to the published model, it was modified to give a model 'which is based on factors comprising elements that have proved to be of importance to the children when learning the violin' (p. 91).

## IMMERSION AND EMERGENCE

A GT does not have a fixed design, as the researcher has to be able to make decisions about data collection as the research proceeds. In GT, there are no distinct steps of data collection and analysis. Rather, data analysis begins as soon as data is collected, and informs decisions about further data collection. Early ideas deriving from data analysis suggest *who* to talk to next, *what* to observe, *what questions* should be asked, etc. This is called 'theoretical' sampling, as the sampling decisions are guided by the ongoing development of theory. (The term 'theoretical' occurs a lot in GT!)

> Theoretical sampling is the process of data collection for generating theory whereby the analyst jointly collects, codes and analyses the data and decides what data to collect next and where to find them, in order to develop the theory as it emerges. (Glaser and Holton, 2004: 51)

GT analysis uses an iterative process of coding ('the analytic process through which data are fractured, conceptualized, and integrated to form theory', Strauss and Corbin, 1998: 3) with several stages. Initial analysis ('open coding') is at a very descriptive level to break down data (such as interview transcripts) into manageable chunks using 'in vivo' codes. In other words, if your students describe the use of statistics in biology as 'sums', then that might be a good label to use to identify (code) those segments of an interview transcript. If your colleagues knowingly refer to vocational courses as 'vacational', then that may be a useful descriptive code.

As data is analysed, the researcher attempts to build up a set of codes that collectively 'fit' all the data. As new codes are generated, previously analysed data is re-examined to see whether the new codes could be a better fit than some of the previous codes. This process of 'constant comparison' continues through the research, at all levels of the analysis, 'forcing' 'the analyst into confronting similarities, differences and degrees in consistency of meaning' (Glaser and Holton, 2004: 58).

In her study of children learning to play the violin, Calissendorff (2006: 85) referred to following 'leads'. For her, a lead 'derives from an interesting event, statement or observation' and is 'followed up, and eventually either forms a category of its own, [or] is placed within an existing category or is rejected'. The analyst also tries to build up concepts or constructs that can start to describe the data at more theoretical levels: applying to *groups of codes* or showing how different codes are linked. Gradually, a scheme for making sense of the data is developed. At first, the scheme may seem to have ambiguities or incoherencies and gaps. Where the scheme does not fit the data perfectly, it is considered to need further adjustment – theoretical sampling and constant comparison being employed until 'the code is sharpened to achieve its best fit while further properties are generated until the code is verified and saturated' (Glaser and Holton, 2004: 58).

For example, consider a GT study to explore your students' experiences of homework. Your analysis may have revealed, among other things, that:

(a) there seem to be gender differences among the attitudes to, and preferred forms of, homework; and

(b) some students find internet-based work very motivating.

However, if you realize that the only students who have mentioned the internet in interviews are boys, then that may (though not necessarily) be because the girls tend to be less enthusiastic about such activities. Theoretical sampling would indicate who you should talk to next, and what you should ask them, to find out whether internet-based homework is one of the aspects where there is a gender difference.

Harry et al. (2005) describe their analytical processes in some depth, as they move from open codes, to categories, to themes – which are then further tested before being interrelated and linked into a final theory. One of the consequences of such an approach is that a researcher cannot plan a definitive timeline for the research in advance, as the fieldwork will not be 'finished' until all such issues are resolved and the final model matches all the data without leaving any gaps.

## CORE VARIABLES AND THEORETICAL SATURATION

One aim of a GT analysis is to identify any 'core variable', 'which appears to account for most of the variation around the concern or problem that is the focus of the study' (Glaser and Holton, 2004: 54), and that can act as the key idea around which to organize the theory.

In my doctoral research, I collected data relating to a wide range of ideas students used to discuss and explain many different examples. However, eventually, I was able to identify one notion (or 'misconception') that all my informants used as a central explanatory principle in chemistry, and which could be seen as a central node for the wider web of ideas (Taber, 1998). This single idea could be linked to a range of learning difficulties in the topic.

The point at which no further data collection is needed (because all new data fit into the model without having to make any more adjustments) is referred to as 'theoretical saturation': 'the point in category development at which no new properties, dimensions, or relationships emerge during analysis' (Strauss and Corbin, 1998: 143).

Only at this point is there a grounded theory suitable for writing up and reporting. For some strict GT adherents, it is only at this point that the formal literature review is undertaken, so that the write-up can offer comparisons with previously published research.

This brief account has not detailed the stages used in a full GT study, but illustrates the iterative nature of the process that allows the researcher to claim a theory that is 'grounded' in the data.

## DIFFICULTIES OF A GT APPROACH IN STUDENT PROJECTS

When a full GT approach is applied to an educational issue, it has the considerable potential to offer insight and improve our understanding of that issue. However, the potential problems of using such an emergent and open-ended approach in student projects (with deadlines, and supervisors demanding literature reviews and research designs) should also be clear. A student is often told that before planning their project, they must review the literature to find out what is already known about the topic. This provides the 'conceptualization' used to start planning research, and to ensure their research report (usually written when it is too late to do any more fieldwork) will not appear naive or ill-informed. Yet, 'to undertake an extensive review of literature before the emergence of a core category violates the basic premise of GT—that being, the theory emerges from the data not from extant theory' (Glaser and Holton, 2004: 46).

Similarly, supervisors commonly require students to have produced a research design, with a plan for how their research will be carried out, *before* approving the fieldwork. Yet, in GT, 'beyond the decisions concerning initial collection of data, further collection cannot be planned in advance of the emerging theory' (Glaser and Holton, 2004: 51).

It is not only students who are required to offer designs for their studies – this is usually the case when professional researchers seek sponsorship for studies: the funding body generally expects plans that include details of the sample and nature and schedule of data collection to be undertaken. Harry et al. (2005: 12) attempted to 'design' their study to meet funding requirements, but to provide phases of data collection that would allow flexibility for a GT approach. However, they faced considerable difficulties in following the principles of theoretical sampling and constant comparison across the full sample of schools they had told their sponsors they would include, and reflected that 'in retrospect, we conclude that we could have achieved a more refined analysis with a sample half this size'.

Finally, students may have very limited timelines for their research, and will usually be expected to provide their supervisors with a schedule for the research that is clearly viable in the time available. Yet, the GT approach 'requires that the analyst takes whatever amount of quality time that is required to do the discovery' (Glaser and Holton, 2004: 60). Again, this limitation does not only apply to student projects. Harry et al. (2005: 12), reporting on their funded project undertaken by a team of researchers, note that 'the complexity of the data set made it impossible for us to pursue the numerous possible connections between all the data within the three-year timeframe of the study'.

## THE SUBSTANTIVE AND THE GENERAL: TESTING THE THEORY

The research by Harry and colleagues was undertaken over a sample of schools in a district. They summarized their GT thus:

> A complex set of negative influences contribute to the overrepresentation of minorities in special education. Predominant contributors are the assumption of intrinsic deficit and the requirement for a disability categorization; inequitable opportunity to learn, resulting from poor teacher quality in lower-SES [socio-economic status] schools and higher standards in higher-SES schools; negative biases against families perceived as dysfunctional; external pressure from high-stakes testing; and subjectivity in referral and assessment practices. (Harry et al., 2005: 6)

Although these findings all derive from one sample of schools, in one school district, the careful selection of a diverse range of schools suggests these findings could well have wider application. (Although, of course, any criteria used to form such a sample imply some preconceived ideas about the range of factors that may be significant.)

However, small-scale studies usually need to have a more specific focus, and be concerned with issues or educational problems in a particular context. So although Calissendorff (2006) was interested in 'young children' learning to play an instrument, her theory is grounded in data from just six children attending particular violin lessons. Her theory is substantially based on that context, and although grounded in data, it cannot be *assumed* to apply elsewhere (Taber, 2007: 111–16).

However, as theory, the outcomes are suitable either for further phases of GT research (Glaser, 1978), for the theoretical sampling of other contexts, or for 'testing' as hypotheses in confirmatory studies (Strauss and Corbin, 1998: 213). My doctoral project was based upon the in-depth study of a modest number of students who studied chemistry in the college where I taught at the time. They each had unique 'conceptual frameworks' for thinking about the subjects, but there were some common ways of thinking among the sample that seemed to be acting as barriers to the intended learning on the course.

It was possible to conjecture that some of these ideas might be common among the wider population of students studying the subject at this level. Survey instruments were designed to test out this idea (confirmatory research), and in this way it was possible to generalize well beyond the original sample (Taber, 2000). Whether this is seen as a further stage of GT, or the use of GT as a starting point for a different type of research is a moot point (the founders of GT, Glaser and Strauss, would probably have taken different views), but either way this is an example of how different types of research techniques can play their part in a *programme* of research (see Chapter 15) developing our understanding of an issue.

**Activity 14.3**

Think about issues that you would like to explore in your classroom context. Identify an issue or problem that you feel would lend itself to GT (issue A), and one where you feel GT would be inappropriate (issue B). Why would GT be more useful in researching one issue than the other? The notion of exploratory vs. confirmatory research may be useful here. Think about the key features of GT discussed in this chapter. How would you go about developing GT to understand and explain issue A in your classroom: how would you operationalize such a study in practice? What might be the challenges that you would have to face?

## BORROWING FROM GT

GT was developed at a time when exploratory qualitative studies were not widely accepted as being 'valid', and Glaser and Strauss (1967) produced an account justifying how such research could lead to a theory for understanding social phenomena that retained 'scientific' rigour. Since GT was 'discovered', the research community has relaxed its view of the nature of scientific research (see Chapter 15), and a range of interpretive approaches to enquiry have become widely accepted as the means to generate authentic knowledge. Some commentators have implied that GT is now rather anachronistic (e.g. Thomas and James, 2006).

Despite this, GT continues to be a popular approach – certainly in terms of the extent to which it is 'name-checked' in research studies. A full GT study is a demanding, open-ended form of research that offers potential difficulties to the experienced researcher, and is a brave undertaking indeed for a research novice! However, there is much to learn from the GT approach with its emphasis on developing theory rather than just offering descriptive accounts. In particular, the type of iterative approach to data analysis exemplified by the constant comparison method has been widely borrowed by researchers looking to make sense of complex data sets. Such an approach will at least ensure that findings accurately reflect the full range of data collected. However, when such an approach is used to analyse data *after* it has all been collected (as in a standard research design), there is no opportunity to refine and 'plug' the resulting analytical scheme through theoretical sampling. This makes theoretical saturation unlikely, so that findings cannot be seen as a completed theoretical model. However, perhaps a pragmatist (such as a student with a deadline) must sometimes settle for a model that is a provisional best fit, and can at least be presented as a starting point for further research.

## KEY IDEAS

This chapter has introduced Grounded Theory (GT), an approach to social research that offers a rigorous set of procedures for developing theory to explain educational (and other social) issues based upon principles of:

- the development of theoretical sensitivity by close and open-minded attention to data sets
- data collection within an emergent design, that employs theoretical sampling
- data analysis that starts from open coding and by the constant comparison method moves to the identification of a core variable
- only being considered complete when further theoretical sampling shows that the theory is saturated.

The demands of GT approaches make it a risky choice for novice researchers. However, an understanding of GT is important when reading accounts of educational research that report GT, and the (more common) studies that claim to draw upon aspects of the GT methodology. GT also offers a model for data analysis in 'discovery' or 'exploratory' studies where previous research does not suggest a suitable analytical framework for interrogating the data.

 *Further Reading*

Charmaz, K. (1995) 'Grounded theory', in J. A. Smith, R. Harrè, R. and L. Van Langenhove (eds), *Rethinking Methods in Psychology*. London: Sage pp. 27–49.

Glaser, B. G. and Strauss, A. L. (1967) *The Discovery of Grounded Theory: Strategies for Qualitative Research*. New York: Aldine de Gruyter.

Strauss, A. and Corbin, J. (1998) *Basics of Qualitative Research: Techniques and Procedures for Developing Grounded Theory*. Thousand Oaks, CA: Sage.

## References

Calissendorff, M. (2006) 'Understanding the learning style of pre-school children learning the violin', *Music Education Research*, 8 (1): 83–96.

Charmaz, K. C. (2006) *Constructing Grounded Theory: A Practical Guide through Qualitative Analysis*. London: Sage. (Sample chapter available at www.sagepub.co.uk/book. aspx?pid=107375&sc=1)

Cisneros-Puebla, C. A. (2004) 'To learn to think conceptually': Juliet Corbin in conversation with Cesar A. Cisneros-Puebla', *Forum: Qualitative Social Research*, 5 (3), Article 32. Available at: www.qualitative-research.net/fqs-texte/3-04/04-3-32-e.htm

Glaser, B. G. (1978) *Theoretical Sensitivity: Advances in the Methodology of Grounded Theory*. Mill Valley, CA: The Sociology Press.

Glaser, B. G. (2002) 'Conceptualization: On theory and theorizing using grounded theory', *International Journal of Qualitative Methods*, 1 (2), Article 3. (Retrieved 9 March 2006 from www.ualberta.ca/~ijqm/)

Glaser, B. G. and Holton, J. (2004) 'Remodeling Grounded Theory', *Forum: Qualitative Social Research*, 5 (2), Article 4. Available at: www.qualitative-research.net/fqstexte/2-04/2-04glaser-e.htm

Glaser, B. G. and Strauss, A. L. (1967) *The Discovery of Grounded Theory: Strategies for Qualitative Research*. New York: Aldine de Gruyter.

Harry, B., Sturges, K. M. and Klingner, J. K. (2005) 'Mapping the process: An exemplar of process and challenge in grounded theory analysis', *Educational Researcher*, 34 (2): 3–13.

Koestler, A. (1982) 'Creativity and the unconscious.' Proceedings of the conference on Brain Function and Learning at the Brain Research Institute, University of California, UCLA Forum in Medical Sciences, 1967; reprinted in A. Koestler, *Bricks to Babel*, Picador Edition, London: Pan Books, pp. 359–67.

Measor, L. and Woods, P. (1991) 'Breakthrough and blockage in ethnographic research: Contrasting experiences during the Changing Schools project', in G. Walford (ed.), *Doing Educational Research*. London: Routledge, pp. 59–81.

Medawar, P. B. (1990) *The Threat and the Glory*. New York: HarperCollins.

Schwandt, T. A. (2001) *Dictionary of Qualitative Inquiry*, 2nd edn. Thousand Oaks, CA: Sage.

Strauss, A. and Corbin, J. (1998) *Basics of Qualitative Research: Techniques and Procedures for Developing Grounded Theory*. Thousand Oaks, CA: Sage.

Taber, K. S. (1997) 'Post-inductive resonance?: The principles of "grounded theory" applied to chemical education research'. Paper presented to the 4th European Conference on Research in Chemical Education, at the University of York, 9–12 September. Available at www.leeds.ac.uk/educol/

Taber, K. S. (1998) 'An alternative conceptual framework from chemistry education', *International Journal of Science Education*, 20 (5): 597–608.

Taber, K. S. (2000) 'Case studies and generalisability – grounded theory and research in science education', *International Journal of Science Education*, 22 (5): 469–87.

Taber, K. S. (2007) *Classroom-based Research and Evidence-based Practice: A Guide for Teachers*. London: Sage.

Thomas, G. and James, D. (2006) 'Reinventing grounded theory: Some questions about theory, ground and discovery', *British Educational Research Journal*, 32 (6): 767–95.

# SECTION 4

## PARADIGMS

# BEYOND POSITIVISM: 'SCIENTIFIC' RESEARCH INTO EDUCATION

## Keith S. Taber

> **Hints**
>
> - This chapter offers the case for considering educational research as 'scientific'. You should consider how this argument may challenge your existing notion of what counts as 'science'.
> - You will find that the argument depends upon a 'demarcation' of what science is that is based upon what might be termed methodological values rather than upon subject matter or the use of specific methods.
> - You should notice that it is not claimed that all education research should be seen as scientific, but only that which is undertaken systematically within an established programme of enquiry.
> - It may be helpful for you to think about whether particular educational research papers you have read would seem to fit the post-positivist criteria for being scientific.

The focus of this chapter is on 'post-positivism' as a guide for carrying out research in education. The chapter will explore what is meant by post-positivism, and so how some forms of educational research may be seen as 'post-positivist' – and so, by extension, a form of 'scientific' research. This is an issue you should take seriously, as those carrying out research in educational contexts, and wishing to have that research acknowledged formally (perhaps by publication, perhaps by a university award), are expected to position themselves in terms of what are sometimes labelled 'paradigmatic' commitments.

## WHAT IS A PARADIGM?

The term paradigm is often used to describe approaches to *educational* enquiry, although it first came into heavy usage after Kuhn's (1996/1962) seminal work on the nature of *scientific* progress. Kuhn believed that science comprised two types of scientific activity: 'normal' science and 'revolutionary' science. As the name may suggest, 'normal' science is what is going on most of the time. In Kuhn's terms, many scientists will spend their entire careers working within an established paradigm or 'disciplinary matrix'. Kuhn used these terms to describe the mind-set and rules (maybe including some unwritten, unspoken and not openly acknowledged) which apply to scientists working within a particular field. The paradigm, or disciplinary matrix:

- forms the theoretical basis of the sub-branch of science
- is accepted by all the workers in the field
- determines what is judged to be the subject of legitimate research in the field
- determines the procedures, rules and standards that apply in the field.

Although Kuhn developed his ideas from looking at the history of scientific ideas, the notion of a paradigm has been adopted in *social science*. Here, however, paradigms seldom have the clear hegemony over a field that Kuhn suggested existed in the 'natural' sciences. For Kuhn, paradigms in science ruled – at least until there was a revolution when a new paradigm would usurp the previous one. An example might be ideas about a geocentric universe being replaced by a heliocentric model. However, revolutions were rare, and normal science was the norm!

In Kuhn's model, different paradigms are potentially 'incommensurable' (as they did not share basic commitments, for example to the definitions of fundamental terms, making meaningful dialogue difficult) so that communities of researchers worked together within a single paradigm. In the social sciences, however, it is quite possible for distinct paradigms to coexist without dominating their field.

A paradigm may be considered as the 'highest' level at which thinking about research occurs (Taber, 2007: 33). If we think of research as being a kind of business (in the widest sense), then paradigmatic choices are made at the 'executive' level. Paradigmatic commitments are reflected in research design: they constrain the selection of appropriate research *strategy* (methodology), which in turn channels the selection of appropriate *tactics* – the techniques for data collection and data analysis.

However, it is important to realize that this is not simply a matter of practical considerations: the adoption of a paradigm is *principled*. It relates to fundamental notions about the nature of (a) what is being researched; and (b) the knowledge that may be produced in the research.

## THE NATURE OF PARADIGMATIC COMMITMENTS IN EDUCATIONAL RESEARCH

Consideration of the 'philosophy' of research is often broken down into the ontological, the epistemological and the methodological.

**Ontology** concerns beliefs about the nature of the things we are researching, e.g.

- What kind of things exist in the world?
- Is there a common reality that we all share?

**Epistemology** (our theory of knowledge) concerns beliefs about the kind of knowledge it is possible to acquire about those things, e.g.

- Is it possible to obtain absolute knowledge of the world?
- Can we find out some things which we can be sure are 'true'?

**Methodology** concerns how we go about acquiring that knowledge.

The first two considerations may seem a little obscure, but actually they are extremely important. A researcher needs to have thought carefully about the ontological and epistemological issues that relate to their research, because the researcher's beliefs here will *influence* research decisions.

### Activity 15.1

Consider two examples – how would you go about undertaking school-based research into:

(a)  how student ability influences GCSE examination performance?
(b)  bullying occurring in a tutor group?

## THE NATURE OF ABILITY

If we consider how student 'ability' influences GCSE examination performance, then we can readily appreciate why ontological beliefs influence research. Anyone researching 'ability' has to have a view of what 'ability' is (see Chapter 1). For example – is 'ability':

- something that is fixed, or that can be developed?
- a unitary quality, that can be measured on a single scale (e.g. IQ), *or* is it the overview of a set of largely independent abilities to be measured on a range of scales, *or* is it a multifaceted and complex set of interlinked factors such that it is better described (than measured)?
- something that can be meaningfully considered in isolation, *or* can we only consider a person's ability(ies) in terms of their potential to perform in a particular task context?

We might even question whether individual ability is actually a meaningful construct, or whether it is better understood as what can be achieved in a particular social context, under conditions that offer a suitable balance of support and challenge. For example, consider Vygotsky's (1986/1934) suggestion that finding out about a learner's ZPD (zone of proximal development) is more informative than finding out what they can actually do unaided (ZAD). The type of entity one believes 'ability' to be determines what it makes sense to attempt to find out about it. If we do not believe that ability is a meaningful construct at all, then we could not research it.

There are many examples of constructs used in education that may not be widely accepted as reflecting the 'same' (or any) thing.

**Activity 15.2**

Consider the following notions – to what extent can they be clearly defined? Pick three examples and attempt to write a definition of what each term means. If you can, ask a colleague to independently define the same terms. To what extent do you share an 'objective' meaning for these terms?

- bullying
- special needs students
- students with specific learning difficulties
- disillusioned students
- gifted students
- challenging students
- a good lesson
- effective school management
- a supporting Head of Department
- a good classroom atmosphere
- poor attendance
- … for a member of staff
- a good homework record
- a suitable professional development activity
- lively staffroom banter
- unprofessional behaviour.

## AN ONTOLOGICAL QUESTION: WHAT KIND OF THING IS BULLYING?

Let us consider the first example on the list. Research into bullying could look at a number of aspects of the topic. For example, it might be possible to explore *how much* bullying is going on – but only *if* we can agree on:

- a *definition* of what is (and is not) counted as bullying
- what indicators would enable us to be confident when we have *identified* an incident.

Alternatively, we might wish to explore *why* bullying occurs. This would assume that bullying was the type of phenomenon that had *causes* (an ontological assumption) and that such causes could be clearly identified (an epistemological assumption).

If we did not believe that bullying had causes, then there would no sense in attempting to investigate what the causes might be. If we do believe there are causes of bullying, but do not believe it is possible to establish reliable knowledge about these causes, then there would be no sense in asking *which* methodologies might allow us to discover them.

It could be argued that we *have* to believe in bullying, as it is the topic of much literature and concern, so clearly must exist in some sense . In the same way, the following entities clearly exist in some sense, as they are commonly referred to, discussed, invoked, etc.:

- fairies
- Superman
- bog-standard comprehensives.

I would suggest that the existence of fairies as something that we can imagine and discuss does not require the existence of fairies in the 'real' world (cf. Popper, 1979). Fairies can populate your imagination even when you do not think they could exist at the bottom of the garden.

However, if some other people give fairies the ontological status of physical beings (i.e. believe that fairies exist as 'real' creatures), then that belief can have effects *regardless* of whether we accept their ontology.

And if this discussion of fairies seems a little obscure, then the same point can be made by substituting fairies with the devil; God; evil; heaven and hell; America as the great Satan; the divine right of kings; destiny; the superiority of the white 'race'; 'naturally' distinct roles for men and women; a fetus as a human being (or not); IQ; giftedness; genius; dyslexia; or many other examples where different people would assign varying ontological status.

We might believe that there is no such thing as bullying per se, but rather that bullying is a construct that has different meanings for different groups. For example, teachers may have an understanding of what bullying is, that leads to the identification of bullies and victims. Those they identify as 'bullies' (or even 'victims') may have very different views of what bullying is, and may exclude themselves from being bullies (or victims). A pupil may consider themselves a victim of bullying, without anyone else considering this to be so. Unless we believe there is a *privileged* view (e.g. that bullying exists, and it is what teachers *believe* it is, regardless of the views of those that then become labelled as bullies or victims), then we are not able to investigate something that has objective existence. This is an ontological issue.

If we take the view that 'bullying' is not a phenomenon that exists in the world as such, but rather a socially constructed notion that allows different observers to construe events in different ways, then we cannot expect research to offer unproblematic answers to questions such as 'how much bullying is going on here?', or 'what are the causes of bullying in this class?'. If 'bullying' does not have an objective meaning, then there is no clear corpus of events about which we might seek objective knowledge.

We might instead ask questions that lead to different *forms* of knowledge: knowledge about the way the notion of 'bullying' is *construed* by different actors in a social context, e.g. teachers and students (cf. Chapter 9). Some of these individuals may well construe themselves as bullies or victims (or protectors against bullying), or construe others as bullies or victims (or protectors against bullying), but these labels and the incidents that lead to them will be construed differently by the different actors. It may be sensible to ask what the different actors see as the causes of bullying, or as the causes of incidents that others identify as bullying. However, *knowledge of people's beliefs* about events is a different kind of knowledge to *knowledge about events* themselves.

## WHY IS IT IMPORTANT FOR RESEARCHERS TO TAKE UP A POSITION ON SUCH ISSUES?

Particular ontological and epistemological commitments underpin any particular study. When reading a study about ability, bullying, classroom atmosphere, effective teaching, student learning, etc., it is important to appreciate the kind of entities the author is writing about: things that can be objectively defined; or cultural entities which are subject to shifts in meaning; or the personal understandings of individuals.

It is also important to appreciate how researchers view the type of knowledge that they are reporting on. An account of bullying in one school class may well offer some tentative explanations of the causes of *that* bullying. If the research was designed to offer a detailed account of one context, it might help us to understand that context, but we cannot consider that the causes of bullying identified may be taken as 'the causes of bullying'. The research may indeed offer insights to other contexts, but a research design that seeks contextualized knowledge of a particular instance cannot be *assumed* to offer general knowledge outside of that research context (Taber, 2007: 111–16).

## EDUCATIONAL RESEARCH PARADIGMS

At an introductory level, we normally think of most educational research studies as fitting within one of two general categories (Taber, 2007: 33), characterized as:

- positivistic, nomothetic and confirmatory; or
- interpretivist, idiographic and discovery.

Positivist is usually taken as a synonym for 'scientific', so that educational research that is considered positivistic is usually considered to be modelled on natural science, and is sometimes simplistically identified with the 'ideal' of 'the randomised controlled experiment or field trial' (Phillips, 2005: 578).

### Positivistic or interpretivist?

Research based on the assumption that it is *in principle* possible to find absolute knowledge is seen as positivist. Research that is based on a view that all knowledge is based on interpretation (for which there is no final arbiter) is seen as interpretivist.

### Nomothetic or idiographic?

Research which sets out to establish general laws about what is 'normal' is sometimes labelled nomothetic. Research that explores the specific nature of individual cases is described as idiographic.

## Confirmatory or discovery?

Research that tests pre-determined hypotheses is referred to as confirmatory, whereas open-ended enquiry that explores a situation in terms of the categories that are ground in the data collected are labelled as discovery (see Chapter 14). These two research approaches are often presented as being competing paradigms (Phillips, 2005), as 'an intellectual either/or situation' (Reynolds, 1991: 194), so that 'researchers with different purposes … tend to see the others as engaged in the same enterprise as themselves, but simply doing it badly' (Hammersley, 1993: xix).

If we accept this notion of education researchers having to choose to work within one or other paradigm, then the choice is something of a stark one – between studies that produce general decontextualized findings, that are usually bound to (and so are dependent upon) the theoretical assumptions the researchers used to design their study, and studies that produce detailed studies of very specific educational contexts, that cannot be assumed to apply to any other context (Taber, 2007).

Phillips (2005: 584) argues that in the USA, government pressure, through the criteria used to fund research, favours research that reflects the positivistic 'gold standard' of the controlled experiment, while 'qualitative case studies, mixed-methods research and ethnographies are beyond the pale'. By such standards, most practitioner research would be considered 'beyond the pale'.

Luckily, some observers (e.g. Carr and Kemmis, 1986: 105) do not think that 'scientific explanation and interpretative understanding are mutually exclusive categories'. Biddle and Anderson (1986) have argued for an integrated, broader notion of how we can come to new knowledge in the social sciences (such as education).

Below it will be suggested that what is a referred to as a 'post-positivist' view can certainly encompass such a broad range of research, by offering a more informed view of how science proceeds (Phillips, 2005). Before we look at this issue, we need to consider two types of 'complications' that make educational research difficult.

## TWO PROBLEMS FOR A POSITIVISTIC EDUCATIONAL SCIENCE

This post-positivist view is welcome, as in practice very little educational research can meet the 'gold standard' of the controlled experiment that characterizes a positivist paradigm.

## Complications of researching educational contexts: the role of the researcher

Positivistic scientific research attempts to be *objective*. This means that, in principle, observers could be interchanged without changing research findings. We should be able to substitute one qualified and skilled researcher for another in carrying out the data collection and analysis without changing the findings of a study. The individual who manipulates the apparatus and the materials is assumed not to interact with them in a way that could be seen as 'personal'.

The way that metals expand on heating, or wires stretch when loaded, or solutes dissolve in solvents, is not dependent upon who heated, stretched or mixed them. New results in natural science are only widely accepted once the work has been replicated by scientists working in other laboratories. A procedure has to be specified closely enough for any competent scientist to demonstrate the same findings.

Social science research, such as educational research, it is argued, is different: it *does* matter who the researcher is. Two different researchers may get very different responses when asking a child why he engages in disruptive behaviour (just as two different teachers may get very different responses). So often in social research, the researcher interacts with the informant(s) in such a way that the data that is constructed is a co-production. A different co-producer will co-produce a different co-production, and so different data will be constructed.

So if our 'demarcation criteria' for what counts as scientific work is based on whether we could substitute another competent researcher, then much social (including educational) research *cannot* be seen as scientific.

## Complications of researching educational contexts: the complexity of the phenomena

A second major complication of educational research concerns the complexity of social phenomena (such as classroom teaching). Science is (sometimes!) able to use a controlled experiment by isolating the various factors that are believed to be the possible causes of or influences on some phenomenon; keeping them constant; and then varying a single factor ('variable') to see what effect that change has. If we get two different outcomes when we have two situations, which are *absolutely identical in all but one respect*, then that difference may be assumed to be responsible for the different outcome. This approach is based on a very important (ontological) assumption: that the world has a kind of regularity where exactly replicating conditions leads to the same outcomes. This is taken for granted (i.e. is a paradigmatic commitment) in scientific work.

In education, we are seldom able to study phenomena in this way. Even when ethical considerations allow us to manipulate a situation, it is very unlikely we can ever compare perfectly matched cases, to have a single relevant factor that is different between the cases. An additional complication in educational research is memory. Often in the physical sciences we can return a test object to its original conditions to then look at the effect of different conditions. Unhelpfully (for researchers), we cannot assume that a student returns to their initial state after some form of educational experience, even if their test results suggest this is sometimes the case!

## THREE PROBLEMS FOR A POSITIVIST NATURAL SCIENCE

So educational research does not often match up to the ideal of the experimental model in science. We can seldom undertake educational research that allows us to draw simple conclusions from carefully controlled experiments. However, the assumption that science has a method that leads to absolute (positive) knowledge of the world is now generally considered to be naive and unsupportable (Phillips and Burbules, 2000).

The experimental method is often presented as a way of uncovering true knowledge of the world: by planning our experiments logically, carefully collecting sufficient data, and then applying our rational faculty to empirical evidence to prove (or otherwise) scientific hypotheses. This is a gross simplification and misrepresentation of how science works, that has been unfortunately encouraged by the impoverished image of the nature of science commonly reflected in school science (Taber, 2008).

Here I will consider three particular difficulties with the assumption that science can offer absolute knowledge, each pertinent to considering whether educational research can be classed as 'scientific'.

### The problem of induction

The first issue is the 'problem of induction'. The natural sciences were long considered to be inductive, i.e. to work by 'that process of collecting general truths from the examination of particular facts' (Whewell, 1976/1857: 5). In his history of the 'inductive sciences', Whewell, who is credited with coining the term 'scientist', suggested that this process of forming general rules 'is so far familiar to men's minds that, without here entering into further explanation, its nature will be understood sufficiently to prepare the reader to *recognise* the exemplification of such a process' (Whewell, 1976/1857: 9). Avoiding 'further explanation' might be considered wise, as although science seemed to depend upon generalization, there is no logically watertight argument to show how one could ever be certain of any general statements based on evidence from only some particular examples.

A famous example concerned swans, and the general statement ('truth') that 'all swans are white'. This generalization was based on empirical evidence, i.e. that no one had ever observed a swan that was *not* white! This did not, however, prove that a non-white swan would never be found … indeed, while this example was being discussed in Europe, the black swans in Australia went about their business not yet observed by Western scientists. So science may tell us (as a matter of fact) that copper will conduct electricity, that ice will melt at 0°C, that penguins hatch from eggs, or that the sun will rise tomorrow, but the 'problem of induction' was that no one could explain how we could possibly be sure of any of these things simply based on observations of only some of the copper, ice, penguins, or tomorrows that have existed and will exist.

Karl Popper (a former school teacher) suggested instead that science works through a process of testing hypotheses, based on the attempt to exclude possibilities by *falsification* (Popper, 1959/1934).

Science does not produce absolute knowledge, but makes progress through the formation of hypotheses that are falsifiable, and preferably bold (not just predicting the obvious), and then attempting to prove them wrong. Scientific knowledge is tentative, and open to review as more evidence comes in. So even the experimental method, the 'gold standard' for research, does not automatically offer generalizable objective knowledge.

> The fundamental difference between positivism and postpositivism is this: ... postpositivists are united in their adherence to fallibilism — the idea that all scientific knowledge is potentially subject to the discovery of error, and thus should be regarded as provisional. (Swann, 2003: 253-4)

## The problem of theory-ladenness

This leads to the question of what *justifies* scientists in telling us that copper will conduct electricity, that ice will melt at 0°C, that penguins hatch from eggs, that the sun will rise tomorrow, or that swans are birds with white feathers. The answer is that these generalizations are as dependent upon theory as observation. Samples of copper or ice behave in certain ways under certain conditions. Theories are developed that are able to offer explanations or models of how the behaviour depends upon the conditions. It is these theories, these models of what is going on, that allow scientists to predict what will happen to *other* samples of copper or ice.

One observation can never of itself lead to a certain prediction. But observations lead to theories, which lead to predictions that can be used to test the theories. The theories are not 'proved' by testing (another white swan proves little) but may be falsified this way (a black swan needs to be explained if we believe that all swans are white). So science is not about collecting 'facts' or finding 'truth', but developing theories and explanations, and then identifying related issues and problems worthy of researching to test and refine the theory.

As Swann points out:

> This conception of science is no less applicable to the study of human social endeavours, such as education, than it is to the study of natural phenomena. (Swann, 2003: 255)

'Science' then is a body of knowledge, but not a body of facts or truths – rather, it is a body of conceptual knowledge (based around concepts developed by humans), that is, of theoretical knowledge. It is objective knowledge, but not absolute: it is always tentative and provisional. Despite that, the methods of science allow scientists to claim *reliable* knowledge (Ziman, 1991) – knowledge that we can have confidence acts as a reliable basis for prediction and action.

Popper offered falsification as the basis of progress in science: that science proceeded by cycles of conjecture and refutation (the 'hypothetico-deductive method'). But Popper was aware that this was not a simple matter. As scientific knowledge is theoretical, refutation may sometimes be avoided by simply changing definition. As a trivial example, if the concept of whiteness is seen as central to the concept of swan, then it is not possible to have a black swan. In this circumstance, a naturalist exploring Australia might well see a 'black, swan-like bird', but could not see a black swan. By definition, the 'black, swan-like bird' would be considered as something other than a swan. In this case, the black swan was accepted (there were considered to be other aspects of swanness that are more central than the colour of the plumage). However, it is said that when Cook first arrived in Australia, the indigenous population did not 'see' the ships approaching shore until they got very close, because they had no past experience that offered a conceptual framework for making sense of their perceptions. This may be apocryphal, but it offers a nice example of the 'theory-ladenness' of observations.

There are many examples of this in science, and indeed much of Kuhn's notion of scientific revolutions was based on an idea that those working within a paradigm take certain things for granted that make it impossible to interpret results as falsifying key beliefs. Although Popper believed that scientists should seek to refute ideas, Kuhn thought that this seldom happened once ideas had become central to a field. When research leads to findings which suggest a central tenet is false, these are likely to be explained away. Only a scientific revolutionary is able to recognize an anomaly as such and offer a new way of 'seeing'.

For example, Uranus was 'seen' and recorded as a star many times before Herschel recognized that it does not behave as a star (i.e. anomalous behaviour), and so *discovered* it as a planet (Kuhn, 1996). Interestingly, he actually claimed that Uranus was a comet, but is still considered to be the discoverer of the planet, unlike his predecessors who identified it as a star. A comet is judged like a planet in the features considered *theoretically* significant here, so Herschel was considered close enough!

It may seem that a scientist must be foolish or dishonest to fail to accept clearly falsifying of evidence in an experiment. Yet much modern science is based on advanced technology. An anomalous result may mean our idea is wrong, or that the apparatus is faulty or miscalibrated. If careful checking and recalibration of the apparatus do not remove the anomaly, then logically we must adjust our theory. However, we can always choose to believe that the fault lies in the theory behind the instrumentation, rather than some key idea we may be committed to.

When Galileo pointed telescopes towards the sky, he saw objects that the then orthodoxy suggested should not exist. Some of those that he persuaded to look denied seeing those objects. Perhaps they were lying. More likely, Galileo interpreted the fuzzy smudges of light as moons around other planets according to his ontological commitment, and other observers saw no more than distortions due to the imperfect lenses available at the time. According to Kuhn's model, the different observers held incommensurable paradigmatic commitments. Those that could not interpret the patterns within *their ontology* of the cosmos made a *judgement* about the limitations of the telescope for showing clear images of cosmic bodies.

Galileo should not have been too smug, as he also saw Neptune through his telescope – but without 'discovering' it as a planet (Bamford, 1989)!

### Activity 15.3

How might the 'theory-laden' nature of observations be used by someone told that 'experiments' on the effect of setting on student learning contradicted their own strong commitment to the effectiveness of set (or mixed-ability) teaching?

## The problem of naturalism

Another problem with Popper's model, at least as it was initially understood, was that if 'falsification' is seen as the demarcation criterion for science, then only experimental approaches allow falsification, and so should be admitted as scientific.

> Simply, a scientist uses a universal theory about how the world is, to predict that, under specific conditions, a particular circumstance can be anticipated ... The next step is to devise an experiment by means of which the prediction could potentially be refuted. (Swann, 2003: 257)

Not all science is based on experimental techniques. For example, Darwin proposed that evolution occurred by a process of natural selection. Darwin's theory was largely based on an accumulation of a great deal of observational data. Darwin observed species, geological formations, fossils, etc. However, Darwin did not undertake any controlled experiments to test his idea of natural selection (although he did draw upon the 'experiments' of artificial selection as an analogy for his ideas).

It is not possible to undertake experimental tests in much of geology, cosmology, etc. These sciences build up theories based on the interpretation of observations, not the results of experiments undertaken to find out what would happen if the tectonic plates were a different size, or the earth's crust was thicker, or glaciers retreated at a different rate, or if the earth was closer to the sun or had two moons, or if the conditions in the Big Bang were different. Under a strict view of falsificationism, topics such as these would fall outside science.

However, clearly, we would normally include naturalistic work such as this as science. It is not just 'nature collecting': it is a business of developing models and theories through systematic observations.

> In science, measurements and experimental results, observational or interview data, and mathematical and logical analysis all can be part of the warrant — or case — that supports a theory, hypothesis or judgment. However, warrants are always revocable depending on the findings of subsequent inquiry. (NRC, 2002: 18)

Science does not all involve 'fair testing' and controlled experiments, for 'one well-conducted case study has the potential to cast doubt on existing assumptions' (Swann, 2003: 260). Indeed, some observers would argue that (natural) science has not proceeded by any specific set of methods (Feyerabend, 1987).

# A POST-POSITIVIST NOTION OF 'SCIENCE' (THAT CAN INCLUDE EDUCATION)

Taking the problem of induction and the theory-laden nature of observations together leads us to the view that, strictly, 'nothing is proved when predictions are fulfilled, nor even when they are refuted' (Swann, 2003: 260). Not only that, but a strict view of falsification as the key criterion of a science would exclude much that is generally accepted as science.

There are many post-positivist critiques of science, versions of what science is really like, which take the view that science makes progress towards more reliable knowledge, without agreeing on what the characteristics of science actually are.

> [Postpositivists] are united in believing that human knowledge is not based on unchallengeable, rock-solid foundations — it is conjectural. We have grounds, or warrants, for asserting the beliefs, or conjectures, that we hold as scientists, often very good grounds, but these grounds are not indubitable. Our warrants for accepting these things can be withdrawn in the light of further investigation. (Phillips and Burbules, 2000: 26)

If we adopt a post-positivist view of science, then we are not using controlled experimental research as the yardstick for deciding if we are being scientific, but rather asking 'has the overall case made by the investigator been established to a degree that warrants tentative acceptance of the theoretical or empirical claims that were made?' (Phillips, 2005: 594). So we do not need to limit 'scientific' research to experimental research.

Rather, 'methods can only be judged in terms of their appropriateness and effectiveness in addressing a particular research question ...' (NRC, 2002: 3). According to the US National Research Council, 'a wide variety of legitimate scientific designs are available for educational research', which 'range from randomized experiments of voucher programs to in-depth ethnographic case studies of teachers to neurocognitive investigations' (NRC, 2002: 6). Scientific studies are those:

- where the design allows direct, empirical investigation of an important question
- that account for the context in which the study is carried out
- that align with a conceptual framework
- which reflect careful and thorough reasoning
- which disclose results to encourage debate in the scientific community (NRC, 2002: 6).

Such criteria allow us to consider *educational* research to be part of an enterprise that could be considered *scientific* in terms of producing 'reliable' or 'objective' knowledge.

> When science is viewed according to the postpositivist model — in which observations are theory-laden, facts underdetermine conclusions, values affect choice of problems, and communities of researchers must examine methods and conclusions for bias — then the perceived gap between social and natural sciences begins to disappear. (Phillips and Burbules, 2000: 65—6)

The careful reader may well suspect that this admission of educational research into the pantheon of the sciences has been bought at a rather heavy cost. The post-positivist vision of conjectures, grounds, warrants and conceptual frameworks offers the potential for a free-for-all that supports eclectic activity, but at a cost of admitting complete subjectivism – after all, a free choice of conceptual framework offers considerable flexibility in selecting what counts as data, let alone interpreting any data that are collected. This does not sound very scientific. One particular post-positivist thinker, Imre Lakatos, can offer us guidance here.

## POST-POSITIVIST, SCIENTIFIC RESEARCH TAKES PLACE WITHIN A RESEARCH PROGRAMME

Lakatos (1970) can be seen as offering a view of how science proceeds – through research programmes – that draws upon the kind of description Kuhn put forward, while having a generally Popperian view of the way in which science may make progress by conjectures and refutations. Lakatos argues that science proceeds through the establishment, and development, of what he called 'research programmes'. Several research programmes can co-exist for extended periods, but to remain scientific, a research programme has to be judged progressive.

A research programme consists of a 'hard core' of central commitments that are taken for granted and assumed to be true for the purposes of the research. Lakatos suggested that there was a mind-set called the 'negative heuristic' that prevented researchers testing the hard-core assumptions. This sounds anti-Popperian, but within a particular programme, research only makes sense if certain commitments are held. Rather, the 'positive' heuristic of the research programme is to develop more detailed knowledge surrounding this hard core (the 'protective belt' of theory). If this terminology makes the ideas seem complicated, then consider Table 15.1 which gives some examples of questions that would be pointless, and questions that could be fruitful, in terms of possible hard-core commitments that could inform feasible research programmes.

According to Lakatos, scientific research programmes were not limited to the natural sciences, but could apply to any field where we are *looking to* develop knowledge that offers models and theories of generality. We can imagine such programmes of research being developed around many different issues, e.g.:

- Is it better to organize teaching in similar ability or mixed-ability settings? Or, if this depends upon context, then what are the contextual factors at work?
- How can ICT be used to enhance student learning? Does this depend upon student age, subject discipline, teaching styles?

As one example of how this perspective can work in education, I have analysed my own main research area – learning in science – in terms of a Lakatosian Research Programme (Taber, 2006). Table 15.2 sets out some of the key tenets of this area of research and some of the questions suggested.

**Table 15.1    How Scientific research programmes work: how the hard core informs research questions**

| Research Programme | Suggested Hard-core Commitment (Inter alia) | Negative Heuristic | Positive Heuristic |
|---|---|---|---|
| What is the research about? | What are the starting points? | What would there be no point in investigating? | What might it be useful to find out? |
| The particle model of matter | That all matter is made up of myriad tiny particles | Is matter made of tiny particles? Can matter be homogenous and continuous on the smallest scale? | How small are atoms? Are they all the same? Do they have internal structure? |
| Defining intelligence | That intellectual ability can be represented by a single measurement | Can intellectual ability be represented by a single value? What are the main factors of intelligence? | Is IQ a good measure of intellectual ability? How can we best design IQ tests? |
| Increasing girls' participation in physical science courses | Girls' under-representation in physics is due to cultural factors, not biological differences | Are girls by nature less capable of studying physics? Are hormone differences responsible for teenagers' subject preferences? | Why do girls tend to drop physics? Do most girls feel physics is irrelevant to their lives? |

**Table 15.2    An example of a research programme in education (modified from Taber, 2006)**

| Hard-core assumptions | Broad general research questions (informing the positive heuristic) |
|---|---|
| Knowledge is constructed by the learner, not received | How does knowledge construction (i.e. learning) take place? |
| Learners come to science learning with existing ideas about many natural phenomena | What ideas do learners' bring to science classes? What is the nature of these ideas? |
| Each individual has a unique set of ideas | How much commonality is there between learners' ideas in science? |
| Knowledge is represented in the brain as a conceptual structure | How is knowledge organized in the brain? |
| It is possible to model learners' conceptual structures | What are the most appropriate models and representations? |
| The learners' existing ideas have consequences for the learning of science | How do learners' ideas interact with teaching? |
| It is possible to teach science more effectively if account is taken of the learner's existing ideas | How should teachers teach science to take account of learners' ideas? |

In this example, the general questions set out in Table 15.2 have led to new concepts and conjectures, that have allowed research questions to be refined, and have maintained the research programme for several decades (see Taber, 2006). As long as the protective belt of theory is being elaborated and developed by this process (so that new theory offers testable predictions, which are generally not refuted), then the hard core is considered immune from question, and the programme is progressive.

However, if a research programme only develops by the use of *ad hoc* adjustments to theory, to make theory match findings, then it is seen as degenerating, and no longer part of science. Lakatos (1978) saw fields such as Marxist theory and astrology as being outside of science, *not* because they concerned topics that were not part of the natural sciences, but because they were degenerate programmes, where theory was bland, and open to *ad hoc* adjustment to fit events, rather than leading to specific testable predictions that helped refine the body of theory.

## KEY IDEAS

This chapter has been about 'science', but about a notion of 'science' that can include educational research. I have reviewed the positivist ideal of scientific research, and indicated why its notion of developing knowledge on totally secure foundations has been shown to be unrealistic. Such naive positivist notions of science have given way to post-positivist perspectives that still aspire to 'reliable' objective knowledge, but admit a broad range of methodological approaches, used within programmes of critical enquiry. The challenge for educational research then is not to be 'scientific' in the sense of limiting ourselves to research designs that are experimental, but rather to ensure that our research is systematic and cumulative, offering theory that supports bold testable conjectures. The interaction between empirical evidence and theory should be seen to make up progressive research programmes, where ideas are refined and developed through the research rather than protected from unfavourable findings.

> At its core, scientific inquiry is the same in all fields. Scientific research, whether in education, physics, anthropology, molecular biology, or economics, is a continual process of rigorous reasoning supported by a dynamic interplay among methods, theories and findings. It builds understandings in the form of models or theories that can be tested. Advances in scientific knowledge are achieved by the self-regulating norms of the scientific community over time, not, as sometimes believed, by the mechanistic application of a particular scientific method . . . . (NRC, 2002: 2)

A key message for the novice researcher wishing to undertake 'scientific', school-based enquiry is to pay careful attention to how the research focus is conceptualized (Taber, 2007) to ensure that your research is supported by, and builds upon, a coherent programme of existing educational enquiry.

# Further Reading

Phillips, D. C. (2005) 'The contested nature of empirical educational research (and why philosophy of education offers little help', *Journal of Philosophy of Education*, 39 (4): 577–97.

Styles, B. (2006) 'Educational research versus scientific research', *Research Intelligence*, 95: 7–9.

Swann, J. (2003) 'How science can contribute to the improvement of educational practice', *Oxford Review of Education*, 29 (2): 253–68.

Taber, K. S. (2006) 'Beyond constructivism: The progressive research programme into learning science', *Studies in Science Education*, 42: 125–84.

# References

Bamford, G. S. (1989) 'Popper, refutation and "avoidance' of refutation"'. A thesis submitted for the degree of Doctor of Philosophy, University of Queensland.

Biddle, B. J. and Anderson, D. S. (1986) 'Theory, methods, knowledge and research on teaching', in M. C. Wittrock (ed.) *Handbook of Research on Teaching*, 3rd edn. New York: Macmillan, pp. 230–52.

Carr, W. and Kemmis, S. (1986) *Becoming Critical: Education, Knowledge and Action Research*. Lewes: Falmer Press.

Feyerabend, P. (1987) *Farewell to Reason*. London: Verso.

Hammersley, M. (1993) *Controversies in Classroom Research*, 2nd edn. Buckingham: Open University Press, pp. x–xxii.

Kuhn, T. S. (1996) *The Structure of Scientific Revolutions*, 3rd edn. Chicago, IL: University of Chicago. (First edition published in 1962.)

Lakatos, I. (1970) 'Falsification and the methodology of scientific research programmes', in I. Lakatos and A. Musgrove (eds), *Criticism and the Growth of Knowledge*. Cambridge: Cambridge University Press, pp. 91–196.

Lakatos, I. (1978) 'Introduction: Science and pseudoscience', in *The Methodology of Scientific Research Programmes*, Philosophical Papers, Volume 1. Cambridge: Cambridge University Press, pp. 1–7.

NRC (National Research Council) (2002) *Scientific Research in Education*. Committee on scientific principles for educational research. Washington, DC: National Academies Press.

Phillips, D. C. (2005) 'The contested nature of empirical educational research (and why philosophy of education offers little help)', *Journal of Philosophy of Education*, 39 (4): 577–97.

Phillips, D. C. and Burbules, N. C. (2000) *Postpostivism and Educational Research*. Oxford: Rowman & Littlefield.

Popper, K. R. (1959) *The Logic of Scientific Discovery*. London: Hutchinson. (Original German edition published in 1934).

Popper, K. R. (1979) *Objective Knowledge: An Evolutionary Approach* (revised edition). Oxford: Oxford University Press.

Reynolds, D. (1991) 'Doing educational research in Treliw', in G. Walford (ed.), *Doing Educational Research*. London: Routledge, pp. 193–209.

Swann, J. (2003) 'How science can contribute to the improvement of educational practice', *Oxford Review of Education*, 29 (2), pp. 253–68.

Taber, K. S. (2006) 'Beyond constructivism: The progressive research programme into learning science', *Studies in Science Education*, 42: 125–84.

Taber, K. S. (2007) *Classroom-based Research and Evidence-based Practice: A Guide for Teachers and Students*. London: Sage.

Taber, K. S. (2008) 'Towards a curricular model of the nature of science', *Science & Education*, 17 (2–3), pp. 179–218.

Vygotsky, L. (1986) *Thought and Language*. London: MIT Press. (First published in Russian in 1934).

Whewell, W. (1976) *History of the Inductive Science*, 3rd edn. Hildesheim: Georg Olms Verlag. (First published in 1857).

Ziman, J. (1991) *Reliable Knowledge: An Exploration of the Grounds for Belief in Science*. Cambridge: Cambridge University Press.

# 16 INTERPRETIVISM: MEETING OUR SELVES IN RESEARCH
## Christine Counsell

**Hints**

- Before choosing or drawing upon a methodology, think about the nature and complexity of the phenomenon you want to examine. In particular, consider the different kinds of *subjectivities* you will be examining. How can the subjective world of other people – whether pupils or teachers – best be understood and represented?
- When framing your project, consider the role of your *own* subjectivity. Is this something you want to push to one side as far as possible? If so, how will you do this? If not, how will you *use* your subjectivity and turn it into a positive condition for enquiry?
- Look to the different intellectual streams of thought for personal *inspiration* and for *insight* into the various possible methodologies, but don't try to cling to one of them rigidly. Reflect and experiment, adapt and blend.

## INTRODUCTION: THREE TEACHERS

Figure 16.1 is a snapshot of three history teachers' thought processes as they assess an essay written by a Year 8 pupil. Let us assume that the essay is a standard piece of history work for Year 8. The pupil was required to construct a causal argument. This involves creative, independent thought, where pupils must select, connect, arrange and prioritize causes in order to make a coherent causal explanation of their own. Our three teachers are looking for a certain kind of causal reasoning in the pupil's argument.

Each teacher is using empirical data – a pupil's work – to try to reach a warranted and useful judgement about this pupil's understanding and progress. Each teacher is therefore engaged, already, in a form of research.

The teachers start off looking *for* something – a something that might act as evidence towards a judgement that the pupil has reached Level 5 of the National Curriculum Attainment Target.

But what happens next?

**Activity 16.1**

Read Figure 16.1 carefully. Find the key similarities and differences between the approaches adopted by the three teachers.

Amidst our various readings of Figure 16.1, some common themes are likely to emerge. I will now highlight those that are pertinent to this chapter:

## COMMENTARY ON THE THREE TEACHERS

**Teacher A** accepts and uses the system of meanings given by the mark scheme. The mark scheme has shown her what to look for. She looks for the language of explicit links between causes. She is being both rigorous and efficient – rigorous in sticking strictly to the manifestation of causal reasoning that the mark scheme specifies ('explicit links'), and thereby ensuring that this piece of work is marked strictly according to the rules applied to all pupils; efficient in that she is using her limited time to go straight to the most readily identifiable manifestation. She rewards only that.

**Teacher B** does the above, but something disturbs her. Something in the pupil's text seizes her. It prevents her from moving on. She senses a possible gap between the reality she perceives and the concept that the mark scheme has of it. The reality of the pupil's work is teeming with possible meaning, some of which may (she feels) be relevant to the business of causal reasoning: perhaps *more* relevant than the surface manifestation she thought she was looking for. But it is partly concealed.

What is concealing it? The mark scheme? But surely a mark scheme helps us *see*. It defines and classifies. And this mark scheme carries much authority, not merely because it is the department's accepted way of establishing attainment and progress (so it is a matter of professionalism to go along with it), but because it is based on tried and tested ways in which the history education community has traditionally defined causal reasoning for the purposes of assessment. Nevertheless, for all its warranted validity, the mark scheme also conceals.

Of course, Teacher B could just make a quick mental note that there was a problem and recommend changes to the mark scheme at the next department meeting. That may turn out to be productive. But we are interested in what she does much more immediately. Notice two things:

## Three history teachers assess the quality of a Year 8 pupil's causal reasoning. Each reacts to a particular history essay in a different way.

Learning objective: to suggest the relationship between causes (Level 5)

| Teacher A | Teacher B | Teacher C |
|---|---|---|
| Finds two isolated sentences in two different parts of the essay where pupil explicitly makes links between causes. This meets the indication on the mark scheme exactly: 'an explicit link'. And it has happened twice, suggesting the pupil's grasp of this aspect of causal reasoning is secure. She notes in the margin:<br><br>*two clear examples – Level 5'*<br><br>She records this and moves on to the next pupil. | Finds same two sentences but thinks to herself:<br><br>'I'm not sure if these examples show that he's really got it. Strictly speaking, he's done what the mark scheme says, but if I look at that first sentence in the context of the sentence before and the sentence after, it seems strangely unconnected. I think he's just parking a formula. I think I need to examine the interplay between the mark scheme and its immediate context'. | Finds same two sentences and reaches same conclusion as Teacher B, but adds:<br><br>'I wonder what this *other* paragraph is telling me though? There's nothing in it at all that directly addresses the mark scheme, but perhaps I'm looking in the wrong places altogether. There is a quality of reasoning in this other paragraph that *may* suggest he's getting closer to causal reasoning than I thought. Perhaps I'm missing crucial signs of learning. But, hang on a minute, what *am* I looking for? As I reflect on this, I seem to be discovering something about my own assumptions about causal reasoning in history. I wonder how pupils are actually interpreting the language I use when I'm teaching this in the classroom? I wonder what assumptions my language embodies? I'm going to forget the mark scheme for a bit and look at this pupil's reasoning again. I'm going to try to decide how best to describe it. It may be that there's a lot more to causal reasoning than 'suggesting relationships between causes' and I just don't yet have the words to capture it. Trying to capture what this pupil is actually trying to do may be a start.' |

Figure 16.1   Three teachers

1. As she looks at the work, her looking is characterized by a moving *away* from the original preconceptions about what she was looking for, and a moving *closer* to the essence of the thing she was really looking for, that thing which was hidden. She is caught up in a pattern of revealing and concealing that is a natural part of her own reading.
2. Focusing on that natural pattern (a pattern that seems to arise from the very reading process itself), she starts to employ a distinctive interpretive process. This requires a continuous movement between parts and whole, a refusal to rest with either constituent parts or whole, but a determination to read each in the light of the other. She is operating hermeneutically, applying a deliberate approach to the movement between parts and whole that her natural interpretive processes seem to lead her towards. She is now sufficiently conscious of it to name this process that she finds herself adopting: 'I need to examine the interplay between …'.

**Teacher C** is doing everything that Teacher B is doing. She, too, is led by what is before her. But she is becoming actively thoughtful about this process itself, and rendering it even more explicit than Teacher B.

Teacher C is wondering if she should re-name 'causal reasoning' altogether. It looks as though Teacher C really is going to be in a position to re-write that mark scheme … or to change the language of the National Curriculum, or even the philosophy of history itself. But, for now, the interesting thing is the effect all this is having on her own approach as an assessor, and therefore on her way of being a researcher and her way of being a teacher.

She is starting to think about how this pupil's written reasoning *appears* to her, but without the concepts and tools of NC assessment standing between her and it. This involves a deliberate and difficult attempt to retreat from those concepts.

It is not that the NC tools are necessarily wrong – rather, that a different interpretive process is revealing something more *essential* (i.e. closer to an essence). This has transferred her attention from deciding if Pupil X matches up to a given marker for progress in causal reasoning into a closer examination of causal reasoning itself. Yet she is still directly using the data provided by Pupil X in order to construct this.

Notice, too, how Teacher C slithers into thinking about language and labelling. She can only think or talk about causal reasoning *through* language and labelling, and yet she is becoming sufficiently self-aware to question the way in which language may have placed limits on her understanding.

Teacher C is now moving constantly back and forth, back and forth, between her existing assumptions and what is appearing to her, between language that conceals and language that reveals, between parts and whole, re-examining each, continuously, in the light of the other. But Teacher C's circular, hermeneutic approach takes her much further than Teacher B. She is:

- beginning to reject a meaning system bequeathed to her (the given ideas about the properties of causal reasoning)
- uncovering possibly hidden indicators of how this particular pupil is approaching causal reasoning
- shining a new light on *herself* as an interpreter, reflecting actively on the possibilities inherent in the interpretation process as it unfolds.

Consider the implications of that third bullet point. Teacher C is now finding out about *herself*, as much as she is finding out about Pupil X's causal reasoning. She has become the object of her own research.

Another way of saying this is to note a shift in the kind of question that Teacher C is now asking. All three teachers are trying to use data to validate a claim that a certain pupil is engaged in a certain kind of causal reasoning. All three teachers know that if they are to defend the view that Pupil X can reason causally, they must ask, in effect, 'How do I know this to be true?' But Teacher C is now asking something else. Not 'How do I know this to be true?' but 'Why do I interpret the truth to be this?'

Teacher C is also noticing a crucial way in which the interpretive process is always moving, dynamic, in a state of flux. It is a circle of movement that she can actively enter and experience more fully and explicitly if she so chooses. She can choose to move into that circle and to learn from it. Indeed, she is already asking – how do things appear to me? What do I need to do to *allow* things to appear to me in their fullness, in their essential features? What is going on when I interpret things and how can I use this to learn more about me as well as about my object?

Teacher C, even more explicitly than Teacher B, has realized that letting a thing appear as what it is becomes a matter of learning how to allow it to do so.

Of course, if Teacher C carries on like this, she will have a nervous breakdown. She is in danger of spending a whole night on one pupil's work. A more constructive way to make use of this experience might be to begin a research project – one guided by this different way of seeing. If she does this, she will be deciding to work within an interpretive paradigm.

Indeed, all three teachers are at the moment of curiosity cultivation that leads to a fascinating research project. Each could successfully build on the processes they are already using. They are anticipating particular ways of working that the interpretive paradigm offers. By exploring an appropriate methodology, they might find that they can augment what they are learning from and about their own practice. Each is ready to take a walk through the various methodologies that interpretivism has spawned.

As you work through this chapter, keep referring back to our three teachers. I will use them as examples to stimulate your exploration of the different practical possibilities offered by various traditions within interpretivist research. This chapter will present a selection of methodologies – the theoretical position sitting behind a researcher's chosen methods. We will focus on how they arose, what they offer and how they differ.

One word of warning. Do not expect the traditions to fit our three teachers neatly. They have not been devised so crudely. Expect surprising convergences. Expect new puzzles. Simply use our three teachers as tools to keep you thinking, and to ground what follows in the practical realities of being an enquiring teacher.

But, first, we need to take a detour by way of the words 'subject' and 'object'.

## RE-THINKING SUBJECTIVITY

Off the top of your head, and before reading on, make up a natural, conversational sentence using the word 'subjective'.

I wonder what your sentence sounded like. It is possible that you used the word 'subjective' in a negative way: 'That's a bit subjective, isn't it?' 'We can't rely on that – it's too subjective.'

While there are times when such usage is appropriate, the word's automatic equation with negative, invalid or inadequate judgements is unfortunate, for much of the word's wider meaning is lost.

Subjectivity is the key feature distinguishing people from inanimate objects. Subjectivity is all about meaning. Our words, actions and other creations hold various meanings for each of us. Thoughts, feelings and beliefs influence those meanings. This issue of meaning has important implications for researching the social world.

Consider two ways to wreck a lesson: an earthquake and mounting pupil disruption. In the case of the earthquake, the researcher could identify physical causes leading to the collapse of the classroom in which the lesson took place. In the case of mounting pupil disruption, the causal chain will have to take account of subjective meanings that underlie the pupils' actions. Why were they not engaged in the lesson? How did they become disaffected? What roles did they adopt? The geologist and engineer have no such interest in the subjective perceptions of the earth's crust or the building (Baronov, 2004: 112–13).

In interpretivist research, subjectivism becomes relevant in two ways:

1. The example above reminds us that subjectivity is our object of study. When examining the social world and trying to understand it, we are trying to make sense of human subjectivity or the subjectivities of a group.
2. But we, as researchers, are exercising judgement and making meaning, too. Thus, to a greater or lesser extent, our own subjectivity, as researchers, is also engaged.

In any enquiry, or any ordinary act of assessment or evaluation by a teacher, you, the researcher, are a *subject* enquiring into an *object*. To clarify this, it is worth recalling some basic grammar. Each sentence in Figure 16.2 contains a subject and a direct object. The subject acts, behaves or reacts to the object in some way. The object is passive in this relationship. The subject is 'doing' something to it, whether eating it, contemplating it or hitting it.

Subject and object are used in the same way in research. You, the researcher, are the subject. *You* are going to have to 'do' something to your object – observe it, count it, listen to it, measure it, engage it in conversation, use it, reflect upon it.

When we hear talk of 'being objective', we are hearing an assumption about the role of *you*, the researcher, the subject. The assumption is that we should minimize what is

| SUBJECT | | OBJECT |
|---------|---------|--------|
| The dog | *ate* | the cat. |
| The man | *considered* | the moon. |

Figure 16.2  Subject and object in a sentence

presumed to be the distorting impact of our subjectivity. According to this assumption, we need to establish that results are untainted by the bias of the observer (the subject). On this line of argument, true understanding results from distancing oneself as one observes. This distancing makes us 'objective' – i.e. object-oriented rather than subject-oriented.

But it is not quite so simple. *You*, the subject, cannot be left out. The object will not research itself. While this holds when researching the physical world, too, it creates particular challenges and offers special opportunities when we are researching the social world of human beings and their webs of meaning.

## Challenge no. 1

What you are researching is, itself, a bundle of subjectivities. You are going to have to make judgements. But what enables you to make those judgements? The answer is: your humanness, the very thing you have in common with your object. If you were not human, you could not make sense out of the meanings made by other humans. So the very thing that supposedly gets in the way – your subjective humanness and its inevitable preconceptions, lenses and biases – is also the very thing that *allows* you to reach across the distance and make meaning out of your object.

## Challenge no. 2

If you are researching a situation in which you are intricately involved, if you are researching your own practice, you are not just researching someone else's subjectivity, you are researching your *own* subjectivity. You have actually become your own object.

What does this mean? Should we give up because we cannot be fully objective?

Some would argue that the only solution is to screen out our own subjectivity in order to limit its damage. We could conceptualize our subjectivity as a problem, and then deploy tools and systems to ensure as much objectivity as possible. This is certainly possible as a *quest* (even if total objectivity can never finally be achieved) and for certain forms of enquiry, it may be both desirable and necessary.

But it is not the only way. If we *always* see our own subjectivity as a problem, we lose the essential advantage our subjectivity gives us in Challenge No. 1 and any attempt to rise to Challenge No. 2 becomes impossible. For teachers researching their own practice, to avoid Challenge Nos 1 and 2 is to give up and go home.

So what is the answer? Interpretivist research offers different forms and modes of researching the social world, each of which handles these questions in different ways. One way of thinking about different types of interpretivist research is to talk about *the extent to which* and *the manner in which* our own subjectivity as researcher is engaged or managed.

So we have choices and possibilities.

Consider Teacher C in Figure 16.1, once again. Her curiosity is leading her somewhere. In her emergent informal enquiry, her own subjectivity is central. It is not something that is getting in the way – it is, itself, both (i) her tool for enquiring, and increasingly, (ii) an object of study in its own right. Increasingly, her focus is as much upon herself, as subject, as it is upon the causal reasoning of Pupil X – her object. She could now decide to pursue an enquiry that makes the most of (i) and (ii) rather than running away from them.

So, has this turned Teacher C away from her original object? No, far from it. What it has done is to create a new kind of *linkage* between Teacher C as the subject and object of her enquiry. Take a closer look at this interesting new linkage:

- She cannot enquire into her *object* without using herself as subject in a very direct way.
- She cannot enquire into herself as *subject* – her processes of seeing, the patterns of revealing and concealing – without using the data that come to her from her object.

This linkage between subject and object is particularly pertinent to teachers researching their own practice. You do not have to be enquiring into or directly using your subjectivity all the time, but you do need to be constructively thoughtful about your role as subject (researcher). Different kinds of project can exploit that linkage in different ways and it is possible to design your research so as to maximize or minimize the emphasis on yourself as enquirer. It is possible to make this work to suit you and the focus of your enquiry. The teacher research projects in Figure 16.3 offer a variety of different ways in which subject (researcher) and object (focus of research) might relate to each other.

As a teacher researcher, the only thing that is impossible to *ignore* is your own subjectivity. At the very least, you will need to reflect upon your own involvement, your starting assumptions, your purposes. You could then make a decision to:

(a) heighten that awareness of your subjectivity in order to reduce its effects and be as object-oriented as you possibly can
(b) involve your own subjectivity and make it a positive condition for enquiry
(c) (more radically) make your own subjectivity the primary object of study.

Teachers B and C are certainly doing (b). Teacher C is perhaps contemplating (c).

**Activity 16.2**

Now look more systematically at the projects in Figure 16.3. Study the three different arrows in Figure 16.4. For each of the titles in Figure 16.3, choose the arrow that best describes the interplay of subject (researcher) and object.

Before we move on, a caution is necessary. The three positions presented crudely in Figure 16.4 are neither mutually exclusive nor fixed positions. They are just conceptual tools, used here to heighten your awareness of the meaning of the words 'subject' and 'object' and to think about these freshly. They represent a possible continuum, ways of

1. 'The trouble with critical cultural geography is that the students just don't care'. Desire for dialogue: how do we know when they are starting to care? An investigation into three modes of student interaction drawing upon a sequence of six Year 9 geography lessons about 'sense of place'.

2. *What* am I really assessing in Year 8's work? A reflexive exploration of the features of Year 8 scientific thinking that I seem to be noticing and privileging across a sequence of three classwork and two homework activities.

3. What does motivation in English look like? An investigation of when and how six Year 9 pupils appear to be motivated while reading, telling and creating traditional tales and stories about fenland life in East Anglia.

4. How do groups operate during a shared project in D and T? Developing a model for small group behaviour in a study of how groups of four Year 10 pupils interact, behave and adopt roles towards each other during different stages of design, realization and evaluation.

5. How can we tell what part imitation is playing in Year 5 creative writing? An exploration of ways of determining whether and how four Year 5 pupils are borrowing rhythms, structures and patterns in their creative writing.

6. In what way do students' prior experiences relate to the take-up of GCSE music? A longitudinal study seeking to examine webs of meaning within which decisions to take up or drop music are made, over two years in two schools.

7. How do students experience early secondary school MFL classrooms? A case study seeking to illuminate the experiences, understandings, perspectives and learning behaviours of four Year 7 pupils in the first year of learning Spanish.

8. What do different forms of assessment tell me about Ahmed and Lech as learners of mathematics? A study of how my own processes of understanding were altered by a series of iterative encounters with different forms and styles of Year 6 pupils' work.

9. Reconceptualizing 'revision': can there ever be any such thing as 'going beyond' an examination specification? Examining the relationship between exploring material *outside* the exam specification and strengthening students' ability to perform *within* it. A theory-seeking case study based on action research designed to improve the revision experience of Year 12 studying British politics 1815–1850.

10. Levels and marks, labels and needs – exploring the deficit model in the concept of Special Needs within English. How do the self-image and the school's image of two Year 9 pupils with SEN manifest themselves in these pupils' experiences?

11. Discovering the power of the word: what is the role of the abstract noun in creating mature expression? A case study seeking to uncover how and what four Year 8 and four Year 9 pupils are engaging with during creative encounters with vocabulary in Religious Studies.

12. Can one concept illuminate another? An investigation into the nature and quality of Year 8's thinking about *historical diversity* developed and demonstrated indirectly during a causation enquiry examining the *historical causes* of early Islamic expansion.

Figure 16.3   Sample thesis titles

leaning in particular directions. It is important not to fix the researcher in each project in Figure 16.3 as 'being subjective' or 'being objective'. We are just talking about *leanings* in terms of the roles that the subject and object might be playing, and how they dance in relation to each other, in any enquiry.

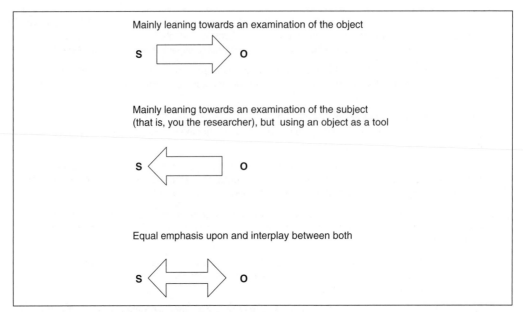

Figure 16.4   Leaning towards subject or object?

Thinking about subject and object is a good starting point for thinking about how interpretivist research arose. To do this, we need to examine how the idea of researching the social world, as distinct from the physical world, first became a focus for debate.

## THE EMERGENCE OF AN INTERPRETIVIST PARADIGM

So how did distinctive approaches to social research arise? A little historical background is useful because it shows us just how fluid and contingent was the emergence of the various methodologies. Such background reminds us that methodologies and methods are not gods to be propitiated; they are merely tools for us to select, adapt, blend and challenge. To do this well, we need to be well-informed about their context and purpose.

The idea that researching human, subjective experience might need some special approaches has not always been commonly accepted. The great German philosopher, Kant (1724–1804), saw things rather differently. Setting out to provide a foundation for *all* knowledge, Kant formulated 'categories' that made *all* enquiry possible, such as *contingency, plurality* and *cause*. For Kant, these categories were equally applicable to the physical and social sciences.

Eighty years later, the German historian Droysen (1808–1884) challenged Kant by naming two types of knowledge: *erklären* (explanation) and *verstehen* (understanding). Droysen maintained that whereas we seek to *explain* physical phenomena by means of causes or universal laws, we seek to *understand* social phenomena through interpretation. Other 19th-century thinkers built on this. For example, an explicit contrast emerged between a *nomothetic* approach seeking general causes and an *idiographic* approach seeking to understand unique, individual cases.

The most influential of these thinkers was Dilthey (1833–1911) and the aspect of his thinking we particularly need to note here was the way in which he defined human beings (Baronov, 2004: 117). He said that humans are not just biological creatures; rather, they are beings that make meaningful things. Humans are defined by their subjectivity. Humans make paintings, puddings and parliaments. They make tables, tubas and treaties. The things we create are expressions or *objectifications* of our subjectivity. Therefore, if we study those meaningful things, we can learn about that subjectivity, about the meanings that make us human.

In a direct challenge to Kant, Dilthey came up with his own categories. He believed that there are categories through which we find structure and meaning in social and cultural experience. His main categories were *purpose, meaning* and *value*. By using such categories to study the things human beings make, the researcher can identify patterns that shape how humans experience and make sense of the world.

Dilthey's basic premise was that physical phenomena – an earthquake or a chemical reaction – have no hidden, meaningful qualities. Human action, on the other hand, is bursting with meaning. Making sense of that human action requires a special kind of understanding, and this is where interpretation comes in.

Research into the physical world involves investigation through observation. Such a process – observing, recording, describing or counting – involves our ordinary understanding. Research into the social world, when it involves observing or measuring human action, also requires this ordinary understanding. But such social research also requires another type of understanding – one that 'allows insight into the hidden meaning behind human action' (Baronov, 2004: 119). This second type of understanding is *verstehen*.

A pupil in your classroom is balancing a pencil on his nose. 'Ordinary' understanding is adequate for apprehending the physical action of balancing a pencil on a nose. *Verstehen* is necessary for establishing that your pupil is showing off, deliberately creating a distraction, avoiding work, enjoying a new skill, obeying a bully's command or simply bored stiff. *Verstehen* thus relies on a type of *interpretation* that ordinary understanding does not require.

Let us think further about this interpretation process. On one level, *verstehen* is an everyday process. We use *verstehen* when we sense a mood, interpret gestures or recognize humour. It can be deployed with little or no explicit reflection. On another level, *verstehen* can be deployed as a data-collection method – a developed, systematic, explicit and self-conscious use of *verstehen*.

**Activity 16.3**

Study Figure 16.1 again. Where can you discern emerging transitions from *verstehen* used in an 'everyday' way into the beginnings of a more self-conscious and systematic use of *verstehen*? Be sure to consider all three teachers. The answers are not obvious.

What we understand today as *verstehen* or the interpretivist approach has appeared historically in many forms. I will follow Crotty (1998) in presenting these as three streams of thought: symbolic interactionism (especially its influence on ethnography), phenomenology and hermeneutics.

## SYMBOLIC INTERACTIONISM

Symbolic interactionism stems from the American philosopher and social psychologist George Herbert Mead. Just as with Dilthey, it was a particular view of what a human being is that drove forwards this branch of philosophy. This view has influenced many basic ideas that many educational researchers take for granted today.

For Mead, what is distinctive about human beings is a concept of the 'self'. People are different from animals because they have selves. Crucially, the self is social. What and who we are comes from our being part of a community. The practices found within any culture thus form the roots of personhood. Mead wrote, 'A person is a personality because he belongs to a community.' (1934: 162)

Yet the term 'symbolic interactionism' was never actually used by Mead. It was Mead's students, especially Herbert Blumer, who disseminated Mead's ideas and who coined the term 'symbolic interactionism':

- 'Interactionist' refers to people's capacity to put themselves in the place of others. For example, it is by seeing ourselves from the perspective of imaginary others that we are able to reflect upon alternative ways of expressing ourselves, and then to select from among those alternatives. This ability to see ourselves as the object of others' attention allows us to direct our actions through self-reflection. Mead said that this process begins in early childhood. It starts with early imitation and develops through play, role-play and games. By putting themselves in the place of imaginary others, children become reflective about how others think and act.
- 'Symbolic' refers to our sharing of symbols (such as language) with others.

Blumer's core propositions were:

- 'human beings act toward things on the basis of the meanings things have for them'
- 'the meaning of such things ... arises out of the social interaction'
- 'these meanings are ... modified through an interpretive process'. (Blumer, 1969: 2)

For Blumer, meaning is not intrinsic to objects, and neither is it a mere reflection of someone's mind. Blumer argued that the meaning of an object for an individual is derived from that individual's manner of acting towards it. Thus, a readiness to use a desk as storage, as a surface to write on and as a personalized space all give the object the meaning of what we call 'desk'. Each object could have an infinite number of meanings. Baert (1998) illustrates Blumer's thinking on this matter:

Grouse are not the same to a grouse shooter, as to an animal rights campaigner. Again, they are different objects for a discerning gourmet who chooses them for his or her main course, a bird-watcher or scholarly ornithologist. This tendency to act in a particular way is in its turn constituted, maintained and modified by the ways in which others refer to that object or act towards it. Within the household, for instance, numerous expectations by husband and children obviously reinforce a particularly meaning of womanhood. (Baert, 1998: 72-3)

**Activity 16.4**

(a) Try to adapt Baert's descriptions with education/school/classroom equivalents to 'grouse' and 'womanhood'.
(b) From your reading so far on symbolic interactionism (and before reading on!), what do you *predict* will be the likely implications of Mead and Blumer's work for an approach to research?

Blumer teased out the implications of the symbolic interactionist perspective for research methodology. These implications might be summed up as follows:

1. The meanings held by those being studied must be taken seriously. The researcher needs to see the social world from the perspective of those he or she researches. This leads to an important place within research methods for dialogue. Only through dialogue can one discern the perceptions of others and interpret their meanings and purposes.
2. Social research should examine the processes of adaptation and re-adaptation. Just as Mead stressed a dynamic relationship between self and society, so Blumer stressed the dynamic nature of social life – human beings continuously re-adapt to a constantly changing world. Many subsequent methodological traditions have developed models for examining how this process of adaptation occurs. The classroom and its many sub-groups and sub-cultures are arguably settings of continuous adaptation and re-adaptation.
3. Researchers cannot exclude concepts that are not immediately observable, such as mind, self or reflection. People's actions cannot be explained, or even described, through a simple, behaviourist view of response to stimulus. Instead, the researcher needs to explore how people self-monitor and self-reflect.

## SYMBOLIC INTERACTIONISM MEETS ETHNOGRAPHY

The practice of researching a culture or a group of people, commonly known as ethnography, was born within cultural anthropology. But researchers influenced by symbolic interactionism adopted and adapted ethnography. It is easy to see why. Think about the emphasis of Mead and Blumer on putting oneself in the place of the other. Now consider how this links with the underlying ethic of all that cultural anthropologists do. Crotty neatly sums up that underlying ethic:

> Culture is not to be called into question, it is not to be criticised, least of all by someone from another culture. Instead one should observe it as closely as possible, attempt to take the place of those within the culture, and search out the insider's perspective. Here lies the origin of ethnography. (Crotty, 1998: 76)

Ethnography is thus the child of both cultural anthropology and symbolic interactionism. Martyn Hammersley, in his work on special educational needs, teases out the relevance of symbolic interactionism for ethnography:

> Ethnography is a form of research in which the social setting to be studied, however familiar to the researcher, must be treated as anthropologically strange; and the task is to document the culture — the perspectives and practices — of the people in these settings. The aim is to 'get inside' the way in which each group of people sees the world. (Hammersley, 1985: 152)

In sum, what does symbolic interactionism contend? First, that to research human life and society is a complex endeavour. The 'objects' we research are dynamic objects and necessarily elusive. Human beings employ all kinds of tacit knowledge, most of which can never be directly observable. Second, that human beings define themselves within shared meanings. Third, that human beings anticipate the results of imaginary actions and, through interaction, constantly *alter* those shared meanings. Like all human beings, pupils and teachers are constantly monitoring themselves, masking bits of themselves and placing the accent on other aspects. What they say, do and write, how they listen or blank out – all these things are meant to convey and conceal who they are.

How on earth do researchers attempt to address all this? The answer is: with great creativity. I will now briefly introduce five examples of methodologies influenced by symbolic interactionism: the dramaturgical approach, grounded theory, negotiated-order theory, labelling theory and narrative approaches.

Each of these can be drawn upon by novice teacher researchers. Each could find a natural home within the projects listed in Figure 16.3.

### Activity 16.5

As you read the following five examples of interpretivist approaches, keep the list of thesis titles in Figure 16.3 close by. Decide which of these five approaches might have particular value for certain titles.

## The dramaturgical approach

Ernest Goffman analysed 'encounters' between individuals by drawing upon metaphors from theatre. For example, he defined individual activities which serve to influence an 'audience' as a 'performance'. Drawing upon Mead's account of the self and role-taking, Goffman argued that in their encounters, all human beings are continuously attending to their actions while adopting other people's views.

Consider the relevance of this to an analysis of learning and students, classroom and curricula. In all interactions, people dramatize their behaviour in order to show that they are performing well or are in control. Sometimes these goals are incompatible. A pupil who tries to convince a teacher that he or she is absorbed in work or can deploy a certain fact might exert so much energy doing this that he or she masks other important learning taking place. Goffman argues that during their 'performances', people tend to express official values. In an education context, these values might be embodied in school or classroom rules, expectations of a teacher or assessment criteria. Sometimes people deliberately play up one aspect of performance that they believe will please others or will foster their own advancement, and so either knowingly or unknowingly conceal others. Sometimes, people quite deliberately play down a quality – such as children showing off to other children in order to present themselves as disorganized, ignorant or non-compliant with an adult's wishes. The 'performance' of non-compliance or the pretence of ignorance is deliberate – the child is trying to show that he or she is in control and cannot be manipulated by the adult. (Goffman, 1970)

Picture people interacting in an education situation (whether family, after-school club, classroom, staffroom, subject department, tutorial, seminar). In these settings, we find people behaving in certain ways: they move 'front-stage', their speeches take on particular forms or they retreat 'back-stage'. They seek to influence an audience by way of costumes, speech styles and props. Goffman's dramaturgical approach is a form of interactionist research which uncovers rituals and investigates their roles and meanings.

## Grounded theory

In *The Discovery of Grounded Theory*, Glaser and Strauss (1967) launched this highly systematic form of ethnographic enquiry. The researcher strives to develop a theory about how people act and respond to a phenomenon. This theory must emerge *only* from the data (mainly interviews and field notes). It is said to be 'grounded' in the data.

In grounded theory, data analysis follows a set format. By segmenting information, the researcher forms initial categories about the phenomenon being studied. Within each *category*, the investigator finds several *properties*, or subcategories, and looks for data to *dimensionalize* by showing extremes on a continuum within that property. The investigator might then assemble the same data in new ways. Grounded theorists often end up producing charts or matrix-like schema, thus creating an abstract 'picture', showing how the elements of their theory relate to each other. For example, the chart will specify *strategies*, identify the *context* and the intervening *conditions* and so on.

Although this sounds complex, it is a logical, rigorous process from which the novice researcher can gain a great deal. If you experiment with grounded theory, you will not waste your time, even if you never use it again. It will discipline your approach to data. Above all, the rigorous stages in the labelling of items will make you newly thoughtful about coding.

I used grounded theory within my own MEd. I was interested in what actually went on in small groupwork when pupils were framing and then supporting hypotheses. What was really going on in the fluid, ephemeral patterns of talk and silence in a small group discussion? I videoed two small groups working in short, 15-minute bursts. I later interviewed pupils about their experiences of cooperating to solve a problem. I wanted to a build a theory – one as grounded as possible in what was taking place in my own classroom – about successful group interaction.

Using the video data, I developed an initial category of 'time spaces' to define the moments when no one spoke. After a series of interviews, I named the *properties* of 'time spaces'. One of these properties was 'waiting'. This property proved fruitful when I tried to *dimensionalize* it. Using the interview data, I discovered how pupils conceptualized and used 'waiting'. 'Waiting' ranged from 'frustrating waiting' ('we're stuck, no one's asking good questions and we're under pressure – this feels bad') to 'helpful waiting' (a positive, comfortable sense of silence, when everyone in the group knew that everyone else was thinking hard; it was a 'waiting without worrying'). This idea of positive or 'helpful' waiting was closely allied to the idea of trust. When the group was trusting itself, this 'good' waiting was possible. This had a relationship with *causal conditions* for such waiting, and so on. Thus, I was able to build an abstract schema fully grounded in the data.

The rigour of grounded theory taught me how to look at my data, and to keep going back to it, again and again. Through *dimensionalizing*, I realized why it mattered that I had not opted for 'silence' or 'inactivity' as my original category. 'Waiting' was rich with meaning, meaning that I found only after an iterative encounter with the data, constantly holding it up against this mirror of 'waiting' to see if it fitted it.

As a classroom teacher novice researcher, I found this experience exhilarating. The rigour of the process taught me to look at my classroom in a new way, and to re-think all sorts of taken-for-granted and intuitive knowledge that I had built up in five years' experience. Above all, it made me critical. I could no longer accept uncritically any superficial guidance on 'how to do groupwork', nor the language in which it was couched.

## Negotiated-order theory

In this kind of interactionist enquiry, researchers examine how social arrangements and processes are constantly adapted and re-adapted by those who live and work within them. In community, school, classroom and group settings, people negotiate tasks, roles and responsibilities, sometimes directly and openly, sometimes tacitly or unintentionally.

Negotiated-order theorists examine this continuous process of adjustment, uncovering the fluid and responsive nature of roles and relationships.

## Labelling theory

All societies have at times labelled certain individuals and groups 'deviant'. Some traditions of social research examine the background or heredity of 'deviants' in order to explore causes and patterns in 'deviant' behaviour. According to labelling theorists such as Becker (1963), however, this kind of study will always tell us very little about 'deviance'. Drawing upon a symbolic interactionism perspective, Becker argues that we should examine the labelling process itself. *Why* does society exclude some people from full membership? *How* does it do this? *Why* does society fear and censure certain behaviours? *How* does this designation of deviant behaviour come about? What processes of adaptation and response lead to this labelling?

## Narrative approaches

Narrative can be thought of variously as a methodology, as a method, as data, as a tool for communicating the results of enquiry or a blend of all these.

This field of narrative research is vast and with many antecedents. But I make reference to it under the symbolic interactionism umbrella because this is one influence that has affected it in direct and indirect ways. Also, to think about symbolic interactionism in relation to narrative can help novice researchers to explore its potential. See if you can think this through for yourself, using Activity 16.6.

### Activity 16.6

Drawing upon the above examples of symbolic interactionist approaches, why do you think that the construction of a narrative might be helpful in educational research?

In Activity 16.6, I hope you came up with 'plot'. You might also have thought about 'time'. Narrative is a tool for exploring the temporal dimension of the social world. You might also have thought of 'perspective'. You might have mentioned, 'meaning'. Narrative makes distinctive contributions to analysis and interpretation.

> A [chronological] map has order and relationships. A story has logic and meaning. ... What makes for convenient generalisation in a chronological map [makes for] uncomfortable coincidence in a narrative, not because everything must be neat and tidy with a complete and perfect explanation ... but because narrative frameworks work with connections: patterns and colligatory generalisations as well as with time and space. [Narrators] construct meaningful

accounts that impute narrative significance to events by means of ... trends and turning points, or intentional and causal explanations. (Shemilt, 2000: 94-5)

Consider the forms that stories of pupils or teachers, of groups or classes, of a school or a professional community, might take. Lieblich et al. (1998) construct life course graphs that treat a narrative holistically. They use these to illustrate patterns of ascent, decline and stability in a narrative. In a progressive narrative, the focus of a story is on advancement, achievement, success. In a regressive narrative, there is deterioration or decline. In a stable narrative, there is neither progression nor decline. To examine phases of a narrative is to employ a practical method by which, for example, the transcript of a biographical interview or a personal diary can be analysed.

But a plot has a narrator. And the narrator changes too. The fact that we change, too, brings us back to subjectivity. A narrative is not something that is found – it is created through interpretation.

## PHENOMENOLOGY

Start by reflecting on this interesting definition of phenomenology: 'Phenomenology is a means of being led by the phenomenon through a way of access genuinely belonging to it' (Palmer, 1970: 128).

That probably sounds a little odd, even a bit mystical. It sounds as though it is almost attributing agency to the phenomenon being observed. Is Palmer really saying that the *phenomenon* leads *us*? Isn't that reversing the subject–object relationship?

Not quite, but it does neatly illuminate the distinctive way in which subject and object are conceptualized for the phenomenologist. This is another reason why it was important to reflect upon subjectivity and objectivity at the start of this chapter.

Phenomenology is such a complex field that one can only gradually move into the circle of its considerations. My aim here is to give a mere taste, to foster a little curiosity about its special value when researching the world of education, especially for the novice teacher researcher.

Let us start with a key thinker and some principles. Our key thinker is Edmund Husserl (1859–1938) and his foundational work is his *Logical Investigations* (1900). Our three principles are (i) a relationship between subjects and objects; (ii) a method of enquiry with twin goals; and (iii) a suspicion of culture and concepts.

## (i) a relationship between subjects and objects

At the heart of Husserl's phenomenology is the relationship between subjects and their objects. Each is necessarily connected to the other. Subjects must have objects because a subject's consciousness must be consciousness *of something*. I cannot just say that I am conscious. I must be conscious of something. Right now, I am conscious of a desk and a keyboard. I am conscious of breathing and typing and the tempting possibility of a cup of coffee. I am conscious of the air temperature and images passing outside the window. These are the objects that fill my consciousness. I, as a subject, must have objects in order to be a thinking subject.

So subjects need objects. But the other way around may seem a little less likely. The computer in front of me or planet Mars are objects. Surely neither needs me sitting here thinking about it in order for it to exist?

But Husserl does not quite mean 'need' in that way. He means that the object cannot be adequately *described* apart from a subject. An *account* of this computer or of Mars is dependent on a human being like me, looking, perceiving, touching, measuring, imagining, remembering. In this sense, an object is always an object *for* someone. Thus neither subject nor object can be adequately described without each other.

This all starts to make more sense when we move on to methods and purposes.

## (ii) a method of enquiry with twin goals

The phenomenologist lifts an object out from its wider context and isolates it for investigation. He or she does this for two related purposes: (a) to identify those features of the object that are peculiar to it, that represent its core essence; and (b) to understand the 'structures used by consciousness' that allow us to constitute the object.

Let's take (a) first. The best way to think of essential features is to think of one thing that has many different manifestations. To take a very simple and obvious example, what is it that makes the concept 'dog' hold together? Although there are many different breeds of dog, the word still holds as an umbrella term. But how? After some enquiry, we would find a set of essential features that characterize all dogs, irrespective of breed. This is why we can tell a dog from a horse.

According to Husserl, once the phenomenon has been reduced to its essential features, we can then return to (b), the quest to understand how the 'structures of consciousness' *organize our experience* of that phenomenon.

But what did Husserl mean by 'structures of consciousness'?

Pick up your pencil sharpener. It has six sides. Each side presents itself to you under different perspectives – if you hold it directly before you, it presents itself as a square, but if you tilt it away from you slightly, it presents itself at an angle; if you tilt it further, that side looks more like a line. If you tilt it a bit further, it vanishes. Let us call each way the side is presented an 'aspect'. If you look at it a few days later, it is a different viewing. The sides and aspects have not changed, but this will be a different moment of looking in time. You will notice different things and 'see' it differently. We can call that momentary presentation a profile. Our perception is dynamic, not static, and we build up ways of perceiving things through sides, aspects and profiles (Sokolowski, 2000).

And these things are real. Indeed, Husserl's slogan was 'back to the things themselves' – this was a realist project, not a project to get lost in the subjective world of ideas alone. This is a common misconception with phenomenology. It is often mistaken for an idealist project because it focuses on the structures of consciousness, but for Husserl, it was a project to do with establishing the nature of things. It is just that the project is carried out through analysis of how we experience and constitute those things in our consciousness. Phenomenologists study *the act of interpretation* by which an object appears to our consciousness.

Sides, aspects and profiles are only the start. Subjects also make sense of objects in presence and in absence. There is a difference between studying the thing before us (the present object) and holding it in memory or anticipation (the absent object). Phenomenology has its own ways of talking about these memories, anticipations and perceptions. It is a very thorough and pure project of *how* we make meaning out of an object.

My use of the word 'pure' becomes clearer when we move to the third principle.

## (iii) a suspicion of culture and concepts

Phenomenology involves concentrated focusing and reflecting upon an object. To do this, phenomenologists argue, we must push out the meanings that we already hold – our preconceptions, presuppositions and assumptions. We must 'bracket' these out, and then to the best of our ability let the experience of the phenomenon speak to us at first hand. This is why we find Husserlian phenomenologists talking about 'primordial phenomena' or the 'phenomena in their unmediated manifestation'. Phenomenology is about the direct and immediate experience of objects *before* we start thinking about them and attributing meaning to them.

According to Husserl, phenomenology invites us to:

> set aside all previous habits of thought, see through and break down the mental barriers which these habits have set along the horizons of our thinking ... to learn to see what stands before our eyes. (Husserl, 1931: 43)

Put more simply, phenomenology is about taking a fresh look at things, but in a conscious, deliberate, disciplined way. At the same time it privileges intuition. It is an endeavour to secure 'a pristine acquaintance with phenomena unadulterated by preconceptions' (Heron, 1992: 164). Another phenomenologist describes it thus: 'Phenomenology asks us not to take our received notions for granted but ... to call into question our whole culture, our manner of seeing the world.' (Wolff, 1984: 192)

You will notice a theme emerging here – it is a sense that a pure perception of the world is somehow sullied or tainted, obscured or distorted by our preconceptions. Our culture – the meanings already given to us – get in the way of seeing.

This is almost the opposite of symbolic interactionism. Crotty (1998) is illuminating here. He presents symbolic interactionism as being 'for' culture and phenomenology as being 'against' culture. They are two different ways of trying to see what is going on:

> Lying behind this attempt to put our culturally derived meanings in abeyance and renew culture in this radical fashion is a deeply rooted suspicion of culture and the understandings it imposes on us. ... Why be suspicious of culture? Surely we owe it our very humanness. Phenomenologists are happy to acknowledge that debt. They recognise that culture allows us

to emerge from our immediate environment and reflect upon it. They agree that it is because of culture – our symbols, our meaning systems – that we know our past and can plan our future. But (culture) ... is also limiting. It sets us free but at the same time sets boundaries. It makes us human but in and through this particular culture, this special system of significant symbols, these meanings. In imposing these meanings, it is excluding others. And we should never lose sight of the fact that the particular set of meanings it imposes has come into being to serve particular interests and will harbour its own forms of oppression, manipulation and other forms of injustice ... Phenomenology is about saying 'No!' to the meaning system bequeathed to us. It is about setting that meaning system aside. (Crotty, 1998: 80-81)

Two implications follow:

- phenomenology is a *radical project* – it is about challenging a system of received meanings
- phenomenology has to be a *first-person project* – 'each of us must explore our *own* experience, not the experience of others: no one can take that step back to the things themselves on our behalf'. (Crotty, 1998: 84)

It is because phenomenologists are cautious about culture that they are cautious about concepts. We all rely on concepts – we need to name things in order to define and classify. However, all too easily, our labels and categories displace what they stand for. Instead of pointing us to realities, concepts can obscure those realities that they were (Crotty, 1998: 84) meant to illumine. Moreover, a concept, even where appositely applied, can never exhaust the fullness of a phenomenon.

Teachers deal with the inherent abstraction of concepts all the time. Our curricula and assessment schema are full of them. One motivation to engage in research can be to transcend or get behind these concepts that can 'stand in' for reality or mask the richness of the phenomenon.

### Activity 16.7

(a) Take another look at Figure 16.4. Which of the three arrows seems best to suit Husserlian phenomenology?

(b) Look again at the three teachers in Figure 16.1. In what ways might Teachers B and C be anticipating aspects of a phenomenological approach?

(c) Think of some concepts that you regularly use in talking about your school organization, your subject curriculum or pupils' learning. For example, 'meeting', 'evidence', 'idea' or 'question'. What kinds of hidden realities might these concepts fail to express?

Our three teachers are finding themselves doing this naturally, but they could choose to do this in a much more deliberate, systematic and sustained way, too. They may find that phenomenology suits them.

## HERMENEUTICS

Hermeneutics is by far the oldest of our three streams of thought. It is hard to say when it 'began'. The word really just means 'finding meaning', or the 'study of finding and conveying meaning', and has traditionally been associated with disciplined ways of interpreting texts, especially biblical and literary texts. Some just use it as a synonym for interpretation. We see biblical scholars developing systematic approaches to hermeneutics around the time of the Reformation, for example, when the trend towards translation of the Christian Bible led to a growing interest in managing ordinary people's interpretation of the scriptures. But approaches to interpreting texts go back much further than this.

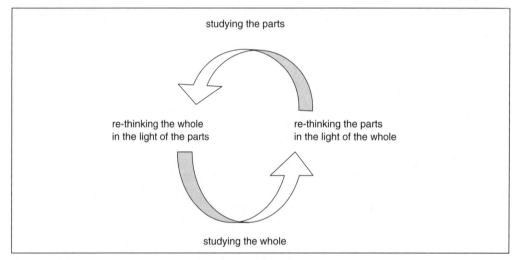

Figure 16.5   Working hermeneutically: an example of a hermeneutic circle

A key theme of hermeneutics, going back to the Greeks, is that of relating the parts to the whole, as shown in Figure 16.5. This is an example of a 'hermeneutic circle'. Teacher B, in Figure 16.1, is starting to work hermeneutically as she decides to relate parts and wholes in the pupil's text. She may not yet be doing this systematically, but she could certainly develop a method for doing this. There are many other kinds of hermeneutic circle, where different facets of human interpretation could be said to be moving in a cumulative, circular motion.

To complete our story here, we are simply going to look at what happened when hermeneutics met phenomenology in the work of Martin Heidegger (1889–1976). The full picture is extremely complex, so we are just going to touch on (a) how his ideas relate to and transformed those discussed above and (b) some implications of all this for how we might use *ourselves* in our own research.

Heidegger's *Being and Time* (1927) made a radical break with a central tenet of Western philosophical tradition since Descartes – the principle that the human mind is a mirror. All positivist scientific enquiry assumes the notion that through observation we can gain an increasingly accurate *reflection* of the world. Heidegger challenged this idea of a mirror. He argued that our minds were designed for creative interpretation of the world, not for objective reflection of it.

If the mind interprets rather than reflects the world, then instead of striving for better and better methods to provide an ever more precise reflection of the world, we should be trying to improve our understanding of how interpretation itself works:

> For centuries the question has been: How do we know this to be true? Now, Heidegger is saying, 'Why do we interpret the truth to be this?' (Baronov, 2004: 123)

Dilthey had thought of the mind as a mirror. For Dilthey, all we are trying to do in social research is find a better way of conveying or representing the world. For Heidegger, this was quite wrong. To understand this, it is helpful (yet again) to go back to how these different thinkers defined human beings:

- Dilthey defined a human being as someone who creates meaningful things. Hermeneutics is a method to understand the meaning behind these things.
- Heidegger defined a human being as someone who interprets or makes sense of meaningful things.

But 'making sense of meaningful things' is just a definition of hermeneutics! Baronov captures the startling radicalism of this position:

> 'Therefore, Heidegger argues that hermeneutics is *not* some abstract method but simply a description of human nature, an account of what we do every day. There is no more need to teach a person the techniques of hermeneutics than to teach a fish to swim.' (Baronov, 2004: 124)

What are the consequences of this line of thought for researching the social world?

## (i) a consequence for the focus of the enquiry

Heidegger is not saying that there is therefore no need for systematic enquiry at all. He *is* arguing for a systematic reflection and analysis. But the focus of reflection is now upon *what it means to be a human, interpreting being*. Heidegger argues that Husserl was wrong to say that the essential structures of consciousness are based on some pre-existing rational, logical order. Instead, consciousness arises from human experience or 'being'. This is why Heidegger chooses to examine something called 'being-in-the-world'. The essential structures of consciousness are generated by a person's *lived experience* and it is that realm of lived experience that we need to study. This quest to find structures within lived experience involves systematic reflection and interpretation.

The focus of enquiry in Heidegger's existential phenomenology is thus rather different from that in Husserl's rationalist phenomenology.

## (ii) a consequence for the role of subjectivity

In traditional forms of science, the conventions of enquiry require us to distance ourselves from the phenomena we observe. We must strive to ensure that no bias of any kind creeps into the observation process. Any such bias will weaken the results. Only by minimizing the effects of observer subjectivity, can we hope to approach accuracy. This kind of scientific analysis therefore strives for objectivity – a deliberate minimizing of the role of the observing subject.

But if the human mind only *interprets* the world, then all of this is turned on its head. True understanding can only proceed from full engagement with the phenomena under observation. So according to Heidegger, *subjective interpretation* is the only road to understanding.

Here is an example of this Heideggerian notion applied to teachers' researching. (I have adapted this from a similar example in the very useful and clear work by Baronov (2004: 124)). Fred is a teacher with long experience of working with pupils who have specific learning difficultires regarding literacy. Freda has never worked with pupils who display such difficulties. They agree to spend a lesson together, working with such pupils. Afterwards, they sit and discuss it. Fred's perspective is biased by the many literacy difficulties that he has worked with and also by his close knowledge of these particular pupils. Freda's perspective is relatively objective; she has no similar prior knowledge to call on, neither of the pupils nor of this type of difficulty. Following our Heideggerian notion, Freda's views will be much less useful in developing shared understanding because she has little basis for subjective interpretation. Understanding emerges from one's subjective biases, not from trying to screen them out.

Thus, while subjectivity was important within Husserl's phenomenology – in that two-way sense explored earlier – with Heidegger, our subjectivity takes on even more importance.

**Activity 16.8**

Using the commentary on Figure 16.1 on page 252, what themes can you detect in Teachers A, B and C that tie in with (a) Husserlian and (b) Heideggerian ideas about phenomenological enquiry?

## KEY IDEAS

Some understanding of three broad streams of thought – symbolic interactionism, phenomenology and hermeneutics – can help us to understand the forms that modern interpretive methodologies have taken. As we examine the ideas behind these methodologies, we can find principles that may guide us in choosing theories and approaches. Crucially, when researching our own practice, we need to be thoughtful about (a) the complexity of the subjectivities we investigate and (b) our own subjectivity as researchers – its role and value. These three streams of thought offer different ways of supporting this task.

None of these are positions I would advise you to pick up and rigidly follow. They are simply insights, ways of thinking about the world. At the very least, they will stimulate you to avoid taking certain things for granted ('objectivity is always good' – 'my own biases are a problem'). At best, they offer radical and exciting roads to systematic enquiry that are particularly valuable for teachers wishing to shine a research spotlight on themselves, on their actions towards pupils, and their own ways of thinking, feeling and being as teachers.

In their different ways, both Husserl and Heidegger remind us that we arrive at our investigations full of pre-conceived ideas and meanings – we layer these onto the way we frame our enquiries, the questions we ask, the goals we pursue. We are foolish to ignore this. Equally, we are short-sighted to imagine that it is necessarily a problem. We just have to know how to use it.

> We carry expectations within us and to an extent we make what we meet conform to those expectations … A raft of largely undetectable assumptions and preconceptions affects the way we perceive and behave in a place. Our cultural baggage — our memory — is weightless, but impossible to leave behind. (Macfarlane, 2003: 195)

What helps us to see the way can also get in the way. If you try to let your own cultural baggage and preconceptions go, stay humble about how far 'letting go' is actually possible. If, instead (or in addition), you try to make yourself the object of study, be systematic and be realistic about what you may attain.

 ## *Further Reading*

Clandinin, D. J. and Connelly F. M. (2000) *Narrative Inquiry: Experience and Story in Qualitative Research.* San Franscisco. CA: Jossey Bass.

Cresswell, J. W. (1998) *Qualitative Inquiry and Research Design: Choosing Among Five Traditions.* Thousand Oaks, CA: Sage.

Elliott, J. (2005) *Using Narrative in Social Research: Qualitative and Quantitative Approaches,* London: Sage.

Etherington, K. (2004) *Becoming a Reflexive Researcher: Using Our Selves in Research.* London: Jessica Kingsley.

Jasper, D. (2004) *A Short Introduction to Hermeneutics.* Louisville, KY: Westminster John Knox Press.

Moustakas, C. (1994) *Phenomenological Research Methods*. Thousand Oaks, CA: Sage.

van Manen, M. (1990) *Researching Lived Experience: Human Science for an Action Sensitive Pedagogy*. New York: State University of New York Press.

## References

Baert, P. (1998) *Social Theory in the Twentieth Century*. Cambridge: Polity Press.
Baronov, D. (2004) *Conceptual Foundations of Social Research*. Colorado: Paradigm Publishers.
Becker, H. (1963) *Outsiders: Studies in the Sociology of Deviance*. New York: Free Press.
Blumer, H. (1969) *Symbolic Interactionism: Perspective and Method*. Englewood Cliffs, Prentice Hall.
Crotty, M. (1998) *The Foundations of Social Research: Meaning and Perspective in the Research Process*. London: Sage.
Glaser, B. G. and Strauss, A. L. (1967) *The Discovery of Grounded Theory: Strategies for Qualitative Research*. Chicago, IL: Aldine de Gruyter.
Goffman, E. (1970) *Strategic Interaction*. Oxford: Basil Blackwell.
Hammersley, M. (1985) 'Ethnography: what it is and what it offers', in *Research and Evaluation Methods in Special Education*, S. Hegarty and P. Evans (eds), Philadelphia, PA: Nefar Nelson.
Heron, J. (1992) *Feeling and Personhood: Psychology in Another Key*. London: Sage.
Husserl, E. (1931) *Ideas: General Introduction to Pure Phenomenology*. London: Allen and Unwin.
Lieblich, A., Tuval-Maschich, R. and Zilber, T. (1998) *Narrative Research: Reading Analysis and Interpretation*. Thousand Oaks, CA: Sage.
Macfarlane, R. (2003) *Mountains of the Mind: The History of a Fascination*. London: Granta.
Mead, G. H. (1934) *Mind, Self and Society*. Chicago, IL: University of Chicago Press.
Palmer, R. E. (1969) *Hermeneutics*. Evanston, IL: Northwestern University Press.
Shemilt, D. (2000) 'The Caliph's Coin: The currency of narrative frameworks in history teaching', *Knowing, Teaching and Learning History: National and International Perspectives*, in P. N. Stearns, P. Seixas and S. Wineburg (eds) New York: New York University Press.
Sokolowski, R. (2000) *Introduction to Phenomenology*, Cambridge: Cambridge University Press.
Wolff, K. H. (1984) 'Surrender-and-catch and phenomenology', *Human studies*, 7, (2), pp. 191–2.

# GLOSSARY

**Coding**   The process of breaking down data by assigning codes that offer interpretation of meaning/significance

**Coding framework**   A structured outline of the codes to be applied to the analysis of data collected

**Collaborative analysis**   The collaboration between interviewer and interviewee in interpreting the issues discussed during an interview

**Conceptualization**   The background understanding of a topic, normally based on a literature review, that provides the rationale for the (need for, approach taken, etc.) current study

**Confirmatory studies**   Research designed to test out well-formed ideas based on claims in previously published literature

**Constant comparison**   A process (in grounded theory studies) of comparing data to codes and codes to data until the set of analytical codes is considered to adequately reflect the full data set

**Context of discovery**   How an idea came about: the 'creative' or sometimes serendipitous aspect of forming a hunch or conjecture

**Context of justification**   How an idea was tested to show that it is a reliable knowledge claim supported by rigorous data collection and analysis

**Core variable**   A grounded theory term for a variable identified as being the most significant in constructing theory to explain the research focus

**Deductive analysis**   The analysis of data according to pre-established themes

**Disciplinary matrix**   See paradigm

**Discourse**   The communication of thought and words through written or spoken form

**Discovery research**   Research designed to explore an issue within a context where there is insufficient guidance from previous research to provide testable hypotheses

**Display**   A visual configuration that reveals the interrelationship between coded themes or contextual factors behind the data generated in a research study

**Emergent design**   A term from grounded theory describing how a research design is flexible and evolves in response to ongoing data collection and analysis

**Epistemology**  The study of the nature of knowledge, and how one can come to knowledge

**Exploratory studies**  Research undertaken in a poorly understood context where there is an insufficient basis to justify the testing of pre-formed hypotheses

**External reliability**  In qualitative research, it refers to the accuracy and consistency of the researched as measured (hypothetically) by the extent to which another researcher doing the same research would reach similar conclusions

**External validity**  The extent of the generalizability of the findings beyond the specific context of the study

**Fallibilism**  A view that all knowledge claims are open to revision and cannot be considered absolutely true

**Falsification**  The process of testing an idea by setting up studies that could show it to be wrong

**Focus group interview**  A group interview, where the researcher is primarily interested in interactions within the group and which produces insights and data that can be linked to other forms of data collected in a study, such as individual interviews and questionnaires

**Generalization**  The process of making general claims about e.g. 'teachers' or 'modern language teachers' or 'teachers of top sets', etc., rather than about 'the specific teachers involved in this study'

**Grounded theory**  A set of procedures designed to offer a rigorous means of building well-supported theory in exploratory/discovery research

**Hawthorne effect**  The inclination of respondents to give answers which they think their interviewer would like them to give

**Hypotheses**  Claims that are specific enough to be tested and can in principle be falsified

**Hypothetico-deductive method**  A method proceeding by a process of conjecture and refutation (setting up hypotheses, and testing them)

**Idiographic research**  Studies that focus on the specific of the individual case, and see the individual as a valid focus of research

**Immersion**  The process (especially in grounded theory studies) of working closely with a data set to allow hunches/hypotheses to 'emerge' in conscious awareness

**Induction**  The (logically untenable) process of generalizing from specific cases

**Inductive analysis**  The analysis of themes in data as they emerge during the process of analysis

**Internal reliability**   In qualitative research, this refers to the accuracy and consistency of the research as measured by the extent to which the same research conducted again by the same researcher would lead to similar conclusions

**Internal validity**   This refers to the credibility of a study's findings by examining the extent to which a study investigates what it claims to investigate

**Interpretivist research**   Research that looks to explore informants' ideas and experiences, and acknowledges the active interpretation of ideas

**In-vivo codes**   Labels which consist of words or phrases used by one or more of the respondents

**Long-term involvement**   The strategy of extended fieldwork over time, allowing the researcher to have a feel for the different influences on the phenomenon being studied and of identifying the specific elements in the situation that are most relevant to the investigation

**Looking for negative evidence**   Looking for evidence that contradicts the main findings in your study

**Matrix**   A display format, with defined rows and columns, that links two sets of variables through the coded data generated by the analysis

**Nomothetic research**   Studies concerned with establishing general laws

**Objective knowledge**   A term used for 'scientific' knowledge, i.e. knowledge that is considered independent of the observer

**Online analysis**   The process whereby an interviewer reflects on responses given to questions during an interview and uses this to generate follow-up questions

**Ontology**   The study of the nature of the things that exist in the world, e.g. which entities (if any) objectively exist in the world independently of observers

**Open codes**   Descriptive labels attached to chunks of text when analysing a transcript

**Open coding**   Coding that uses 'in-vivo' codes based on the data, rather than applying a preconceived analytical framework

**Paradigm (or disciplinary matrix)**   A term used to describe the norms of a field of study in which certain researchers work, concerning inter alia beliefs about the nature of what is being studied, the kind of knowledge that is possible, and suitable procedures for coming to knowledge and reporting it

**Positivism**   Now usually taken to mean a belief that appropriate ('scientific') procedures can lead to objective knowledge that is not open to revision

**Post-positivism**   A term applied to the various models of science that see it as encompassing procedures for developing objective knowledge that can be considered reliable, but which are never 'water-tight' and so are open to revision

**Problem of induction**   The problem that induction is (a) needed to make assured generalizations, but (b) logically non-viable

**Progressive research programmes**   Programmes of research studies that build upon each other in ways that are considered to make progress within a post-positivist perspective where all scientific methodologies are considered fallible

**Semi-structured interview**   This includes predetermined questions and topics to be covered, but also allows the interviewer to be flexible and to follow up new ideas and issues that emerge during the interview

**Substantive theory**   A theory based upon the study of specific contexts (i.e. not a general theory)

**Thematic codes**   Inferential labels grouping different open codes in relation to interpretation

**Theoretical sampling**   A process (in grounded theory studies) of using ongoing data analysis to direct decisions about further data collection

**Theoretical saturation**   The point (especially in grounded theory studies) when further data collection will not provide any additional input to the building of theory

**Theoretical sensitivity**   The state of mind to be developed in grounded theory studies that allows the analyst to be open to the possible significance of data for suggesting hunches/hypotheses to be tested by constant comparisons and/or theoretical sampling

**Theory**   A coherent set of propositions that collectively models or explains a phenomenon of interest

**Theory-laden observations**   The way in which what we see and hear, etc. is always interpreted in terms of our existing conceptual frameworks for making sense of the world

**Triangulation**   Drawing conclusions on the basis of different sources of information, or of different methods of data collection, or from different investigators in the same study

# INDEX

Added to a page number 'f' denotes a figure and 't' denotes a table.